CONTENTS

	GREG CRAVEN Prologue	1
	Preface Robert Falzon	3
	Editor's remarks About the Contributors	10 11
1	ROBERT FALZON What is not resolved will be repeated	19
2	DANIEL ANG Pilgrimage in fatherhood and faith	33
3	DOUG BLACK A life turned around	53
4	JOHN BRADY Solidarity, not sympathy, is what men need	71
5	STUART BRADY Brady Bunch 101	97
6	MICHAEL FORBES There is no normal	117
7	PETER GABAUER "You have what it takes"	133
8	JUDE HENNESSY The spark of the infinite	157

9	Torrien Lau	
	Let's call this one Grace!	195
10	Steve Lawrence	
	Fatherly approval is a very liberating reality	215
11	Warwick Marsh	
	Turn the hearts of the fathers to the children	239
12	Brian Sullivan	
	Only the sacrament of the present moment	261
	Robert Falzon	
	Conclusion	283
	Bibliography	291

RAISING FATHERS

FATHERING FROM THE FRONTLINE
12 MEN'S STORIES

AUTHORED BY ROBERT FALZON

DANIEL ANG, DOUG BLACK, JOHN BRADY, STUART BRADY, MICHAEL FORBES, PETER GABAUER, JUDE HENNESSY, TORRIEN LAU, STEVE LAWRENCE, WARWICK MARSH, BRIAN SULLIVAN

connorcourt
PUBLISHING

Published in 2020 by Connor Court Publishing Pty Ltd

Copyright © Robert Falzon, as a collection, 2020

All rights reserved. No part of this book may be reproduced or transmitted in any form or by any means, electronic or mechanical, including photo copying, recording or by any information storage and retrieval system, without prior permission in writing from the publisher.

Connor Court Publishing Pty Ltd
PO Box 7257
Redland Bay QLD 4165
sales@connorcourt.com
www.connorcourt.com
Phone 0497-900-685

Printed in Australia

ISBN: 9781922449184

Front cover design: Ian James

Front cover picture: Kelli McClintock on Unsplash

Prologue

In his famous, "Sermon of Hope", St John Vianney is said to have preached, "If God took the name Father, it was to inspire us with a greater confidence in him." This observation delivered to his congregation of farmers in the village of Ars in France must have seemed to the good Curé one that was entirely free of controversy.

Yet fast forward to today, to our postmodern world, and many social commentators would disagree with the saintly priest from Ars. Fatherhood, whether one is referring to God, priests, or laymen, is no longer easily and agreeably associated with confidence. But the very notion of fatherhood should inspire us with confidence. A child takes the hand of his father, the communicant receives the Eucharist from the priest, the believer prays to "Our Father who art in heaven".

Pope Francis, in meditating on the passage from Genesis in which God promises Abram the joy of a child, along with descendants as numerous as the stars of heaven, rightfully observed: "When a man does not have this desire [for fatherhood], something is missing in this man. Something is wrong. All of us, to exist, to become complete, in order to be mature, we need to feel the joy of fatherhood: even those of us who are celibate. Fatherhood is giving life to others." As Pope Francis has quite rightly reminded us in this meditation, the modern acceptance of the disconnect between fatherhood and confidence must be healed and fatherhood restored to its original wholeness. This is critical if fathers are to play their rightful role in our society and our world.

This book, inspired by the real and lived experience of twelve fathers from all walks of life and circumstance, serves as a call for all men to reflect on the unique and critical role the relationships that our fathers have with us and that we have with our fathers, have in forming who we are, and who we will become. While reading through the contributions, I was reminded of my own father and the memories of his influence on my life, on who he was and who I was to become as a man. He was a simple man of family and faith, who boldly modelled for me the very essence of fatherhood with all its trials, tribulations and celebrations.

Quite unexpectedly, as I walked more deeply on the journey of each chapter – each written with an honesty and sensitivity that is often absent or hidden in men these days – I was also drawn to reflect on my own role as father to my children, and the impact I have had on their lives. Questions about how I did or could have done things as a father came to mind as I recalled the memories of my children growing up at a time when the very notion of fatherhood was being challenged by contemporary western thinkers. Now as a new grandfather, I am drawn into contemplating what wisdom I can impart, and what role model I will be for my own grandson who has entered a world completely different from the one I grew up in, and even different from the one in which I raised my own children.

St. John Vianney boldly proclaimed that fatherhood and confidence are inseparable. His humble and prophetic words, spoken almost as a lone voice in the wilderness, have more truth in them than anything that can be found among all the postmodern thinkers who today are fervently trying to deconstruct fatherhood on every level. It is my hope that this book will go some of the way in proving the Curé d'Ars right in his proclamation and inspire a new generation of men to greater confidence in their vocation as fathers.

Professor Greg Craven
19th August 2020

Preface

I'm writing this piece on the 10th anniversary of my father's death.

I'm sitting here at my computer at home, where I have mostly been since the onset of the Coronavirus pandemic, in its fourth month now. The image I have is one of hungry bears making an appearance after hibernation. Many of us are slowly emerging from the lockdown, rejoicing in going out and excited by newfound freedom. Perhaps I should say 'fearfully rejoicing'. I have found things that I want to keep from the Covid-19 confinement experience and much that I must leave behind. It has been a radically enforced, refreshing time of reflection and recalibration. Others may not have had this experience. Many have suffered terribly in so many ways. Some have died.

The cadence of these times has enabled and accelerated this writing project. A different tempo has offered the time to be in touch with our histories and record our stories.

The contagion's character has many negative aspects but it has taught me something I hope I don't forget in the return to 'normal'. My living and loving has a new rhythm that feels right, as opposed to the manic banging of the drum in the boat I was rowing. Some would say I needed to learn this new rhythm!

My relationships seem more human. I see people differently;

less functional/operational and more relational, more human. I really want to say I listen more – and I need to listen more! Over the past 20 years I have come to understand a deeper journey. I am aware that there is much more going on than I expected. Through life experience, reflection, working on myself and learning to manage my own life, I have become cognisant of the journey of a man. Furthermore, the significance of this has materialised in my work with other men, with the processing of our pasts so that we may approach the future more informed and less encumbered. I have been privileged to have access to many men's lives.

Through this I have discovered that the role of the father (fathering) and the experience of being fathered are among the most significant relational experiences a man will ever have. I wanted to capture the truths and evidence from the social sciences that conclusively support this hypothesis. What emerged in 2014 was my first book on this captivating and socially defining topic. In *The Father Factor*, co-author Dr Peter O'Shea and I specifically wanted to prove the importance of fatherhood based on the evidence and the research.

We had the idea that fathers mattered in terms of the key drivers of success and happiness. In fact in our research we discovered that there are four factors that determine success and happiness: The Father Factor, The Mother Factor, The Relationship/Love Factor and The Addiction Factor. We touched on all of these in our book but focused on the Father Factor because it is in most need of social attention.

We claimed that children perform better in every social indicator if they have an involved, nurturing and loving father. Children with this advantage will experience greater happiness, health and success.

We also exposed what happens when fathers are absent,

angry, alcoholic, abusive, addicted and anonymous: increased poverty, lower educational performance, increased crime, increased drug abuse, increased mental health problems, increased child abuse and increase in physical health issues including obesity etc.

We referred to over 170 peer-evaluated research papers and books, we included 50 case studies and stories and we were rigorous in only communicating what can be supported by evidence. The material and findings in *The Father Factor* are supported by convincing, compelling and cogent evidence. "This is The Father Factor. It is real, it is relevant, and it is destiny shaping." It was written, in part, to help fathers to be better informed about their vitally important vocation/role. *The Father Factor* has also been written with a view to helping sons, daughters, mothers and society restore the ground lost from poor father-child relationships.

"Based on evidence, data and the insights provided by pertinent case studies, this book will argue that fathers and father-child relationships matter." *The Father Factor* began as an exposition of the problem of fatherlessness. Statistics and data suggest that:

- One in three families is fatherless.
- Approximately 40% of our teenagers grow up in a home without their biological father.
- Over a million Australian children will go to bed tonight in a home without one parent – usually the father.

What does this yield?

- Approximately 60% of teen suicides come from fatherless homes.
- Approximately 70% of violent rapists come from fatherless homes.

- Approximately 80% of children with behavioural problems come from fatherless homes.
- Approximately 70% of all high school dropouts come from fatherless homes.
- Approximately 70% of all adolescent patients in chemical abuse centres come from fatherless homes.
- Approximately 80% of all youths in prison come from fatherless homes.

In *Fatherless USA* (1994), author David Blankenhorn states, "Fatherlessness is the most harmful demographic trend of this generation. It is also the engine driving our most urgent social problems. Fathers form an indelible impression on the lives of children. Good fathering grows healthy children, fosters stable marriages and forms the scaffolding of a robust and strong society."

I want to say also that for every absent, angry, abusive, addicted and anonymous father, there is usually a mother doing the hard yards of raising children. I want to shout out to heroic hard-working mothers everywhere!

So, why write another book about the importance of fatherhood? Why write this book?

The overwhelming feedback from *The Father Factor* was that most of the readers loved the stories and case studies. The evidence was compelling but the personal experience of fatherhood was the connection point. Real people loved reading real life stories and feeling their impact.

It is said that, 'Those who tell stories rule the world.' Even before the advent of writing, people and peoples would tell their stories, establishing an oral tradition before the written history. You need only to sit around a fire at night with others to watch the mystery unfold.

PREFACE

"You're never going to kill storytelling because it's built into the human plan. We come with it." said Margaret Atwood, author of *The Handmaid's Tale*.

Life is a story. Which character do you play?

I believe story is the power behind the fascination these days with ancestry and binge watching epic tales. Some industries depend on our deeply ingrained need to enter the story, even if on the surface it is simply escapism or entertainment.

"Once upon a time...." has us sit up, lean forward, take a breath...

So I invited a number of men with various business interests, family histories, careers, educational backgrounds, qualifications, ethnicity and upbringings to write a chapter for this new book, *Raising Fathers (Fathering from the Frontline: 12 men's stories)*.

What has eventuated through effort and emerged through imagination is twelve brave men who tell it all. Nothing is held back. Their stories are raw, radical, relevant – and each is unique. The goal is to allow the stories to reveal the message.

While these are narrative accounts, there is no fiction here. Each story is by nature distinctive, individual and sometimes idiosyncratic. The characters are personal and not polished, not necessarily professional and definitely not perfect. Just like you and me!

The message of the stories, however, is the same: fatherhood really matters! Done well it is world-changing. Done badly it is catastrophic.

> *The crisis of fatherhood we are living today is an element, perhaps the most important, threatening man in his*

> *humanity. The dissolution of fatherhood and motherhood is linked to the dissolution of our being sons and daughters.* Joseph Ratzinger (Pope Benedict XVI) in an address to a congregation in Palermo, Italy.

> *We know the statistics – that children who grow up without a father are five times more likely to live in poverty and commit crime, nine times more likely to drop out of schools and 20 times more likely to end up in prison. They are more likely to have behavioral problems, or run away from home, or become teenage parents themselves. And the foundations of our community are weaker because of it.* Barack Obama, Father's Day speech 2008.

This book is not designed to be read from cover to cover. As each story stands alone, I suggest you read a story at a time. Then spend some moments thinking about your father and your experience of him and with him. You might like to make some notes or even begin a journal and reflect on what these memories do to you. What do you feel? You might also like to look at your own fathering experience. What sort of relationship did you have with your Dad? If you are a father or grandfather, how has that experience impacted you?

At the end of the chapters there are some fathering tips you could take on board and use as guidance for the days to come.

There are also some recommended references from each author. These include poetry, movies and other authors whose work has had an impact.

You have purchased a treasure that my generation – and many generations before me – did not have: men on the fatherhood journey who have told their stories for other men sharing the terrain. I needed a map and a compass to traverse this territory.

Without these, many of you are faking it till you make it, just as I did. Not sure what to do? Where to start? Let these men mentor and guide you in the way you should go. Receive the life skills and experience the love.

At the very least, these stories may entertain and that might be enough for now. However, they may also be enlightening and even transformative.

Know that each author wrote his story with you in mind. He wrote knowing he would be exposed.

You can do this thing called fathering. If you do it well, you will change the world. You will become a better man and father, and your children will grow up better humans. We sure need more of them.

We want to stay in touch with you, so why not email us and let us know how this book has been for you? Tell us what's going on for you. I look forward to hearing some of your story. You can direct your email to a specific author, to all the authors or just to me.

You can reach us here: robert@raisingfathers.com.au

Robert Falzon

Editor's remarks

Everyone has a father.

Most people know their father, and have a relationship with him. Some never know their father, or their relationship is little more than one of acquaintance.

Whatever your situation – and whether or not you are a father – you will be enriched by reading this book.

My father went to heaven many years ago, and these stories deepened my love and appreciation for him. He would never have read a book about being a father – but he could have written one.

I was privileged to immerse myself in the stories of these men and I am filled with admiration for their searing honesty and penetrating insights.

In many ways our Australian culture doesn't make it easy to father well. Often, the role models presented embody rugged individualism; workaholism; fondness for alcohol, if not alcoholism, and reluctance to engage at a deeper level. The nation pays a high price for this, and yet, Australia offers so much to families who live and grow here.

Read and weep and laugh and then accept the invitation to reflect on your story of being fathered and – if you are a Dad – fathering.

Tracey Edstein
August 2020

About the contributors

Robert Falzon

Robert Falzon is a husband, father, businessman, co-founder of menALIVE and writer. He is married to Alicia and they have four adult children. Robert received many business accolades including Australian Marketing Institute Marketer of the Year and Australian Institute of Management and Owner Manager of the Year. In 2007 Robert sold his primary manufacturing business to focus in a full-time volunteer capacity on ministry to men through menALIVE, a national Catholic ministry to men. Since 2003, this ministry has delivered 450 events in 26 dioceses in Australia and New Zealand for more than 30,000 men. The purpose of menALIVE is to bring men together, to renew their faith in God and to encourage them to become an active force for renewal in the Church. In 2011 Robert saw his first book, *How to Grow a Men's Ministry*, published. His second book, *The Father Factor*, co-authored with Dr Peter O'Shea, appeared in 2014. Robert has a passion for finding effective and powerful ways to bring the message of the Good News to the good people in the parish pews and the street.

Daniel Ang

Daniel Ang is the Director of the Sydney Centre for Evangelisation in the Archdiocese of Sydney. Entering the Church as an adult, Daniel worked for the Daughters of St Paul for some years in editing and marketing before serving in faith formation in the Diocese of Parramatta. He was then appointed Director of Pastoral Planning in the same diocese before taking up the role of Director of the Office for Evangelisation in the Diocese of Broken Bay. He holds a Bachelor of Arts/Commerce from the University of Sydney and a Master of Divinity from the Sydney College of Divinity, undertaken at the Catholic Institute of Sydney. He is a member of the Executive Committee for Plenary Council 2020 and the Australian Catholic Council for Pastoral Research. Daniel has been published in a number of peer-reviewed journals in the areas of ecclesiology and pastoral theology and maintains a blog at www.timeofthechurch.com. He is married with two children.

Doug Black

Doug Black grew up in Newcastle, NSW. He graduated as a veterinarian in Melbourne in 1978, specialised in birds and became a pioneer of ostrich medicine and surgery in the 1990s. After introducing microchip identification of companion animals to Australia, he now works in two microchip-associated businesses. Doug is married to Malia and they live on the Murray River. They have three daughters, Jess, Claire and Emma. Doug was introduced to the Catholic faith by Malia and they are both significantly involved in St Mary's parish, Echuca. They are passionate about parish renewal and evangelisation. The experience of a menALIVE weekend in Ballarat had a massive impact on Doug's faith journey and, shortly after that encounter, he joined the Victorian menALIVE team in an effort to bring that same opportunity to others.

John Brady

John is married to Linda and they have five children and six grandchildren. He has been with MATES in Construction Queensland since 2008 and helped develop the national award-winning Mates in Construction program in suicide prevention. John strongly believes that suicide is a preventable problem, particularly if we can get Mates helping Mates. The effectiveness of this approach has also seen the creation of MATES in Energy and MATES in Mining. John holds a Master's degree in leadership and a Bachelor of Education and has undertaken considerable postgraduate study in organisational psychology, theology, biblical anthropology and suicidology. John comes from a diverse work background, having spent 20 years as a Catholic school principal and supervisor of schools; owned a wine company, owned a leadership and management consultancy and spent many years coaching young men in sport. John spends several weeks a year in central Africa conducting collaborative leadership programs and establishing micro economic projects in poor communities.

Stuart Brady

Stuart is a serial entrepreneur, having established some seven businesses during the past 20 years in the transport, film and funeral industries. After successfully retiring at 43 he found himself at a menALIVE weekend looking for answers, both spiritually and figuratively. He has been a part of his parish of St Joseph's Moorebank for 46 of his 49 years, serving the community initially as an altar server and later as an acolyte and parish council member. He has been married to Jenny for 20 years and has two stepdaughters, Elise and Kaylee, and a son, Harrison. Stuart found retirement not to his liking and currently runs three businesses just to keep him from getting bored. He is passionate about men's ministry and also Fathers and Sons connecting on a deeper and more spiritual level. He is heavily involved in the Growing Good Men weekends conducted annually by menALIVE Ministry and is one of the NSW menALIVE team members.

Michael Forbes

Dr Michael Forbes is a mathematician and entrepreneur. He was for many years a partner in Opcom, a successful Brisbane-based software company. From 2009 to 2014 Michael was part of the management team at NET (National Evangelisation Team) Ministries. Through his NET connections he travelled to Uganda and has become involved in many startup companies there. In 2014, as part of the Biarri Networks/NBN team, he was a finalist in the prestigious Edelman Prize. Michael is also a senior lecturer at the University of Queensland. He and his wife Lisa have three children and four grandchildren so far, and love going on (very) long walks. Recently, Michael has become more serious about running, including running marathons.

Peter Gabauer

Peter graduated from the Australian Catholic University in 1995 with a Business Degree majoring in Marketing and Management. He has held a variety of national marketing roles working across the four-wheel drive and marine accessories markets. In 2003 Peter started a marketing consultancy business servicing a diverse range of clients from luxury boat builders to the Catholic Church. Peter was involved in youth ministry between 1990 and 2000 and in 2003 joined the founding team of menALIVE, a ministry to men in the Catholic Church. The team at menALIVE has run events across Australia and New Zealand for over 25,500 men. Peter initiated menALIVE Xtreme, a weekend adventure experience for 18 – 35-year-old men and the Catholic Man Breakfast Series designed to reach out to men in the business sector. For 15 years Peter served on the board of NET Ministries Australia, a peer to peer Catholic youth ministry. Peter also serves on an advisory board for Emmanuel City Mission (ECM), a grass-roots Catholic ministry devoted to journeying with the most vulnerable in our society. ECM has a drop in centre for the homeless in South Brisbane. Peter is a sought after public speaker with a wonderful sense of humour. He lives in Brisbane with Jo, his wife of 25 years. They have two daughters, Sophia, 20 and Olivia, 18. They think Peter makes pretty good pancakes. Peter enjoys adventure motorcycle riding, road cycling, mountain biking, surfing (trying anyway) and good coffee.

Jude Hennessy

Jude Hennessy is married to Kerrie and they have two daughters, Tara and Rachel. He loves God, the Church and his family. In his role as the Director of the Office of Renewal and Evangelisation in the Catholic Diocese of Wollongong, he endeavours to support parishes in the formation of missionary disciples. He believes that church renewal hinges on bringing people to a powerful encounter and personal relationship with Jesus Christ and each other, and that men's ministry plays a strategic and impactful role. Jude had over twenty years' experience in teaching and leadership in Catholic schools before commencing work for the Diocese of Wollongong. He is the host of Journey Catholic Radio, a weekly program aired widely on a growing number of Christian radio stations around Australia and as a podcast. He is a 'sports nut' who has been accused of completely losing the plot when watching important games of rugby league – particularly State of Origin. He loves playing guitar and singing – especially around a campfire with a nice 'red' and good friends.

Torrien Lau

Torrien is a husband, younger brother of two boys, a father to five girls and a grandfather to two boys and a girl. Born to Chinese and English immigrant parents, he is a proud first generation Australian. Currently Torrien is the CEO of one of the largest not for profits in Canberra after working in the Disability, Consulting and Hospitality sectors. Torrien contributes as a volunteer to Christian radio and Catholic men's ministry through menALIVE and runs his own website posting prayer reflections.

Steve Lawrence

Steve Lawrence is a passionate speaker and storyteller whose mission is inspiring and equipping good leaders to become great. He played twelve seasons of professional Australian football with Hawthorn, was the Player of the Finals series in the 1991 Premiership team, and had a pivotal role in the 2008 Sydney World Youth Day as its Director of Evangelisation and Catechesis. Steve's adventures include living on three continents, running an international school of Mission in Rome with the Emmanuel Community, transforming Catholic educational institutions and starting his own leadership business. He is married to Annie and they have six children. As a couple they have run programs for married couples and families for many years. Steve has degrees in Humanities, Education and a Masters in Theology (John Paul II Institute), and has published two books. His second book, *Make Your Mark: Five Hidden Keys to Great Leadership* (Wilkinson) was launched in May 2019. His third book, *The Tiny Book for Giant Men*, is due to be published in late 2020.

Warwick Marsh

Warwick Marsh is married to Alison and they have five children and eight grandchildren. They live in Wollongong, NSW. Warwick is a family and faith advocate, social reformer, musician, TV producer, writer and public speaker. In 1988 Warwick and Alison founded Australian Heart Music.

In 1990 they travelled extensively throughout Australia, performing in many Aboriginal communities, country towns, schools, pubs, gaols and churches. From 1995-98 Warwick worked with Indigenous Australians whilst co-ordinating the Praise Corroboree, an annual event featuring prayer and reconciliation held in Parliament House, Canberra. In 2002 Warwick and Alison established the Dads4Kids Fatherhood Foundation to encourage fathers and promote excellence in fathering. Warwick is a leader in the Men's and Family Movement and is well known in Australia for his advocacy for children, marriage, manhood, family, fatherhood and faith. Warwick passionately encourages men to be great fathers and to know the greatest Father of all.

Brian Sullivan

Brian has been married for 20 years to Elisa whom he met at University in America. They were married in Rome in 2000 and returned to Australia in 2001. They have two teenage children. His faith, marriage and family are his priority and his domestic violence intervention career takes up much of the rest of his time. Brian has worked as a secondary teacher, school counsellor, in ministry and academia, as practice manager of a men's domestic violence program and has now returned to university teaching and research. His research interests include accountability in the domestic violence sector, effectiveness of collaborative community approaches to domestic violence intervention, identifying and managing unintended consequences of domestic and family violence interventions and working with men for change. Public health, human rights, social justice and hope are at the core of his work.

Robert's parents, John and Lucy Falzon.

The Falzons, (l-r), Shem, Isaac, Chiara, Alicia and Matthias.

1

Robert Falzon
What is not resolved will be repeated

Growing up with a distant father was confusing. It spurred and stirred me to try to do things differently. I made a vow, with myself as witness: "I am not going to do it like that!"

Now I look tenderly at that young man, barely a teen, trying to navigate life, the last years of school, home, sex, girls and the perennial question: who am I? What will I become and what will I do with this one life of mine?

Come with me, let us go back. Let us go back so we can grow forward. Let us revisit the past so we can make peace with it and forgive those who need forgiveness, even though they may well have gone from the family or passed from this life like my Dad.

Let us go back to learn, to discover truths about why we do what we do now. Why do we make these choices? Our family history speaks abundantly, not just of our DNA, but also into our present, with an insistent challenge to understand my self, my life story, by relating to history – his story – my story!

There is an ancient saying that has become one of my antiphons: "What is not resolved will be repeated."

My parents, John Falzon and Lucilla (Lucy) Maria Rubinich, were born between the two great World Wars. Dad grew up in Perth, Western Australia, and Mum in north-eastern Italy and then in Perth. They lived in a fearful and frantic time. Their parents experienced two world wars and survived the Spanish Flu pandemic. This was a seriously good effort considering that 500 million people were infected, about one third of the world's population, and an estimated 50 million died. It was an anxious, dangerous and uncertain time.

My Dad's parents, Joseph Falzon and Margaret Clech, found each other during World War II and married in Perth.

Joseph was allegedly of Maltese origin and worked as a chef in the merchant navy. Margaret's father was allegedly of Hungarian origin, migrating via London to set up a new life in Adelaide, South Australia. Margaret was purported to be a nurse. They had three children: Joseph (Joe) and the twins, John (my Dad) and Mary. Their lives were difficult, fearful, poor and sometimes violent. Much has been left unsaid about those days.

Mum's parents. Ferruccio Rubinich (a captain in the Italian Navy) and Darinka Mandic, married somewhere near Fiume, northern Italy, and had five children: Carlo, Lucilla (Mum), Hugo, Franco and Tulio. They migrated (ran away) after the war to Fremantle, Western Australia, and built a simple and reasonably happy life together. Wars, dislocation, language difficulty, uncertainty, financial insecurity and being the only girl in a large family left Lucy with a lingering anxiety, which from time to time escalated.

John and Lucy married in Perth and quickly proceeded to have five children: Robert (me), Stephen, Peter (deceased), Maria and Anne.

They also raised their children in a difficult environment and economy. They were good people and they tried hard, but with five children to feed, clothe, school and care for, there was never much time nor enough money.

My memory of those times was that Dad was rarely home because of working two jobs; typesetter for the *West Australian* newspaper at night and during the day, a brickie's labourer. When he was at home, he was exhausted and emotionally absent. We did not have a close relationship in those childhood years. I thought he loved me, and I loved him, but we did not do many things together to reinforce or communicate this. We did not play or talk much. He was not present for special events or my sporting activities and achievements. Dad was the boss; he provided, protected, and punished. He did these tasks diligently. The discipline was sometimes harsh and physical.

The lack of a strong father-son relationship left me with many unanswered questions, confusion about who I was and what it was to be a man. I believe that I was searching and longing for affirmation, validation, modelling and instruction. It did not come, and I was left incomplete and strangely ashamed. To be fair, I did learn a great work ethic from my Dad.

I do not blame my father for any of this. It was not his fault. He did the best he could, given the times and the circumstances. His own upbringing left him significantly impaired and unfinished as a man. His father, Joseph, was a cook in the merchant navy. It was the era of steam and sail-driven vessels and long hazardous voyages across oceans and seas. Joseph was absent for most of Dad's life, coming home for only a few weeks a year. Joseph's past is substantially a mystery.

My recollection of my grandfather, Joseph, was a one-off meeting. I think it was mid-afternoon, he was sitting at the small Laminex dining table in the little kitchen of his very part-time home, rolling his own cigarettes for that evening. I remember the dusty light and the lino floor.

It seemed to be an important event; judging by what we wore, the very rare event of being the only child on an outing with Dad and his obvious nervousness. I like to think my Dad was presenting his firstborn to his Dad. This would be a big occasion in most men's lives. I cannot remember what he said, if anything. I do not recall Dad saying anything much either. The only thing communicated in the silence was distance. It seemed to define the destiny of a generation.

I think of those lost opportunities with sadness. My Dad and I were strangers, as he and his Dad had been. I knew almost nothing about him; what he felt, how he thought, what made him happy or sad. Did he have dreams and hopes? I wanted and needed so much from him. He held something unique for me – and I for him.

I left home straight after completing school at 17 years of age. I was probably running away. The journey of nearly 4000 kilometres from Perth to Canberra, ACT, with two train changes then a car ride to Galong, was a challenge and a great adventure.

I felt called to join the Redemptorist Fathers and become a Catholic priest. After one year in Galong, I took the next step in the training/discernment process and went to Edmund Gleeson House in Maitland, near Newcastle, NSW, to begin my academic training. After about two years, having decided I was more interested in girls and football (AFL), I left priestly training and moved into a share house. These years were full of discovery: girls, music, sport, learning how to make friends, navigating studies and various part-time jobs.

It was the late 70s and early 80s. The fashion was big hair for men and women, flares and florals. Significant musical influences were David Bowie, The Cure, Prince and Bob Dylan. The Aussie bands I liked were The Angels, Midnight Oil, ACDC, Men at Work and INXS. It was a politically incorrect time, and that suited me.

I changed my degree from Philosophy and Psychology to Arts. I loved literature, poetry and film. I graduated with Honours.

At this time Dad and Mum made a huge decision to move from Perth to Brisbane. They drove from the west coast to the east coast. When I graduated, instead of going back to Perth I went north to Brisbane where I lived with Mum and Dad for a while, then made my own way.

The change of direction meant that I met Alicia Belle Clarke in early 1982. We fell in love and married on 5 February 1983. We have built an amazing life together and now in our sixties we are more in love than ever and have a really great friendship.

Alicia was a hairdresser and I was a budding business owner and entrepreneur. I worked as a marketing manager for a furniture company and then began my own business,

Furniture Manufacturing Company of Australia (FMCA). It was a small business with a big name!

We made money, lost money, survived a huge fire, experienced some ups and downs and made a great life, with everything on the line most of the time. Along the way we built and sold several family homes.

We now live in an inner city apartment which we enjoy very much. Alicia has her own practice as a clinical therapist while I do volunteer work for menALIVE, some public speaking and writing.

It's a boy!

"My son, you're a Dad. Congratulations Robert."

My father, John, enthusiastically spoke these words like a blessing over me on 17 April 1987. It was on the morning of Good Friday that my first child, Isaac, was born. What a profound moment in my life! It was a dramatic, painfully traumatic experience, especially for Alicia as the big baby was pulled into the world by high forceps delivery.

It was at the same time a triumphantly terrific event. "It's a boy!" A son was born. The whole experience was exceptional, This was the beginning of something momentous. It was a significant transition in my journey as a man. In that instant I was changed. I became a father. I had arrived too!

Incapable of containing the tears, joy and relief, I looked at my son. I saw him, touched him, held him, smelt and kissed him, marvelling at the miracle and revelling in the mystery of the moment. Look what I/we made! So many feelings and sensations were swirling in those minutes. From somewhere deep a new place within me was opened up with a strange surge of tactile, tangible warmth, a form of love I had never experienced before.

In the 37 years I have been married to Alicia, we have given birth to four children – Isaac, Matthias, Chiara and Shem. The joys of fatherhood have been many.

When I set out on the great adventure of fathering, however, I had no comprehension of what it would take to be the father I dreamed of being. Nor did I know how I would go about fulfilling the great responsibility of raising sons and daughters into men and women. I had no idea!

I was ill-equipped, idealistic and naïve – no training, no plan, no method, no instructions, no tools and no real sense of the staggering impact and generational imprint I would make in the most important task and vocation ever assigned to me.

I received more instructions on how to set up our new blu ray DVD player with its two manuals (one written in five languages), warranties, a helpline and a 30-day return policy than on how to be a father.

It seems to me now that I was not alone in my lack of training and equipping for effective fatherhood. How about you?

As I've said earlier, my father was absent from home much of the time. The experience of longing for my father, of needing a primary male figure in my life in my first 20+ years and the pain of not experiencing that, has been one of my greatest personal struggles. My desire and deep need for approval, validation, boundaries and initiation into manhood were not met. Some writers call this the Father Hunger and/or the Father Wound. There is an ancient saying, origins unknown, "What is not resolved is repeated." Richard Rohr has stated something very similar: "If the pain of your story is not transformed it will be transmitted." I acted out of my wounding and several times nearly lost it all. I felt I was on a path that was almost impossible to correct.

So, what did I do when it came time to raise my own family?

I repeated the historical patterns and pain of the past. I started a furniture manufacturing business in 1986 and over the years became extremely busy and stressed. The demands of a growing business and a growing family were more than I knew how to balance, so my family suffered. I traded down on them and up on my business. My fathering was accidental and dissipated. I was frequently physically absent from the home and when present, I was emotionally spent and angry. Sounds familiar?

In the late 1990s and early 2000s I had a wake-up call; a mid-life crisis. I ran into the wall of my own inadequacy. I noticed that my children were growing up without me and I was missing out on them. I was not the father (or husband) I dreamed of being; far from it!

It was time for change; I needed to modify my life direction, grow up, man up, reject passivity, accept responsibility and live courageously in order to become a better father, a better husband and a better man.

I began to read about parenting, manhood and fathering. I realised I needed to repair the wrongs of the past and I sought forgiveness for my failings, from both my children and my wife.

I thought parenting was the three Ps – provide, protect and punish. I learnt that from my Dad. Was this not the way to love?

One of my discoveries was that I love others in the way that I need to be loved. I loved my wife and my children the way I needed to be loved. It was the only love I knew.

Conversations that I call '30 seconds of madness' began with Alicia. I would ask a dangerous question and stand back for the response. One day I asked her, "Are you happy, and if not, how could life be better? What sort of a husband am I?" Much was said, over many weeks. There was a need for change. I needed to grow up and we needed to grow closer. Together we worked through hurts, tears and historical patterns. We agreed on changes, we made plans for the future and we made a weekly time to check in.

Eventually we fell into lasting love. This relationship is not something I can ever take for granted and even now I need to check in regularly.

At the same time, I created conversation moments with my eldest son, Isaac, a teenager at the time. "What sort of a father am I?" "You're an OK Dad." That gutted me – I didn't want to be an OK Dad, I wanted to be a great Dad!

I asked him how I could be a better father. The response went something like this: "You have a big life Dad working in a big business, travelling all around the world and sometimes you even invite me up into this life, and that's fun, but you have never come down into my small little life to do with me the things that I like to do."

He was right. He spoke the truth. I was choosing everything but my son.

Again, there was soul searching, reflection and decisions to change.

Around that time, I also began to take time for silence, solitude and stillness each morning. It was a time to talk with God and a time for God to guide and instruct me. What began with ten minutes has grown. This has helped me make the necessary change process a journey, rather than a one-shot event. I found a mirror that showed me the real me. It is a long game and some of the progress is punishingly slow. However, the trajectory is in the right direction. The place I am in now has taken generations to create, and as I look forward, I know there is still some way to go.

An interesting and very important consequence of our differentiation process was that as I began to change and possibly grow up, I also noticed Alicia changing in her own right. She began attending the University of Queensland as a mature student; firstly, completing a Bachelor of Arts and then Master's degrees in Counselling and Psychology. She now has her own practice as a Clinical Therapist specialising in Family Therapy and is highly regarded.

Life, grace and circumstances provided new opportunities for a real relationship with my Dad in his later years. I was in my thirties when we intentionally sought each other out. We became reconciled and built a warm and meaningful relationship. He made efforts to reveal his heart and mind. I made efforts to listen, learn and love. Eventually, he said the words that I needed to hear:

"I love you Robbie. I am so proud of you my son. You have what it takes to be a great man."

It was a blessing: necessary, irreplaceable, delicious words that became flesh, that became a man – me! Dad and I enjoyed each other, did things together, grew in relationship, laughed and cried. I grew as a son and man, he grew as a father and man. At this emotional banquet there was much healing, nurture and nourishment.

In Dad's last years his humanity, life and vitality drifted away. He was afflicted with the debilitating disease, dementia. It was excruciating to watch someone I had grown to know as a great man, my Dad, fade away. At the same time, it was exquisite, as I had some of my warmest and dearest moments and conversations with him.

John Falzon died on 16 June 2010.

I needed my Dad and he needed me. This father hunger, this father factor has been pivotal in my life.

It drove me to seek a better relationship with my Dad. I am certainly fortunate to have been able to find resolution in my relationship with my father in his lifetime and be transformed in the process. My Dad has helped me understand how destiny-defining is the relationship between a father and his children.

The truth is, it is never too late!

The Father Factor
As I have already stated, I struggled with my childhood relationship with my father and with fathering my own children. As I started to confront important issues, I began sharing my experiences with some trusted men. In the process I discovered that many struggled with similar issues. Each of them was searching for integrity, intentionality and authenticity, just as I was. I thought I was the only person in the world struggling with these issues and problems. I was wrong. Isolation and distancing are not just something that happens in a pandemic!

I found that most men who were prepared to be vulnerable expressed similar wounding and pain. So in 2003 a few brave men and I began working with and for men, and we called it menALIVE.

Since then we have worked with men in every state of Australia and in New Zealand and Uganda.

During the past 17 years we have come to the realisation that the overwhelming majority of men have father wounds, due mostly to absent fathering. Some men have been seriously damaged, not only by absent fathers but by fathers who were also angry, abusive and driven by addictions.

There have been men who never knew their biological fathers, either because their fathers died early in their lives or because the fathers left the home and them and became anonymous fathers.

The work of menALIVE has sought to create a fellowship and community of life and nurture for these men. It has also sought to encourage men to rise to their calling to be good fathers, husbands and leaders in their families and communities.

The incredible response to menALIVE is a testimony to the significance of the father wounding pandemic and the need for the restoration of fatherhood in our society and churches. As of September 2020, about 30,000 men have participated in one or more of the 450 menALIVE events and programs. For more information go to www.menalive.org.au.

In my work with menALIVE the teams have had the privilege of going to many places and working with many men. What we have discovered is that men struggle with life – with happiness, success, health, relationships, marriage and raising children. None of this is news. However, what we have encountered is that fathers play a major role in influencing the outcomes of an individual's life.

So now I'm in the last quarter of life. My children are finding great partners and moving towards marriage. They are responsible and mature adults and so much fun to be with.

One day I will be a grandfather to my children's children! Some say this is the best time of life and a tremendous blessing.

Alicia and I are looking forward with much hope and joy to the days to come. Our task is not finished, just changing. How incredible is it that if I lift my eyes and look, there is a new rising, a new horizon, a brand new day? These days belong to new generations of Falzons.

Thank you Joseph, thank you John (Dad.) I love you both, very much.

Thank you Lucy (Mum), who is still with us.

Thank you Alicia, Isaac, Matthias, Chiara and Shem – you taught me how to love.

Thank you God – Father, Son, Spirit, Lord and Giver of Life.

Fathering thoughts

1. Do the work on self. Look in the mirror and observe self. Begin the adventure of Life Change.
2. Resolve your past, especially with your father.
3. Ask the hard questions; '30 seconds of madness'.
4. Learn to love others the way they need to be loved.
5. Generously give your life away. This means individual time with your children.
6. Be the fun Dad. Laugh lots.
7. Find and cherish a band of brothers (friends) with whom you share life deeply.

8. Cultivate a regular contemplative time of stillness, solitude and silence.

Some books that have influenced me:

1 John Eldredge *Wild at Heart/Sacred Romance*

2 Gordon Dalbey *Healing the Masculine Soul/Sons of the Father*

3 Richard Rohr *Adam Returns/The Naked Now/Eager to Love*

4 Ronald Rolheiser *Seeking Spirituality/Against an Infinite Horizon/The Holy Longing*

5 The Bible

6 Dr Peter O'Shea & Robert Falzon *The Father Factor.*

2

Daniel Ang
Pilgrimage in fatherhood & faith

I write this on the Feast of Pentecost in the strangest of years, huddled in the home where I have spent much of the past few months on account of the global Coronavirus pandemic. It has been a time of disruption and reflection as everyday realities – schedules, plans, interactions, habitual ways of living – have been swept aside by a most unexpected phenomenon and only now are starting to regather. Life before the Coronavirus seems a distant memory.

However, just a week before Covid-19 shut down our best-laid

(Above)Daniel Ang with his father, Keong Heng.

(Below) Daniel with his parents, Keong Heng and Kah Chin, his wife Sara and his children, Noah and Isabella.

plans, my family was fortunate enough to celebrate the fiftieth wedding anniversary of my parents, my 76-year-old father, Keong Heng Ang, and my 73-year-old mother, Kah Chin Chong. It was a surprise celebration that brought together fifty of my parents' closest friends, replete with a traditional nine course wedding banquet. There were Chinese lion dances, speeches, memories of yesteryear and of course dancing – for my parents, always dancing.

It was an opportunity to give thanks for the marriage of my parents upon which family life for my older brother and I was built, and which still today shapes our own marriages and families. The longer we live and the more our families grow, the more of their presence we find layered within our lives. This is tradition in its best sense, the handing on of those things that are precious, the sacred gifts that make us who we are, from one generation to the next.

As I was preparing my salutary speech for the occasion, it struck me how much each of my parents, but especially my father, has contributed to my faith and outlook as a Christian and a father of two children, now eight and four years old. Though my parents are not Christian and come from practising Buddhist and Taoist families, and while the cultural outlook of my Malaysian-Chinese parents is quite different from my own experience, being Australian-born, their influence on my faith and life commitments has been palpable. I trace this pilgrimage in fatherhood and faith to my paternal grandfather, Ang Lian Kooi, though in memory he serves more as foil than example.

Origins

My grandfather was born in Johore, in the south of Malaya, on 23 November 1912, broad and heavy-set though only 5'3" tall. With thick black hair combed back from a wide and intimidating face, his serious demeanour was punctuated by large, thick eyebrows that made him look severe. However, despite this appearance he was in character a social man, so outgoing that my father barely remembers him ever being home.

As a young man, my grandfather moved to settle in Taiping, an understated township in Malaya's north, situated in the shadows of Mount Larut (then called Maxwell Hill), between the dividing hill ranges of Peninsula Malaysia in the east and the waters of the Straits of Malacca in the west. Tin was discovered in the town, then named Klian Pauh, in the mid-1850s and soon mines populated the region, feeding the demand of the emerging tin canning market and the Industrial Revolution in Europe.

The rich sources of tin brought an influx of miners to Taiping, including thousands of Chinese labourers from southern provinces of China such as Fu Jian and Guang Zhou. A series of wars soon broke out between rival Chinese groups in the 1860s and 1870s before the British intervened, eventually renaming the town 'Taiping'; Mandarin for 'everlasting peace'.

Another consequence of this mineral wealth was the opportunities it provided for merchants to sell and trade their wares, including linen and crockery. It was this trade that brought my grandfather to Taiping. His older sister, Kim Muan, had set up a small crockery shop on Jalan Kota, the town's main road, and the young Lian Kooi soon joined her, assisting with inventory, sales, deliveries and the general upkeep of the store.

With a working knowledge of Malay, Cantonese, Mandarin, Hokkein, Tamil and English, my grandfather made friends quickly and widely, and spent long afternoons riding around the edge of the Taiping Lake Gardens on his motorcycle, stopping at roadside stalls for cups of *teh tarek*, strong black coffee, and tailored cigarettes.

This idyllic period was shattered when the Japanese arrived on the beaches of Kota Bahru in December 1941, just a few hours before the bombing of Pearl Harbour. Exporting vast quantities of rubber and tin to markets both near and far, Malaysia was a country of strategic importance for the American, British and Dutch freeze on raw supplies to Japan in July 1940 quickly turned Malaysia into a precious jewel in South East Asia. With Britain preoccupied defending itself from the threat of German invasion, the Japanese quickly overwhelmed the British forces and by February 1942, both Malaysia and Singapore were firmly in Japanese control.

It was this event, above all others, that was to shape our family's life for it was in the midst of the Japanese invasion of Malaysia that Lian Kooi came to marry my grandmother, the 19-year-old Khor Lai Fong, originally from Penang.

Upon their arrival at Kota Bahru the Japanese armed forces moved south to Kuala Lumpur, occupying or destroying small towns along their course. The young girls from these towns were frequently taken captive by military units and either raped, murdered or turned into *ian'fu* or 'comfort women' whose sole purpose was the sexual gratification of their captors.

In Taiping, hundreds of families immediately fled to the relative safety of the surrounding jungle, entrusting themselves to these difficult depths. Lian Kooi and Lai Fong were among the hundreds of fleeing villagers and, fearing the advancing Japanese army, the young family friends were hastily married in the hope to protect Lai Fong from the threat of capture and exploitation.

Eventually separated by the invading forces in 1944, my grandfather would endure torture at the hands of his captors while my grandmother was imprisoned with her newborn son, my father, before the war came to its welcome end.

Home away from home

In the years that followed, the Ang family grew to a total of 11 with eight more children born in quick succession. However, as time went, on Lian Kooi was rarely seen at home. It is sadly one of my grandfather's legacies that he was conspicuous by his absence, a lesson that was not lost on my father who determined to build a different kind of future, to seek out a life and education through the guidance of friendships rather than the counsel of family.

The small wooden shack in which the growing family lived is still there today, at the start of Thompson Road on the west side of Taiping. Without running water, the cabin was set on the side of a long block of land dominated by the landlord's mansion that stood at its centre. The cabin was made entirely of vertical wooden planks and roofed with a piece of rusted corrugated tin that covered one bedroom and a small kitchen leading out to the neighbouring property.

At night, Lian Kooi, Lai Fong and eight of the children would sleep in the only bedroom while my father took to sleeping alone in the corridor on a fold-up canvas bed. Even in these early days, his place within the family was as one set apart rather than one at home within.

Much of the daily routine of family life centred on collecting firewood and drawing water from the landlord's supply. As the oldest child, my father would collect the water and pour it into a massive urn used to wash the vegetables and cook the rice. Fallen trees and wood from the roadside were valuable commodities and the Ang children would gather as many scraps as they could while running errands for the neighbours at a rate of 20 cents a time.

Home life was a chaotic mix of cleaning, cooking and survival. Amongst it all, Lian Kooi rarely shared a word with his children when present and left the day-to-day care of the ever-expanding family to my grandmother. He worked various jobs with mixed success as a salesman and then a store owner and finally as a taxi driver. It was this last enterprise that would eventually cost him his life.

In those beginning years the Ang family moved from Thompson Road to a modest home near the area known as Pokok Assam. Pokok Assam was a suburb planted with rows of low-cost housing built by the local town council. Still, the modest income Lian Kooi brought home as a driver became increasingly stretched as the family grew in number almost every two years.

The financial pressures brought tension to the house and my grandmother would often reprimand my grandfather for their grim situation, one that he frequently escaped by coming home late into the night. Rumours of womanising and infidelity surfaced but were never aired inside the home and, when he was home, Lian Kooi would often sit down in a corner of the home, somewhat detached, playing a small mandolin and singing songs that echoed through the house.

My parents

It was in the Taiping Green Valley dance hall that my father and mother met on 29 February 1964 at a dance celebrating the leap year. My mother was 17, in only her second year in Taiping, having moved there from the Kinta Valley in Perak, and had only attended the dance at her cousin's insistence. After being introduced through a mutual friend, Keong Heng and Kah Chin joined in the dances that filled the hall with throngs of activity and laughter.

Soon after the dance Keong Heng was helping Kah Chin with

her schoolwork and they set out on their first dates at the local cinema house where they watched *The Sound of Music*, *The Ten Commandments* and westerns starring John Wayne and other American luminaries. My mother enjoyed these outings all the more for they were, in part, a resistance to her aunty's best efforts to match her with young suitors of her own choice. In this way their partnership was born of both love and resistance.

After graduating from school, both my mother and father sought work though opportunities in Taiping were rare. For a while, my father sold encyclopaedias door-to-door and tutored primary school children in maths and English. Other times he would be paid to write letters or complete government forms for friends or neighbours, and later took a part-time job selling insurance policies for American and Chinese companies.

This variety of work continued until the prospect of migration to England emerged as friends undertook the passage with fervour. London had a reputation of offering well-paid, steady work and a number of others from Taiping had already taken the journey as students or nurses. It represented an opportunity for financial security and adventure, far from the limits of small town living.

Soon enough, my father borrowed eight hundred dollars from a cousin and made an application to train as a student nurse at Harperbury Hospital in Hertfordshire, an institute for adults with learning disabilities. His application was approved and in September 1966 my father set sail, leaving behind Kah Chin for whom he hoped to open up a future and realise the promise of a new life together in London.

At the age of 22, it was a momentous time in my father's life. It marked the beginning of a new life. It also marked the last time he saw his father who died not long afterward in an automobile accident.

My father does not speak of his own father very often. There is no hint of resentment or nostalgia for lost days, however, only the facts. The ultimate legacy of this upbringing and these events on my father was a keen sense of self-reliance and responsibility for his eight siblings, a widowed mother and for his own uncertain future. In many respects these fates were intertwined.

His entrepreneurship was not the product of choice but of circumstance. Whether it was catching fighting fish to sell at market or collecting leftover copper wire from building sites in Taiping, or selling ice creams from a van between hospital shifts at Harperbury, his industriousness and creativity were a necessity, not a luxury. These were traits sorely lacking in his own father from whom it seems my father inherited very little, not only materially but by way of example.

Over the years I have only grown in admiration of my father's independence and capacity for hard work because it has opened a world of possibility for us and for others, his brothers and sisters included. I have no doubt that this role as provider and shepherd of the family came at some personal cost to him for he was inevitably seen by his brothers and sisters less as a sibling and more as a father figure whom they feared as much as they respected.

After being joined in London by my mother in July 1967, Keong Heng and Kah Chin were married in the St Alban's Registry Office on the afternoon of 6 March 1970 in the company of 20 friends and neighbours. My mother wore a white mini-skirt, blouse and jacket while my father wore a new suit bought from a London department store, driving a car borrowed from their neighbour to their reception in a local Chinese restaurant.

My brother Desmond was born four years later and another two years on my parents made the decision to migrate to

Australia following the cessation of the White Australia policy in 1973. When the family of three landed at Sydney Airport in October 1975, my father pulled out a pen and wrote in his pocket diary, "New life starts today."

Fast forward four decades and I remember my father saying as much to me across the kitchen bench at a crossroads of my life, reminding me of the opportunity that is always there to make choices that usher in a new future. How radical this piece of advice is for a man who remains even today the beacon of stability, consistency and security in our own family! Then again, this was the lesson of his life, demonstrated in his ability to make a home wherever he was planted – that it is a requirement of life to change in order to remain faithful, to ourselves, our families and, for the Christian, to the Lord our God.

Born and raised

Following a stint at what was then the Villawood Migrant Centre, and then in a Commonwealth Government unit in Merrylands, our first settled home in Sydney was in Toongabbie, a small suburb in the west of Sydney that drew its name from the Aboriginal word for 'meeting of the waters'. The land there had been owned by the Marist Fathers and later sold to developers from whom my parents purchased their first home in May 1976. This was the home that greeted me when I born in January 1979.

The three-bedroom house on Vianney Crescent was a small but comfortable home with marbled white and brown carpet and open white walls. The living room was just large enough to fit a small orange lounge suite and a television unit fitted with tape deck and record player. At Christmas a small tree would stand proudly in the corner, adorned with reams of tinsel, baubles and even plastic snow that feebly evoked the memories of an English winter.

From the outset in our new home, my parents befriended families from Greece, Italy, Ireland and others from Malaysia too. My earliest memories are of dinner parties in our Toongabbie home, with visitors seemingly from all corners of the earth. My father was able to value that which was outside his own experience and in primary school we were encouraged (almost *ad nauseam*) to 'mix' with others of different backgrounds. At a time of new beginnings and insecurity, when it seemed understandable to cling to the familiar (and many other families we knew did exactly that) we were encouraged to reach outwards and discover new traditions, new ways of being and new ways of living.

In their synthesis of traditional Chinese values and the great variety of Western culture, my parents brought together distinctions with natural ease and I believe nourished us to openness without fear and a freedom without judgement, in essence, to realities beyond our own preference.

It is true that my father could be impatient with my brother and me at times and even severe. Perhaps fuelled by the stresses of work and an acute sense of responsibility, my father's seriousness dominated the atmosphere of the house and his discipline of both Desmond and me meant that at times we surely feared him more than we felt we knew him. However, it is also true that he would mellow with time, a phenomenon noticeable not only to us but to our uncles and aunties who saw my father lighten as the weight of the world seemed to lift with the growing security of our extended family in Sydney and abroad.

In many respects our lives were typical of the migrant experience for our parents worked hard to obtain the financial security they never enjoyed, laboured to provide for our needs as well as those of family members back home. As I shared on the occasion of their wedding anniversary, though it is a journey of economic migration that is not uncommon in Australia it demands personal courage, risk and determination. It demands faith in the assurance of things hoped for, to realise a future that is never so definite before it is actually reached. Largely unconscious of itself, it was a pilgrimage that met the challenges of the moment with the promise of better days and the plain hard labour that such expectation demands. I believe this is one of my father's greatest forms of witness to my brother and me – the virtue of hope and the resilience to work towards that future.

The stories we live by

Of course, there will always be lessons we learn from our parents that, in time, we unlearn or amend as we live out our own paths in circumstances that are inevitably different. It was natural that the ghost of scarcity lingered in the experience of my father and my mother and while relative abundance and opportunity was our gift, it was underwritten by their hardship.

It was their experience of poverty and fear of its return that, looking back, sedimented into a culture of achievement within our family, not as satisfaction of a job well done but almost as a means of escape from life's uncertainties. As many Chinese Australians are taught, directly or implicitly, it is achievement that will hold us back from the precipice.

What's more, in the Asian-Australian experience the ancient Confucian stress on effort as the source of success can find itself aligned with the 'new heaven' promised by a Western culture of consumption and accumulation.

However, as we grew into our senior years at school, my brother and I learned that a high-performance culture inevitably exhausts and the promise of this new heaven rings hollow. The ethic of mere life enhancement can leave one feeling empty and restless. Mere addition can be no substitute for personal growth.

As was made clear from the experience of other Chinese families we knew, staying on the allotted treadmill would prove too much for some. In these cases sheer effort and dogged discipline did not deliver *shalom* but defeat, quickly followed by the onset of shame. Others more resilient would run the race and attain social respectability but at personal cost. This cost was progress without presence, making without meaning.

I think it is true, on account of the circumstances of poverty experienced by past generations, that the emphasis in childrearing in those times fell more heavily upon the questions of how to earn a living over and above the art of learning how to live.

While the discipline of hard work ran through my bones, inherited from my father's diligence, it was this privileged hunger for a larger story by which to live that ultimately led me to the Gospel of Jesus and to the Catholic faith. This is not to say my father's influence did not shape that faith for he planted the seeds of hope and self-giving love which I now recognise to be of Christ. However, faith has placed that inheritance within a wider perspective, within the divine assurances expressed by Psalm 18, allowing us to feast on its fruit while tempering its utopian or more excessive tendencies.

I see in the Word of God – embedded as it is in the story of the patriarchs, a nation, a people – a story of a family also anchored in a past. It is also a story that is located in a people's longing amidst poverty of spirit and hostility of circumstance.

In this story, however, the risks and contingencies of history are not overcome by performance or accumulation. These contingencies are not overcome at all in fact but are instead engaged by a form of trust and divine knowing called faith. This knowing burst the boundaries of calculated ends and progress bordered by fear. The Gospel offers instead a plenitude that is accessed by our surrender of any veneer of self-sufficiency.

Perhaps differing from my father, my entry into the way of faith enabled the discovery that our own worth lies not in self-sufficiency or promethean effort but in an encounter with a divine other. For the Christian finds and grounds life in the reception of divine gifts, not the gaining of social acceptability.

Jesus, in his life, death and rising, reveals authentic progress to be neither self-development nor a program of action. The Gospel stands as an invitation to enter into the achievement of God's promise in the risen Christ, he who loved us first and who is our abiding hope and stay.

So as I give thanks for the hard-won legacies of generations past and the opportunities they have enabled for our family, I also recognise that this gift need not terminate in a desperate ethic of performance and accumulation. Achievement is not the basis of self-worth. The lessons and legacies of their toil and exertion, hardship and heroism, can be received as a summons to give of ourselves to others with the abundant love that underpinned their sacrifice. The undeserved graces of our forebears are invitations to live by a story bigger than even their imagination, to live for him "who by the power at work within us is able to accomplish abundantly far more than all we can ask or imagine" (Ephesians).

Embracing the way

Attending public schools, both primary and secondary, and with virtually no contact with Christianity throughout this time, I was an unlikely candidate for religious faith and ignorant of its reality, to the extent that I was not aware that there were denominations or divisions within it. To be honest if I had been schooled in God, between mathematics and history, trigonometry and geography, I sense I would have shown him equal disregard.

Though my grandparents were avowed Buddhists and Taoists, my parents did not bring any religious conviction to Australia or to our family life. While not averse to religion, the subject was not a topic of dinner table conversation and so life went on without such considerations.

As I journeyed through adolescence and began to 'kick against the goads' I grew in self-imposed distance from my family. Immaturity, self-absorption and dissolute living were a part of this story which is better left implicit.

It was at the age of 20, beset by a somewhat hardened heart and unforgiving exterior, that I came to consider Christian faith. What had set off this possibility was my attendance at the baptism of a friend whom I had known since high school, in the parish of St Bernadette, Castle Hill, in Sydney's northwest.

It was in the pews of this parish at the Easter Vigil that I heard the Litany of the Saints for the first time. I did not know much of Mary, or St Francis, St Joseph or St Peter, or the roll call of other names that followed, but I could assume that each had done some good in their lives, had undoubtedly lived for others on account of their beliefs. I had no sense of the personal source of their faith but I was nevertheless moved by their impact and the conviction of their living, now celebrated and recalled by this community of faith. They had truly lived, not for themselves but a greater horizon which I would learn to be a person, the beloved Son of the Father.

Over the coming months, I would ask gentle questions of my newly baptised friend whenever we crossed paths, a Thomas prodding at the truth of his experience. I began to attend Mass once in a while as a spectator and then as an observer, and sometimes even found myself there for weekends in a row.

The parish priest was a kind and welcoming man, possessing a charism of care and dedication that endures to this day. He fostered and worked hard at intentional relationships and invited people to become involved in the life of the parish with an audacious persistence which usually won the day.

When I disappeared from the pews for weeks or even months, I would receive a call from him, with an invitation to drop by for a coffee if I was in the area or simply to ask about my welfare. He encouraged me to connect with the youth leaders he had fostered in the community but this for me seemed a stretch and, living in the inner city as I was, the drive to the suburbs for church was not yet convincing. At this time, I occupied a middle position, open and curious, even attracted by the Christian life, but well short of any formal commitment.

What brought forward the decision for faith in the following new year was, as for many, the immediacy of an encounter with Christ that was personal, irreversible and uninvited. The embarrassment of such an experience is that it can ring with an air of irrationalism or illuminism.

Nevertheless, in the early hours of a morning, while driving home from a night of indulgence with friends, on a regular road near my parents' home, there was an overwhelming experience of divine friendship and embrace, a vivid sense of presence, a commanding grace. In the quiet of that morning, typical in all other respects, I prayed for the first time, "Thank you for waiting for me for so long."

Sometimes we are granted an experience that we spend the rest of our lives catching up to and entering into – in this case a sense of intense presence paired with the gift of tears which I have since come to know as the fruit of love. If it is any assurance of my usual sobriety, I have not had such an experience since.

The journey to baptism was difficult as it demanded a turn towards a new future that again differed from family expectation and a turn away from illusions of self-sufficiency and misplaced desire. The Australian Cistercian, Michael Casey, memorably shares this process of conversion. "It is not faith in God that is hard, but the renunciation of illusory faith in myself. To turn toward God means, first, turning away from whatever is untrue or delusory – no matter how much comfort it brings."

With the relationship with my father and mother somewhat strained at the time, I struggled to find even the most basic words to tell them of my decision to be baptised and when I did, on its eve, they fell out with awkwardness and insecurity.

My father, as was his tendency, did not utter a word while my mother reacted with slight surprise and gently inquired when it was all going to take place. In the end, my mother, a nurse, had to work the following night while my father stayed at home. I still wish I could have explained myself better.

I was grateful for the small group of friends and sponsors that gathered for my baptism that drizzly Wednesday night in November 1999. I took the Christian name 'Matthew' because he was a disciple not in spite of, but because of, his being a sinner.

The following years saw my involvement in parish youth

ministry, a commitment that endured for some fifteen years and brought treasured experiences of prayer, friendship and service that remain important even today for what they taught and gave to me. I soon discovered the spiritual masters including Thomas Merton, read Scripture with eagerness, the Gospels and the psalms above all else, and explored other spiritual luminaries and practices in a haphazard plunge into the Catholic tradition. Eventually I enrolled in night classes in theology at the Catholic Institute of Sydney to learn more about my new-found faith, Christ and the Church which proclaimed him.

In time I was married in the church of my baptism, to my wife who also entered the Church as an adult. In the years that followed I worked in media and advertising before taking up my first Christian role with the Daughters of St Paul and seven years later with the Diocese of Parramatta, in Sydney's west.

It was during this time that our son was born, along with some anxiety about my preparedness to be the kind of father that I sought to be. Of course, this romantic ideal of parenting was unclear to me but surely lay between the best of my own father and those influences which by this time had left their deep impression on my outlook – my godfather and best friend, the parent couple of our parish youth ministry and priest friends who were spiritual fathers and companions.

When our son was baptised at the same font that initiated his mother and father years earlier, I committed my new fatherhood to Christ and to the prayer of Mary and of the newborn saint Arielle, my god-daughter who had been born on the same day as our son but who lived only eleven precious days on this earth.

Reflecting on who I have sought to be for my son and daughter as a father, I have been striving above all to ensure that they take confidence in my presence and love. Standing on the shoulders of my own father, I am able to offer our children more time and attention than perhaps past generations. Like my father I am striving to provide for their material needs but also offer them a witness to the ordinary, often understated joys of Christian living before they inevitably encounter its suffering and self-emptying demands.

I try to speak to my children about Jesus on the way home from school. I have had the good fortune to take them to Rome and Florence, places where Christ has been met and saints have walked, and to offer our constant gratitude to God for the blessings of the opportunities we have and the challenges we have been able to meet. My prayers as a father are of course for their present and their future, and for my own father and mother who are unwell.

In the past years my father and I have grown in intimacy and through the inevitable ups and downs of relationship we have emerged closer than ever. This growth in our relationship has in no small part been enabled by my Christian faith which has opened up a new horizon of appreciation with me for what is good though imperfect, whether that be my father, the life of the Church and my own Christian fatherhood which grows in its depths and changes in its demands.

At the celebration of my parents' wedding anniversary just weeks ago, I could share with my father that I love him and that my brother and I, and their circle of friends, have been recipients of fifty years of marriage which has given them more than they could have expected and more than for which we can give thanks. My mother's care and daily dedication to my father and our family have been paired with the presence of integrity, dedication and love embodied by my father who nurtured our lives and my Christian faith. He has taught me the gift of being a father by being, first of all, a faithful son.

Tips for fathering

Pray for the gifts of discernment, courage and resilience, to step fully awakened into the opportunities of relationship we have in our lives as fathers, to forgive where forgiveness is needed, to love when the loving seems hard and to praise and surrender to God with thanksgiving and expectation for what he seeks to accomplish in our lives.

The future is shaped by our past and present as fathers – it can be a great gift to explore more of our own father's history and that of our families to anchor ourselves in their good and make changes in our fatherhood to avoid or amend their limitations.

Create small moments of connection with our children, say to them those things that matter, tell stories about faith, challenge and adversity with the virtue of hope, and be patient in times of challenge, with our children, our wives and ourselves, knowing that the Lord is patient and loving with us.

Four books

St Paul's Letter to the Ephesians
Michael Casey *Toward God: The Ancient Wisdom of Western Prayer*
Henri de Lubac SJ, *The Splendour of the Church*
Thomas Merton *New Seeds of Contemplation.*

3

Doug Black
A life turned around

I remember driving my expectant wife Malia to the hospital – just two of us that later suddenly became three. The birth of our first daughter, Jess, was life-changing in so many ways but I remember holding Jess for the first time as a father, feeling an overwhelming love for her and knowing, from that point on, I would do everything to love and protect her ... no matter what!

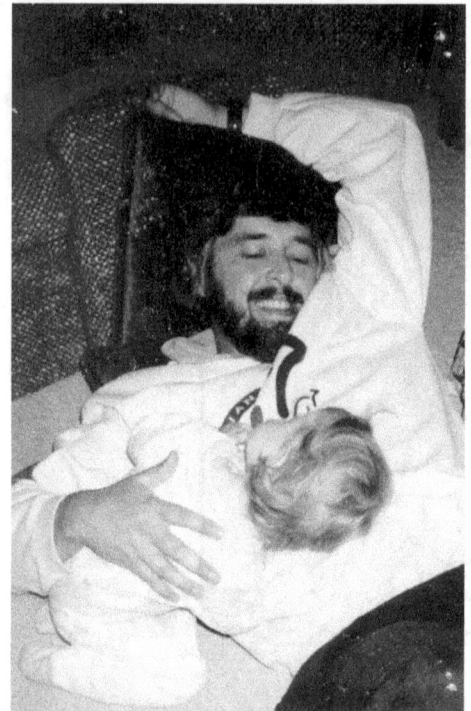

Doug and baby: Doug and his daughter, Jess.

Doug, his wife Malia and their daughters, Claire, Emma and Jess – and the dogs, Sunny and Walter!

But how would I convert this innate feeling of love and protectiveness into action so that, for Jess, and later Claire and Emma, I would be the best father I could be? I'm afraid to admit that I hadn't really thought about this in great depth before Jess was about to be born. I hadn't read any books on the subject of fatherhood. I just assumed I'd 'wing it' based on my own childhood experience of my father and the experience I had gained in life over the previous 34 years.

Little did I know that by taking that approach I would be destined to repeat some paternal behaviours that would not be conducive to my aim of being the best father I could be for my three beautiful daughters. It took help from my patient and understanding wife and the experience of a life-changing event to help me get closer to my aim of becoming a good father to the girls.

So, what were some of those childhood and later life experiences that were destined to influence me as a husband and father?

As a child and teenager, I had a wonderful life; some would call it a blessed life. Until I was about 16, our family (my parents and my older brother, Graeme) lived in Toronto, on the shores of Lake Macquarie on the central coast of NSW (yes, there is another Toronto outside Canada). My school life was generally trouble-free, I had lots of friends and I had the privilege of being able to go fishing, snorkelling, sailing or surfing after school and on weekends. Life for this growing boy was literally a breeze.

My parents, Hamish and Isabel, were Scottish and both born in the early 1920s. My father was an accountant and was fortunate to avoid having to fight in the Second World War because of his poor eyesight. He courted my mother when they were both living in a town near Glasgow called Bishopton and a few years after the war they bravely left their homeland as young newlyweds to come to Australia and make a new life.

Since you are reading this book you are well aware of the enormous influence parents have on their children. I inherited some things from my parents that I was very glad about but also some that were not helpful to me as I grew up.

Let me explain. Many Scots of my parents' generation were not very open with their emotions.

In fact, a photo of my parents holding hands is a very unusual thing for me to reconcile because I can honestly say that I never witnessed my parents showing any obvious outward signs of affection at any stage when I saw them together.

I believed they did love each other. They rarely fought but neither of them was comfortable in outwardly expressing their love for each other or their love for my brother or me. My father was an honest and hard-working man whose life centred around providing for my mother and his two sons. In my later life I would read a book that I found incredibly enlightening and helpful, *The Five Love Languages* by Gary Chapman. Chapman describes the five ways to express and experience love as "love languages". These five ways are words of affirmation, acts of service, receiving gifts, quality time and physical touch. Clearly, after discovering this, I realised in retrospect that my father's love language was definitely "acts of service". Unfortunately, because of his strong work ethic and dedication to his company and those he worked with, he was very often occupied with work or away on business trips.

Communication within our family was never very open or common and I struggle to recall any significant family discussions, particularly if it involved an emotional or controversial topic. Emotion was best kept hidden and topics like love and religion were never discussed – and certainly nothing to do with sex!

I assumed that my parents discussed these issues between themselves but even that assumption came into question based on one experience that I recall when I was in my second year of university. I was still living with my parents in Melbourne, just the three of us, and at some point, my mother stopped talking to me and my father for over a month! She cooked our meals, washed and ironed our clothes but she just would not talk to us. There was no known argument or issue and her response to several queries from me or my father as to what was wrong was either that she would shrug her shoulders and walk away or simply ignore us! I'm sure, my father in private would have been trying to ascertain the reason for this behaviour but at one point, after at least a couple of weeks of this, my father came to me and asked me, "Doug, do you know what's wrong with your mother?" I thought "Really!?" Was the level of their communication so bad that he had to ask me what I thought was going on with my mother ... his wife? In retrospect, I think it was maybe a menopausal issue for Mum but eventually she began speaking again. The episode was never discussed and to this day, I have no idea what it was all about!

So, following my parents' example, I simply learned to hide emotion and keep my deeper thoughts to myself while maintaining an exterior that divulged little of anything that was going on inside. I just assumed that this was normal behaviour and it was with this background that I was brought up.

My idyllic lifestyle came to an abrupt halt as I was approaching puberty when my father had a career move to Melbourne in the early 1970s. I was forced to leave my life at the lake and a co-ed high school in Toronto where I had many friends and had just begun noticing girls to a life in suburban Melbourne at a large boys' school without any friends at all. As my older brother had just finished secondary school, he stayed back in Newcastle when we moved to Melbourne and so, without knowing anyone near my age and my father heavily involved in the demands of his new career path, I was left to work out what life was all about by myself.

I loved and admired my father and I know he loved me, despite my putting him and my mother through some trying times later in life, but I don't recall any time that he actually told me that he loved me. And equally, I don't think that I ever really told him that I loved him.

He helped and supported me in my pursuit of sport and my academic efforts and took me to a number of local soccer matches when I was younger. In the early stages of our new life in Melbourne when I was yet to establish a group of friends, he and I would go to a VFL game together once a month or so. We even built a boat together which is a challenge to any relationship, but the conversation was always about superficial things - we never talked about any 'deep' issues. This was by no means just his fault because I didn't raise any of these issues myself. He was a generous and caring man and, despite our relationship not being as open and deep as, in retrospect, I would have liked, there was an unspoken love, respect and guidance that helped me in the development of my ideals, beliefs and work ethic. He was devoted to his family but was also devoted to his work and his responsibilities to those he worked for and those who worked for him. Consequently, I simply accepted my relationship with him as one of respect and assumed love but not one in which I could discuss sensitive and personal issues. Ultimately, my father's wealth of knowledge and experience went untapped and my own life experience and advice from my immature and inexperienced mates had the greatest influence on my early adult development.

Later in life, my parents lived in a house on the Murray River that we built, joined to the house where my wife, Malia, and later our three daughters, lived. It was a conscious decision to share the property with my parents as my father's eyesight was failing and we thought he would need support in the future. We had no idea that this support would be needed a lot sooner because, not long after moving into the house, Dad was diagnosed with lymphatic cancer. After two courses of chemotherapy and nursing him at home, it eventually became too much for us to look after him, particularly for my mother. Malia was pregnant with our third daughter and surprise, surprise, I was generally away with my work.

We finally had no choice but to have him cared for in hospital. Initially, for the pain, he was given morphine but he suffered major hallucinations and would often behave like a little boy telling me that there were people who came up from under the hospital at night trying to scare or even kill him! He was genuinely frightened and so we eventually elected to take him off the morphine but then nothing helped him with the pain. I recall one day when I visited him, he said to me, "You put down dogs all the time so why can't you do the same for me?" It was a distressing time.

He deteriorated while I was in Africa at an ostrich vet meeting (see below) but he kept asking Malia and my mother when I was due back home as he wanted to "tell me something". I remember pondering and anticipating the "something" that he wanted to talk to me about on my return, thinking this will be a watershed moment in my deeper relationship with my father. On my way back home from the airport, I called in to see him at the hospital late in the evening. I was the only one with him at that hour and I could see that he was greatly relieved that I was finally there to see him. Despite being very weak he managed to update me on some minor financial issue that, to me, was really of no consequence at all but, being an accountant, to him, I guess it seemed very important.

I was torn between the disappointment of the subject matter and my overwhelming concern for his condition and well-being. For the first time that I can remember in my adult life, I told my father that I loved him that night but I'm not sure if he heard it as he had fallen asleep. He died a few hours after I left him. I wasn't there. He was alone but I cling to the belief that God was there to comfort and welcome him.

As a young adult, I was always very good at writing words of great gratitude and praise on cards at Christmas or birthdays but, until that night in the hospital, I had never actually told my parents how I felt about them face to face. Do you know the first time as an adult that I told my mother that I loved her? It was after attending my first menALIVE weekend only a few years ago (more of that later). I'm not sure she remembers that time because unfortunately, she doesn't remember much at all anymore. Alzheimer's is a cruel disease for the loved ones of the sufferer.

Since that time I try to tell her that I love her every time I see or talk to her and amazingly she now responds by telling me that she loves me and, whether she remembers my last visit or not, that is enough.

That is my story as a son but how did that affect my life as an adult? I had a materialistic value system, I was independent in my thinking, quite ego-driven and ambitious and living life 'according to Doug'. Religion was not part of my life and I rarely pondered the meaning or mystery of life.

I graduated as a vet and, soon after, I naively married a girl I had been going out with during the last few years of university. We had broken up before I graduated; the pressure of my final year of university and the obvious flaws in our relationship took their toll. But, several months after graduating, I met her at her brother's birthday party, and we rekindled our relationship – largely driven by my feelings of loneliness. I had no idea what love really was but many of my friends were getting married and we seemed happy enough together – so why shouldn't we get married? Given my family history, I didn't consult my mother or father about any of this, simply informing them of our decision to marry. I think in retrospect even if I had asked them, I probably would have ignored their advice.

Within a few months of marriage, I realised that I had made a very grave mistake, and with the lure of another woman, I walked away from my marriage and 'followed my heart'. To this day, I feel ashamed that my stupidity and immaturity in wanting to be married and my betrayal of her trust had such an effect on the life of my totally innocent wife, Mandy. My behaviour also caused my parents great pain, embarrassment and anguish.

I believed that, after putting that mistake behind me, I had now finally found the 'love of my life' and life would be great again. I was even able to declare privately how I felt about my new partner even though I was still awkward in outwardly showing affection in public. I eventually married her and we seemingly had a great life. We spent several weeks snow-skiing in America and Canada, bought a ski boat, took up karate together and finally purchased a sports car for her…all these material things and exciting times! Life was fun and our love seemed 'perfect'.

We had been married for three years when, very suddenly she became quite distant from me and relatively non-communicative. My inability to discuss personal issues and my determination not to show how I was feeling led me just to let this ride, hoping it would get back to normal very soon.

But, after two weeks, I decided to confront her and try to find out what was wrong. The memory of my experience with my mother not talking for a month was probably a subconscious incentive not to let that happen again. So I 'cut to the chase' and asked her what was wrong, and she simply replied, "I am leaving."

I thought that she meant that she needed to get some food or supplies from the shops – a reflection of how oblivious I was to the fact that we had an issue at all. Once I finally realised the true meaning of those words I was in disbelief and after constantly questioning her as to why this was happening, I discovered that she had begun an affair with our black belt karate instructor! I had not seen any of this coming and it had all taken place in the previous couple of weeks. I was in shock and pleaded with her to stay. She didn't.

I grieved badly; it was like she had been killed in a car accident. I even prayed to a God I didn't believe in but that didn't work, or at least not according to my plan. I can't describe how painful it is to be left alone as a result of infidelity – unimaginably devastating, and added to that, for me, was the realisation now of the effects my actions would have had on my first wife when I walked out on my previous marriage.

My life fell apart. I really struggled to find a reason to get up each morning because there were times when I couldn't see the point of going on. I could see no light at the end of this dark tunnel. I couldn't converse with my parents to any degree because I never had in the past and now I was ashamed of how my life was unravelling. Fortunately, I had two friends … angels … who slowly, patiently and lovingly helped me through this time. I am forever in their debt as I was as low as I had ever been.

Once I started to feel that I could function again and have

another go at life, I just felt shame. I felt like I had a tattoo on my head telling everyone that this idiot has had two failed marriages!

More than two years later, tired of a life of being alone, I built up the courage to ask someone to go out with me. This short relationship was a monumental disaster and it just confirmed my determination never to marry again.

But then I found Malia! Well, in retrospect, God had put her in front of me some time earlier but finally my eyes were opened!

I asked her out for dinner, but we didn't eat anything. We were discussing deep issues that I had never discussed with anyone else before that time. We even talked about a life together and marriage .... yes, marriage!! I couldn't believe it myself. Unfortunately, she told me that we could never be married as she had a strong Catholic faith and, because I had been married twice before, we could not be married in the Catholic Church and so we could not be married at all. I couldn't accept this – not now that I had finally discovered what love really felt like, so I investigated and found that my second marriage was not recognised by the Catholic Church. What a relief! But then I discovered that, to be eligible to marry the person that I finally realised was my life partner, I had to have my first marriage annulled by the Catholic Church. This involved statements from family, friends and even my first wife (an incredibly selfless act for which I am eternally grateful). There were many interviews and questions. It was a long, drawn-out process, a harrowing and stressful experience that took over 12 months, all the while knowing that if an annulment didn't happen, we would never be together.

I was so impacted by the commitment she had to her faith that I decided that I needed to learn more about it. She inspired me and opened my eyes to God. I started to learn about Catholicism over red wine and lamb roasts with our wonderful Irish parish priest and friend, Fr Paddy O'Reilly! I asked questions that Malia had never thought of and we started to grow our faith together – a journey that continues today.

Finally, an annulment was granted and we were free to marry. God, through Malia, turned my life around!

Our life together since has led me to believe strongly that a shared belief in God is a key ingredient to a successful marriage and effective parenting.

A year later Jess arrived, then three years later, Claire and a further two years later, Emma; three beautiful daughters. Coinciding with their arrival, my career had taken a significant turn. My veterinary speciality in birds had somehow led to my becoming one of the few vets worldwide with recognised skills and experience in ostrich medicine and surgery. Despite all the lessons in my life, my ego was being fed once more and I pursued this career path passionately. As a result, I travelled all over Australia and to many countries overseas treating ostriches or delivering talks to vets, ostrich farmers and governments. But that, of course, meant that I was largely absent from home, my wife and my three growing daughters. I guess my father was not the only one with "acts of service" as his language of love. Had I learnt nothing along the way or was the influence of my experience of my own father so strong that it just seemed natural to do this?

I also believe that another key to a beautiful marriage and successful parenting is selfless love and a commitment to a strong partnership.

Malia has both those qualities in spades and particularly in those earlier years she helped make up for my absence. We discussed what was happening and agreed that the ostrich phase would not last for too long and it may be the last opportunity for us to secure our financial future. We decided that I would leave my partnership in a veterinary practice in Melbourne and pursue the 'ostrich path'. She, more than me, knew the consequences that this would have on my role as a parent and her amazing maternal relationship with the girls was such that the negative effects of the temporary absence of their father were lessened. With my mother living (eventually alone) on the other side of a door, the girls also developed a beautiful relationship with their Gran – something that was vital to my mother and the girls and was a great help to Malia in my absence. Because of this our family to the girls was always "Mum and Dad and Gran". Sadly, with the advent of Alzheimer's, the girls have lost the Gran they grew up with some years ago, but her impact will be lifelong for them.

The ending of the ostrich phase was a stressful time for us; even, at one point, threatening our home ownership. We had little income and I began doing locum work for a local vet clinic to try to meet our commitments. Again, my effectiveness in my role as a husband and father was challenged by a feeling of depression that was starting to envelop me. Many days, when there was no work, I just wanted to lie in bed and not face the almost overwhelming difficulties of reality. I knew that I could get a job as a veterinarian in Melbourne but our love of life on the river on our beautiful property and our country lifestyle were too much to give up. The work slowly increased, enough for us to survive but the owner of the local vet clinic where I was working announced that she wanted to sell the practice.

As much as we did not want to do it, we realised that, if we didn't buy it, I would have no work and we would have to sell up and move to Melbourne. We borrowed more money and purchased the clinic and proceeded to turn what had been almost a 'hobby' practice into a viable business. Malia did all the administration for the clinic and I proceeded to build it up. As in the ostrich phase of our lives, we worked incredibly well in partnership but this again meant endless hours for me at the clinic and answering calls at any time of the night and on many of public holidays – even interrupting Christmas Day and birthday celebrations. We also seemed to be constantly under financial pressure to develop the business and pay wages for our growing number of vets and vet nurses but at least I was at home more and could finally spend more time with the girls.

I developed a ritual of taking them with me to the vet clinic on Sunday mornings to treat any animals and answer any calls. This gave Malia a chance to have a little time off from the demands of being a busy Mum and it gave me some quality time with the girls. The girls played in the clinic while I worked and afterwards I would buy them a soft drink and a Yowie chocolate treat (that contained a plastic toy of an Australian wildlife animal that had to be assembled) and, as long as an emergency call didn't interrupt us, we would chat and play in the local park before driving home. These were special times for us and helped me stay close to the girls despite the demands of building a veterinary practice. I cherished my time at home with Malia and the girls, but they witnessed my feelings of anger and frustration when an after-hours call dragged me away. I tried to hide the effect it had on me, but I know there were times when they had to witness my venting my frustration and I deeply regret that.

I believe that parents must be consistent and unified in their approach to decision-making and discipline when bringing up their children.

This may sound ridiculous, but Malia and I modelled some of our parenting on how we approached puppy training. Our daughters always knew where the boundaries were, and they were not constantly shifting depending on whether it was Mum or Dad who was defining those boundaries.

One of the other keys to successful parenting for us has been the involvement of the whole family in activities.

We are truly blessed that we could allow the girls to pursue their love of horses and we would all (if I wasn't on call) load up horses and head off to a weekend event. We would camp together and eat meals in the horse float, walk courses together, support each other and laugh and cry together. Looking after the horses also taught the girls a sense of responsibility and discipline that benefited them in their immediate and later lives. We are also lucky enough to live on the river and share a love and passion for water skiing. This bonded us as a family and allowed the girls to invite their friends to come and stay and learn to ski and have fun on the river. This is still something we all do together and they are always special times.

The real love in our family is not only based on a love for each other but, together, we also share a love and passion for many things like animals, nature, the river, skiing as well as spirituality and helping others.

Despite all of these great things happening in my life, my marriage and particularly my relationship with the girls continued to be affected by the influence of my upbringing in that I still struggled to express my true and deeper feelings. Instead, I buried them and avoided the embarrassment of appearing vulnerable and openly affectionate. I struggled to overcome this, despite really wanting to be more expressive with them. Again, I had no trouble in writing how I felt about them in birthday cards but frustratingly, I found it difficult to verbalise those feelings.

Despite rejecting several attempts by a friend to get me to

attend a menALIVE weekend in Ballarat, Victoria, I finally relented and accepted the invitation to attend. The impact was life-changing! I remember coming home from this weekend event, being greeted by Malia and the girls at the door and declaring in a loud voice, "I'm alive!" Malia had introduced me to God but menALIVE kick-started my next level of faith awareness and commitment. Since that day, I now feel free to tell Malia and the girls (and my mother as mentioned previously) that I love them! Best of all for me, they all tell me how they feel about me! They are all amazing and inspiring women who make me proud every day.

It's never too late to tell them that you love them!

I have come to realise the power of a father's influence on a daughter. As a son, I should have told my father and mother that I loved them far earlier in life, but it is never too late – even if they are no longer around to hear it or they may not comprehend it! I knew that my father loved me, but I will always regret that he was unable to tell me that to my face and that I failed to do the same for him. I am determined not to make the same mistake again. I want and feel compelled to affirm my wife and daughters in their beauty and their worth, to express the immense pride I have in them and to declare that I am prepared to stand up for them and protect them – no matter what. This has enormous reward for me, but it also significantly reinforces their self-esteem and will have long-lasting and deeply positive effects on their lives as well. We can also now regularly discuss deep emotional and spiritual issues and, through this, they have all helped me become a better man, a better husband and a better father. Most important of all, I now have no problems in telling each of them that I love them deeply. I hope never again to miss an opportunity to do that.

I have made some bad life choices in the past and, despite

feeling beaten at times, God has always given me new life and a new path and reason for hope. There are, and always will be, challenges and I continue to make mistakes, but I know that my life is blessed. The love for, and of, my family is evidence of that.

Doug's fathering tips
- A shared belief in God is a key ingredient to a successful marriage and effective parenting.
- A beautiful marriage and successful parenting are based on selfless love and a commitment to a strong partnership.
- Parents must be consistent and unified in their approach to decision-making and discipline when bringing up their children.
- Try to foster a shared love of many things together as a family.
- Never miss an opportunity to tell your children, your spouse and your parents that you love them … it's never too late!

Doug's recommended reading
- Meg Meeker *Strong Fathers, Strong Daughters: 10 Secrets Every Father Should Know*
- Gary Chapman *The Five Love Languages: The Secret to Love that Lasts*
- Richard Rohr *The Universal Christ: How a Forgotten Reality Can Change Everything We See, Hope For and Believe.*

John Brady and his wife, Linda.

Family: John Brady, his wife Linda, and their children, Joshua, Shane, Michael; (front) John, Caitlin, Lara, Linda.

4

John Brady
Solidarity, not sympathy, is what men need

To write one's story should simply be a matter of recall and some disciplined writing – right? Oh, how I wish it was that simple! We suppress so much of our story, so our recall becomes some form of success script where we are the hero – or at least a warrior who is still standing, having fought off the demons.

For me, this was not the case. Recalling the story I have lived has brought back incidents and events I had suppressed in the backrooms of my memory, thinking I would never visit that room again. The hardest aspect was opening the door to those long-forgotten rooms. The feelings associated with those particular times, both pleasant and horrible, erupted with the same force and presence as when they occurred.

I started to write this story in late February and now it is 4 May and the first words are hitting the paper.

My first learning, or perhaps it is more accurate to say 'wisdom' I have had to learn over and over again is, "Unresolved issues never die; they just lie buried to surface in an uglier way at another time."

I don't know what it is about blokes. We handle difficult issues lightly and put them behind us as quickly as we can so we can get on doing life, rather than thinking about or reflecting on life. What does this particular event mean or what is it trying to teach me? If you live long enough, and I am 63, you can end up with a lot of unresolved stuff left behind you. It's just waiting for the day you are going to stop and deal with it. If you are too slow, it deals with you!

Much of this chapter will be stories where I wasn't the hero – in fact, I created shit storms. How did I deal with them and what lessons have I learned? I'm continuing to learn. This is a collection of stories on my journey to maturity as a man. A journey I am still on!

I take solace from the line in the film, *The Best Exotic Marigold Hotel*: "Everything will be alright in the end so if it is not alright it is not the end."

So here goes.

I was born on 17 March 1957 in the small Victorian goldfield town of Castlemaine. The 17 March is St Patrick's day. This Irish theme, a link to my heritage in County Cavan, has followed me all my life; sometimes in joy and celebration; other times in melancholy and anger. But more about that later.

I was born the eldest of five children to loving parents. They were the product of an Irish Catholic Australian upbringing in the first half of the 20th century. My parents were poor, hardworking, community-minded, politically involved and they enjoyed a cold drink on a hot day. Actually, it didn't have to be that hot!

While the birth of their first child should have been a moment of unbridled joy and pride, it was also a crucible that brought many difficult issues to the surface. My mother had lost her sister to rheumatic fever only a few years earlier and her father to a stroke only a few months earlier. Being the eldest girl of nine children, the household demands left little time for grieving. I was a honeymoon baby who fortunately didn't arrive prematurely, as my mother was certain it would have caused a scandal with the old ladies at St Mary's Castlemaine who were very good at maths.

My birth was particularly difficult and triggered a severe dose of post-natal depression. This, coupled with the unresolved grief, proved to be a volatile cocktail, spiralling Mum into a decade of poor mental health. It came with a side dish of stress-related epilepsy. Several times my mother had to be hospitalised.

Before I talk about the impact this had on me and my father, it is important to note this decade of poor mental health did not define my mother. It was a difficult season of her life, but she went on to live a joy-filled life of contributing and much love. It was an important lesson I learned from Mum. We all have winter seasons in our lives, but spring does come. The cold desolation of winter melts away to make room for new growth. Difficult times don't last but to get through them, we all need a mate/family member/mentor. They don't need to save us, but also, they won't let us drown, as we navigate our way through difficult times. Solidarity, not sympathy, is what men need during difficult seasons in our lives.

So back to the story; what did this difficult birth and its aftermath mean for a little John and a young father and husband – my Dad? My mother once told me it was six days before she had a chance to hold me and swaddle me. Interestingly, I spent so much of the first 20 or so years of my life looking for affection and attention. I have learned that an unmet need is a powerful motivator. It does not determine us but if we remain unaware, we can operate from our animal brain. This means we forget we have the power to choose our response to feelings and thoughts which might be racing through our mind and body.

Dad was by nature compassionate and very pragmatic. His father was a veteran of World War II, so sharing of feelings or showing weakness was not part of the modelling Dad received from his father. It was more, "You have made your bed son, so you have to lie in it." My grandfather was a tough man and yet incredibly generous. He was 49 years secretary of the St Vincent De Paul conference as well as MC at dances and weddings and other such community events. When I was in my late teens, he asked me how I could think clearly with so much hair hanging from my head. He also told my mate Bluey, who was a gifted guitarist, to learn to play a real instrument like a trumpet!

So, Dad did what he was taught by his father. Work hard and do what has to be done. Look after your family, be of service to your community, keep your troubles to yourself and have fun when you can. This is what I remember Dad doing. When I was only a year old, Dad accepted a promotion to a shoe store in Shepparton and moved there immediately, leaving Mum to cope in Castlemaine. He would return on weekends to see us. Dad was doing what was necessary to set up the family to be able to live. After several months my mother and I joined Dad in Shepparton where I spent the rest of my childhood and teenage years and where Mum and Dad lived for 40 years.

Dad had a clear focus, or to me seemed to have a clear focus – make the family secure. Dad worked two, sometimes three jobs at a time so he could provide food for the table, pay for medications and get a deposit on a home. I remember when we moved into our first home in the number three housing commission area in north Shepparton. Dad took such pride in the presentation of the house. There were always fresh flowers growing in the front yard, the lawns and edges were well kept, our vegetable garden was prolific, as well as having generous fruit trees. There was always a project on the go, whether that was renovations, painting, wallpapering or just cleaning up. I often complained about having to do the work, but Dad would always reply with, "It's work we do as a family – and you're the oldest so you need to do more." While I would complain, underneath I loved spending the time with Dad. Dad worked hard but always finished the day with a cold drink and a thank you. I loved those moments with him.

However, these times were far too sparse for a young John who wanted to know if he was a man or at least growing into one. Dad worked so hard that he often didn't arrive home until seven o clock at night. His energy levels after a big day working were often depleted. I did not have too many times of just fooling around in the back yard with him. The occasions he would play cricket with us kids or kick the football were fantastic. I think he enjoyed them as much as we did.

Life was difficult for Mum with enormous swings in energy and consequent swings in moods. She also had frequent blackouts and the occasional epileptic fit. Being a new young mum in a town where she knew no one must have been difficult initially. Young children never understand the complexity of the human situation and I know we added to Mum's stress with childhood shenanigans and tantrums, especially when we didn't get our way. At times Mum used to complain to Dad about our behaviour, and so instead of having some moments of peace with Dad, we'd get a scolding and were often sent to bed.

Dad was a vivacious man who made friends easily. Dad instantly gets involved in the community. The friends made in these early times at the local parish and local football club were to become family friends for life. During the really difficult times with Mum, these friends would bake, babysit or take us kids for a week to give Dad some respite as well as Mum. Times spent with these families, who incidentally also had a tribe of kids, were some of our best times. I would see Mum and Dad relax, often laughing and singing Irish ballads and feasting on shared casserole dinners or barbecues. For me, and obviously for Dad, having a circle of friends who know the crap you are going through, and who support you, is essential. It was through being part of a community, that Mum and Dad, and consequently we children, survived the wintertime of Mum's life.

As I look to my life as a father, to a certain extent, I duplicated what my father modelled. As a young family, we threw ourselves into the local community, be that church and school, local sporting clubs, or similar. The friends we made then are still some of our closest friends today. So much of what we learn from our fathers is not taught but caught.

Much to the chagrin of my parents, I found secondary school

to be a distraction amid sport, my mates and girls. I went to a Marist Brothers all-boys college with an all-girls secondary college, run by the Mercy nuns, directly across the road. The road between us was like the Korean demilitarised zone, patrolled diligently by the brothers on one side, and the nuns on the other side. Our role, or at least the role I took on, was to get through these watchtowers and connect secretly with one of the girls. Inevitably, I (we) would get caught and be hauled before the principal. It always amazed me that the brothers only seemed to know my surname. I would be caned, my parents informed of my misdemeanour and I would be punished at home. For Mum, this was a major sin to bring our family into disrepute, while Dad, who was cornered between Mum's wrath and his amusement, would scold me, generally without too much conviction. I suspect I was more like Dad than Mum realised.

I was bright enough at school but much to my parents' disappointment, I did not qualify for a scholarship in form two or form four. It didn't mean much to me at the time but as I look back, any financial assistance for Mum and Dad was a big deal. Raising five children and sending them to Catholic schools in those days, as it is today, was expensive so every little bit helps.

My children for the most part found secondary school a distraction as well, but I always tried to give them the big picture around family resources, so they knew what things cost and how they could contribute. We insisted they all get part-time jobs once they were of appropriate age. We paid for their school costs. We also paid the costs associated with one summer and one winter sport and learning a musical instrument, as well as food and basic clothing. If they wanted designer jeans or an Xbox or whatever luxury item, they had to pay for it out of their savings. It was an important lesson for them and for the most part they learned it well.

Year 12 was an interesting year for me. It started with a school retreat at Harrietville up in the snow country. As a cohort of boys, we were looking forward to it for two reasons; firstly it was the only retreat we were to attend in our entire school lives, so we had a curiosity as to what it might entail; secondly, the girls from across the road were to attend also. The retreat was to last five days. The boys had more plans than an architect as to how to fill those five days!

What was to unfold was nothing like we had planned.

For the first session, we all went into a room that was small in size, with a u-shaped set of benches with multicoloured cushions upon which we sat. On the whiteboard in front of us was written the following quote;

"There is a page that aches for a word which speaks on a theme that is timeless."

This a quote from a little-known Neil Diamond album called *Jonathon Livingston Seagull*. This was to be the theme of our retreat. The retreat was run by a Redemptorist team while our teachers, including the two principals, watched on, presumably as wardens.

Even 45 years after this retreat, I still find it hard to explain what happened. For the first time, people dropped their well-maintained egos and masks, and talked honestly about their lives, their insecurities, their hurts and their fears. Not since then have I ever been with a group of people who were prepared to be so honest and vulnerable with one another. When we brought this vulnerability to prayer and singing, something happened. This was 1974, and we did not talk about the Holy Spirit or any of that stuff. We were still trying to be released from a religion that was all about pray, pay, and obey – something with which I had always struggled.

This retreat team talked about the gifts of the Holy Spirit; about a loving non-judgemental God who is always looking for the lost and those on the fringes, and a call on our lives to follow and do the same. Wow! What a power was unleashed; at least for some months and in some cases for a lifetime.

As for me, I tried to play the cool dude for a few days, but the energy to keep up that mask eventually became too much, and I dissolved. All the hurts and insecurities from my early childhood just bubbled out. Much to my surprise, I felt so much better talking about it. I had a sense of support from my mates, not the judgement and ridicule I expected. We so often underestimate our mates' compassion for us. Perhaps the most profound experience for me was a sense of being loved completely, by a power much greater than me. Some called it God, but this was far more extensive and intimate than any notion I had of God previously. The God I was taught about was small and judgemental; this experience was big and overwhelming. My life was to change significantly over the next decade, but this experience never left me. Even as I write today, I can still feel the enormity of that time as if it is fresh again. My closest friends today were in that group of Year 12s, and I am pleased to say we are still able to be honest and vulnerable with each other.

For many in the group, the effect lasted about two months before we got back to the business of completing Year 12, much to our parents' relief. The rest of the year for me revolved around two highs and a low. Despite distractions, I was able to become dux of the college. My marks weren't outstandingly high but in a group with a low bar of academic focus, I jumped the highest.

The second high was a premiership in my under 18 football team. We played in a high standard competition, so to win was a massive team effort. I think we celebrated for weeks.

The low came when a girl I was dating, and with whom I was smitten, though it was best we break up. This blindsided me and sent me into a spin for about a month. The side benefit was that it occurred about six weeks before exams, so study became the way I coped with this big hit. I don't know what it is about us men, but when our relationships break, we always seem to be blindsided somewhat. It often sends us into a spin. It's not just the relationship that breaks, but our sense of self-worth takes a hit as well. We do not deal well with rejection.

These days I work with men who are doing it tough, many thinking of suicide. The number one presenting issue with many of these men is a relationship breakdown. It hits young men particularly hard, but old men also struggle to deal with rejection. I have learned these feelings of rejection don't last, but in the first four to eight weeks they can be intense. If you know a mate going through a breakdown, stay close. You can't fix him (and don't try and set him up with another date!) but you can walk with him until his emotions settle down. This solidarity can be lifesaving.

As a result of doing well in Year 12, I was offered two scholarships; one to Melbourne University to do law and another to Bendigo Teachers' College. My parents were delighted after my having missed the two previous scholarships; this was a big win. I chose law in Melbourne. On the Friday night before I was to leave for university, I was having a few beers with my close mate Paul, who was going to Bendigo. He was trying to convince me not to do law and come to Bendigo with him. I said to him, "Give me three good reasons." He said firstly, "We have a house with a spare bedroom, and we need another boarder so we can afford the rent." I laughed and said, "You will need to do better than that Paul." Secondly, he said, "You are a country boy, you will get lost in the city and it's not really your scene." I told him I was prepared to give it a go and thanks for the vote of confidence. Thirdly he said, "Girls outnumber boys ten to one." I went to Bendigo!

Sometimes the decisions we make in an instant can have lifetime ramifications.

Teachers College provided all the freedom and excitement a young man could desire. Unfortunately, one needed to study as well. I scraped through the first year but by the time the second year came, my life was in a downward spiral. To qualify to pass, you needed an attendance record of 80% in each subject as well as a successful teaching practicum. It is often said, "If you remember the 60s and 70s you weren't there." There was some truth in that for me. I was involved with a group of fun people who loved partying but weren't so big on college. Nights were full of parties with copious quantities of alcohol and drugs as well as girls and lots of music. Sometimes these parties would last for days. When I wasn't partying, I was in recovery. Occasionally, I would go to class.

I found myself losing energy for life and some days I wouldn't get out of bed. To the outside world, I was full of life and fun, but underneath I was flat out paddling, just to stay afloat. I chose not to share my internal struggles with anyone. To this day I am not certain why, but it is one of my regrets as it almost ended my life. You are always perfectly aligned to get the results you get. I failed second-year college, five of the subjects on attendance. My teaching practicum had been outstanding. I guess it was one of the few times I had a clear focus and felt a sense of purpose. I was eventually given a pardon by the Board of Studies to repeat second year, on the proviso my attendance record was at least 80%. I also had my scholarship suspended which meant getting a part-time job to pay for my rent and bills. I picked fruit and carted hay in the early part of the summer before my mate Paul got his Dad to hire me at SPC on the palletiser line. Work was monotonous but the pay was good. We had T-shirts printed, "You don't get much wiser when you work a palletiser."

My return to college for my repeat year started poorly. The partying and late nights had started early, and our house was the party house. My life was in a downward spiral and I felt overwhelmed by feelings of despair and hopelessness. Thoughts of suicide were starting to become more frequent, especially during periods of drug use. One night in early February 1977 I was completely overwhelmed. I left the party and wandered for some time before ending up on the steps of Bendigo cathedral. It was two o clock in the morning and the church was closed. I remember crying out, "God if you really do exist, save me because I am drowning." I woke about an hour later, glad no one had seen me, and went home as if nothing had happened.

On the following Tuesday night, there was another party at our house. A young, attractive first-year college student had come to the party and was sitting in my favourite chair. I used a line on her which had never worked previously; "What if I sit in my chair and you sit on my knee and we will both have a seat?"

I have been married to that girl for over forty years.

A few weeks later it was my birthday and we went on a date. When we returned to my house, a party was underway. Some friends had come with a special joint as a gift for my birthday. It had been laced with a narcotic and it put me into a deep trance. To my surprise, when I awoke many hours later, Linda was still there. She said in loving but firm words, "You can have drugs, or you can have me, but you can't have both."

I have learned that you can't change your circumstances

overnight, but you can change your direction. That morning the direction of my life changed for the better. God did hear my cry and sent his angel to save me – corny I know but so true!

I finished my teaching degree as did Linda and we both took jobs with the Victorian Education Department. At the start of 1980, we married and moved to Melbourne. It was a great time with lots of friends, football, and fun. In October of 1981, our first daughter, Lara, was born. We started what was to be a series of moves in country Victoria and then eventually to Queensland. Over the next seven years, Linda was to give birth to Joshua, Shane, Caitlin and Michael.

Our first move was to Edi Upper in the King Valley, a beautiful part of the world. Linda was raised a city girl and was now living in a remote farmhouse with a newborn baby and no friends. I was teaching in Wangaratta, coaching football, playing tennis and cricket, and fishing in my spare time with my neighbour Fred. Linda eventually made friends, some of which remain friends to this day. For my part, I thought life couldn't get any better. It was only years later when I was saying what a fantastic time it was, that Linda shared that for her, it was the worst of times. I didn't realise because I didn't ask! My life was so full of me that I did not see Linda was struggling. There were glimpses, but I didn't go for the deeper conversation. This was to bite me a few years later.

In 1987, I was offered a role as a school principal in a country Queensland town. I was to be one of the youngest principals ever appointed. Despite being professionally competent, I should never have been appointed to that position as I had not 'gotten over myself'. Nothing strokes the ego like power and influence. The ego can develop its own momentum and it does not like to hear contrary voices. While I did some good work professionally, I became so engrossed in the position that I neglected my marriage, my health and my deep inner life. My professional life was on a steep ascent while my personal life was in a steep descent.

Remember early in the story I said, "Unresolved issues never die, they just lie buried to surface in uglier ways later on"? Now was their time!

After three years in the country, I took a position as principal in Brisbane of a larger school with a history of recent dysfunction. My job was to sort it out. In my mind, I was the man for the job. Gandhi once said, "You can't do right in one area of your life and wrong in another area because life is one indivisible whole." My marriage was under strain as I was giving it no attention – I had become married to my work. Issues from the past started to surface; Linda was crying out for help and attention as were the children. A wave of anger commenced growing inside me which I tried to settle through having a few drinks. Anger and alcohol should never go together. My anger was actually a deep sadness, but I didn't realise that at the time. For men it's OK to show anger, but sadness is a non-approved emotion. Like my father and grandfather before me, I simply sucked it up and tried to cope by drinking. It was a lousy solution.

In 1992, Linda and I separated. We had five young children, all still at primary school or home.

As Dickens said, "It was the best of times and it was the worst of times."

You can't talk yourself out of a problem you have behaved yourself into! This is what I had done for many years without taking an axe to the root of the problem. My desire for attention, a basic need which was unmet as a young child, was being satisfied with my professional life as a school principal as well as other significant positions to which I had been appointed. The sadness I felt as a young child left without attention had turned into anger as a young teenager, then into depression and drug use at college. Now, when I thought I had the world at my feet, my life was starting to unravel.

Initially, I blamed Linda for my situation. We often use those closest as a projection screen of our crap, especially when we will not own it ourselves. I would run miles at night in the dark. Somehow the running gave me peace and for a short time at least, a respite from the constant chorus of inner voices. It was over four months of separation before I finally admitted I needed help. It came in the form of a priest friend and a bohemian nun. They helped me see the root cause of my malaise was actually unforgiveness. I needed to forgive Mum for not being the mother I needed when I was little, and surprisingly, my Dad for not being there when I needed him to help me deal with life as a young boy. Mum and Dad did the best job they could as parents and were, I suspect, totally unaware of the impact these times had on me. Confronting them would have been both cruel and incredibly ungrateful. However, I did need to deal with this issue of forgiveness. With the help of my two friends, I wrote down all the issues on paper. Then, in prayer, I forgave my parents. I then burnt what I had written. It is hard to believe such a simple ritual could be so powerful, but it changed my life.

I learned that one of our first tasks as adults is to forgive our parents for not being perfect. Failure to do so destines you to live your adult life from childhood scripts. This will eventually punish you.

From there I was now ready to work on my marriage. We had been separated for over nine months. Linda had also been getting some help. We came back together. We put together a sort of plan so we would never go back to that place again.

In the plan was a weekend away each year, without children. Apart from being respite, this weekend was to look critically at our progress as a couple and set goals for the next year. We also looked at what our children needed from us over the next 12 months. As was the case previously, you can't change your circumstances overnight, but you can change your direction. Coming back together was a change in direction and we steadily changed our circumstances.

Over the next few years, we made some significant decisions about raising children at these annual weekends away. Without going into the complete context, I've listed them below. These decisions had a profound effect on our children and their growth, as well as on us as parents and especially me as a father.

1. **Adopt our children's friends.** It was important for us that our children's friends felt at home at our place even if we did not particularly like them. We trusted our family culture would impact them, rather than our children being at the homes of people whose values or family culture we did not know. It did mean lots of late-night feeds; purchasing a billiard table and table tennis, lots of camp mattresses, listening to all sorts of music and late-night pickups – and it was worth it!

2. **Raise them to be independent.** It is clear that only independent people can choose an interdependent relationship. If we wanted a long-term adult relationship with our children, they first needed to be independent. This meant having part-time jobs and paying their way some of the time; travelling by public transport; not rescuing them from the consequences of their poor decisions; teaching them to cook, iron, wash; having chores for which they were responsible. The outcome of this was that all our children left home early to go out into the world – sometimes across the world! Now, the relationship we have with them as adults is more precious than gold or silver!

It made the hard yards worth it.

3. **Girls with girls and boys with boys.** As much as we did lots of family stuff, there had to be times when I went with my sons and we did "secret men's business" and Linda went with the girls for "secret women's business". These were special times as a Dad. It ranged from camping trips to interstate adventures, football and movies. Dads need to spend time with their boys so they know they are becoming men.

4. **Be of service.** We needed to help our children understand that service to the poor is the rent we pay for living on the earth. We always sponsored an overseas child. We had an arrangement at Christmas where we had to give the same amount to St Vincent De Paul as we gave to one another. We would pack Christmas hampers and help deliver them. We took any opportunity to serve the community. I am pleased to say all my children are community contributors as adults. It is often flavoured with a strong social justice streak.

5. **Spend time together.** I learned very quickly that children spell love, TIME. We put time aside every school holiday to go on a family trip. When you have five children, there is only one trip you can afford and that's camping. We had regular winter and summer camping trips often with other families. As adults our kids still tell the stories from these trips.

6. **Have dinner together as a family with the TV off.** This was the time when we shared our day, talked about what was coming up and sometimes just laughed together. We always started with grace and included a prayer for the poor. For our children's friends, who were at our place for dinner, this was a very unusual ritual. It was one which had a positive effect on them. Even today, some of our grown-up children's friends comment on how they loved having dinner at our place. Linda was a great cook and that helped!

My life has taken a series of turns that have been both surprising and profound. Nothing would have happened if I had not learned the earlier lessons. I have found if you are faithful in little things, then gradually you are trusted with greater things.

I enjoyed 20 years as a school principal before sensing I was called to do more with my life. I left schools to work in leadership in our parish and in the broader church. It opened up many opportunities that I could not see while I was still in the schooling system. As happened all those years ago on the steps of Bendigo cathedral, God still hears my cry and answers me in surprising ways.

One of those ways was an opportunity to go to Uganda. The lead-up was very unusual. In 2004, I was waking up in the middle of the night after a vivid dream where I was in Uganda. This is surprising, as of all the places in the world I did not want to go, Uganda was number one. In Year 11, my biology teacher, Kanti, was one of the Asians given 48 hours to leave Uganda by Idi Amin. He used to tell us tales of how the guards used to eat the prisoners and other horror stories. I thought that won't worry me because I will never go to Uganda. These dreams went on for several weeks, with my waking up in the middle of the night. Eventually, I gave up and said, "God, if this is you giving me these dreams, will you stop it. I will go to Uganda if I have to, but please stop waking me in the middle of the night." The dreams stopped!

At this stage I had no intention nor invitations to go to Uganda. A board I belonged to had sent the CEO to Uganda to investigate a youth ministry. I was aware of Uganda but thought it had nothing to do with me.

The next month after the dreams stopped, I received three invitations to go to Uganda. I took the least scary, which was to go with the CEO of our board. Without going into all the details, Linda and I went to Uganda, taking our 15-year-old son Michael. It was, to my mind, our one big African adventure and that would be it – tick the 'go to Africa' box.

As I write this paragraph, I have been back to Uganda 23 times. It has changed my life forever. Something happens when you stand with the poorest of the poor and look back at our privileged life in Australia. You cannot look at your life the same way again. It gives your life both perspective and humility. I have also had the honour of taking others and watched them be changed in the process of standing alongside the beautiful Ugandan people.

I mentioned early in this chapter about my Irish heritage. My story would not be complete without acknowledging its impact on my life and the life of my family.

Every year, our family would celebrate St Patrick's day regardless of health or financial situation. Friends and family, near and far, would come to our house for the celebrations which always included lots of singing of Irish songs; dancing the Irish jig; mountains of Irish stew and dumplings with lashings of mashed potatoes; and of course, lots of drinks. Everybody would be dressed in green or at least have a piece of green fitted to their attire. It was my birthday as well, so it took on extra significance for me. We lived in Australia, but we never forgot our Irish roots. In our boys' bedroom was a small sculptured alcove in which a statue of St Patrick sat watching over us. In Mum's words, he was "protecting us from the devil". During a robust pillow fight, St Patrick took a hit and his head fell off, revealing he was hollow inside. While rapid repairs occurred to save us from Mum's wrath at such sacrilege, St Patrick did become the perfect hiding place for our contraband smokes!

In 2003, I went to Ireland for the first time. I remember vividly flying into Dublin airport and being overwhelmed with emotion, as if I was coming home. I have been to Ireland many times since and I always have a similar experience. On that trip, I was able to visit the family farm and the cemetery where my ancestors were buried and go to the local parish church where the Bradys for decades had been baptised, wedded and buried. Ironically, when we were there, the parish priest's name was Fr Phillip Brady.

Our family trees are full of wisdom, death and tragedy. Wisdom from the lessons we have learned along the way, as well as habits we developed to cope with the tragedies and death. At birth, these are passed down, often unknowingly, through the family gene pool. They become our default program. Our Brady family tree has centuries of persecution, disenfranchisement, war and starvation. It is the fruit of English colonisation in Ireland. So, what was our default program?

It can be compared with the two sides of a coin. On the light side of our ancestral coin is singing, dancing, writing and social activism. All positive traits. On the flip side of our ancestral coin, the dark side, lives melancholy, non-compliance and anger that often spills over into aggression and alcoholism. We are by nature anti-authoritarian, fiercely independent, creative and good fun – what a cocktail! We are more fighters than lovers; however, we are extremely loyal to those we love.

Alcoholism runs down both sides of our family tree back many generations. It's a damaging default program and one which I became sensitive to in the nineties when I was struggling to hold my marriage together. It was the way I (we) numbed the pain, both past and present. Sometimes we drank out of the bottle and other times the bottle drank out of us.

In 1994, I gave up all alcohol for six months. It was my effort to show myself my ancestral default program was not in control – I was! During that six months I was inundated with offers to corporate boxes at key sporting events; invitations to be a guest at lavish functions at wineries and breweries as well as some special dinners at classy restaurants. I was pleased I did not give in to temptation! Unfortunately, these sorts of invitations have been very sparse since that time.

In 2015, I went to Belfast with Linda and my eldest son Joshua. We had the opportunity to visit the peace wall separating the Shankhill from the Falls area. It was the flashpoint of much of the recent troubles. We were able to write our message of peace on the wall. I found this both emotional and cathartic. The fruit of this visit produced inner healing for me. Both our recent past and our ancient past play a role in us all. Once we are aware of how it plays out in our lives, we have the opportunity to do some healing of the family tree. This helps prevent negative default programs from being passed on to the next generation. This was such an important lesson for me.

I am currently the deputy CEO of MATES in Construction. It is a charity working to prevent suicides in the construction, mining and energy industries. Its founder was a man called Jorgen Gullestrup. Ordinarily, we would have little in common. He is a Danish Communist and I am an Irish Catholic. We were brought together by my squash partner, who was Jorgen's nemesis at the industrial level. Jorgen was a union leader and Wayne was an industrial advocate for an employer association. Wayne saw a natural synergy between us which we did not see. He also knew that a good bottle of red over a Breakfast Creek Hotel steak was the perfect bait. Our differences were overcome by our passion to support broken men. Our values were the same even though we came from different backgrounds and philosophies. Our differences, over time, became our complementary gifts, brought together by shared values. From the humble beginnings of just the two of us, and a research report showing we had a problem with suicides, we have grown to sixty staff across Australia and New Zealand. We have trained over 250,000 workers in suicide prevention.

Our message is simple. Most men will not ask for help, so when you see they are struggling, you need to offer help. Persistence and being non-judgemental are essential. It's not your job to fix them, just walk with them. This approach has reduced suicides in Queensland construction by 8% and numbers continue to fall.

This work was never on my radar. When you take time to listen to your deep inner voice (I call that God), you end up in some amazing places, doing some amazing things, with amazing people.

I am now a grandfather of six. I take great joy from supporting my children to be parents and fathers themselves. It is a lot easier being a Pop than a Dad once you let go of the need to control and advise! All Dads, and indeed all parents, need support, but they must be allowed to walk their path. Initially, like a grandad, I thought it was my role to help them not make the same mistakes I made, and of course, give them sage advice. My children are good people, so they didn't oppose me directly, but they did start to exclude me from activities or key decisions. I found things out after the fact. I admire their parenting. They are doing a much better job than ever I did. I realised my role was not to be the parent but to be a grandparent. For me, this means no judgement; advice only when asked; some babysitting; attending key events and being an encourager. I also have lots of fun with the grandkids and do very little discipline – I even have Pop's special lolly jar!

Once I understood I was no longer the parent but the

grandparent, and behaved accordingly, I started to be included in lots more family events. Yes, they do ask for advice at times. My general response is, "What is your intuition saying? Have you had time to pray and reflect on this? Then go with it and you can expect 100% support from me." Interestingly, many of their difficult decisions are well made without any direct advice from me.

One of the activities I love is when the boys have a day out. There is something special at play when generations of males in the same family are together.

Socrates once wrote, "An unreflected life is a wasted life." Writing this has helped me reflect more on my roles as a man – husband, father, grandad, and mate. I wish I could say I have it 'nailed', but the truth is I am only just starting to understand who I am. The journey inward is the longest journey!

Like Albert Facey I can say, "I have indeed had a fortunate life."

A couple of principles and books have shaped my growth and I would like to finish by mentioning them.

1. Love is a verb. Love is a decision which means doing loving things for each other whether we feel like it or not. Feelings come and go but the decision to love is constant.

2. If there is no quiet space or quiet times in your life, you do not have time to learn life's lessons. This means you will have to keep going through the same crap over and over again.

3. No one on their death bed wishes they spent more time at work. If you do not intentionally make time for your loved ones, time will run out.

4. Thich Nhat Hanh, the renowned Vietnamese Buddhist

teacher once said simply, "We are here for such a brief time." Say what needs to be said, do what needs to be done, be who you need to be – and do it today as you may not have tomorrow.

5. Even if you parent perfectly, not every child can receive love perfectly. Every parent stuffs up their kids! You can't help it so don't beat yourself up over it. One of the first jobs your children will need to do when they become an adult is to forgive you for not being perfect. For some this will be easy and others will need help to perform this task.

6. In giving we receive. This is an old proverb but the truth of this is profound. Throw yourself and your family into service to others, be it the community of the church, school, local clubs, service to the homeless, visiting old people. It doesn't matter what it is; the rewards will surpass your wildest imaginings. The purpose of life is to give yourself to a purpose greater than yourself.

6. Mahatma Gandhi once wrote, "You must become the change you want to see in the world." I have this above my office desk. If I want men to be better, then I must become a better man first. This saying empowers me to take action in those things over which I have control, rather than fantasise about what I wish would happen or others would do.

Being a man and especially a husband and father is unbelievably rewarding and unbelievably hard. You need to call on all the wisdom living in your family tree, as well as the wisdom of others. Books can help you do that. Here are some that helped me.

- Stephen Covey, *Seven Habits of Highly Effective People*
- Ron Rolheiser, *Forgotten Among the Lilies*
- Richard Rohr, *Adam's Return*

- Gary Chapman, *The Five Love Languages*
- Brene Brown, *The Gifts of Imperfection*
- M Scott Peck, *People of the Lie*
- Bill Hybels, *Who You Are When No One's Looking*
- Wayne Bennett, *Don't Die with the Music in You.*

Stuart with his parents and his brother.

3 kids: Stuart's children, Elise, Kaylee and Harrison.

5

Stuart Brady
Brady Bunch 101

When I was asked to participate in the writing of a chapter for this book, I did mention to Robert that I never really read books, let alone contribute to the content of one. He assured me that this is how JK Rowling started, so here we go.

When I was a kid there was a saying that went something like this. Nobody loves me, everybody hates me, I think I'll go and eat worms. I'd like to say I don't know what worms taste like but that would be a lie. They're awful. Just like my childhood.

My wife can remember her first day of primary school and even aspects of her life before school. I struggle to think of anything noteworthy from my time as a child. The things that I can remember, the ones that bring joy to my face, are almost instantly overtaken by the painful memories that now and then pop into my mind.

I went to St Joseph's Primary School, Moorebank, when it was a brand new school with only one grade above mine when I started kindergarten. A very special moment for me was when all three of my children went to the same school. That was cool. My two favourite subjects were recess and lunch. I was a show-off, the class clown and I couldn't sit still. Some say I still can't. The more my classmates laughed at what I was doing, the more it spurred me on. Maybe I was too young to work out that they may have been laughing at me, not with me.

I was always being sent to the principal's office or made to stand in the corner. Detention was the first word I could spell without hesitation. All my report cards said the same thing: if Stuart spent the same time and energy on his schoolwork as he did on being the class clown, he would be a genius. One teacher said to me that I wouldn't amount to much.

18 October 1970 was a wonderful day in the life of the Brady household. My birthday. Two became three; Mum, Dad and me. Three years later, three became four with the arrival of my little brother. Very early on I became aware of my Mum's drinking problem and the impact it had on our family, on me and on my childhood, requiring me to grow up fast – way too fast. I couldn't foresee the train wreck that was ahead and how I would go from being a passenger on that train to the one driving the train.

Dad was a travelling salesman so he would be away for days at a time, sometimes for as long as a week, leaving my brother and me at home with Mum. I hated it when he would leave because I knew what was in store while he was away. Mum would start drinking while she made dinner and then once that was done, drink more and more like she was drinking glasses of water. The more she drank, the more abusive and violent she became, lashing out at whoever was there at the time. When Dad wasn't there it was me. The worst part of it all, apart from my Dad not putting a stop to it, was that the next day when she sobered up, she had no recollection of what was said or done the night before. She would spend hours every night calling people and abusing them until ultimately, all those people who were once our friends stopped being our friends. Who would blame them? There was never the opportunity to have a school friend come over to play because I wouldn't be able to predict what state she would be in. More than likely their parents wouldn't let them anyway. I spent most of my childhood scared, alone and unloved.

Long before the mobile phone was invented, the school bus broke down one afternoon so my brother and I had to walk home. I had no way of letting Mum know what was going on so by the time we arrived home she had been drinking and worrying for way too long. As I walked through the front door, she hit me in the face with a frying pan and chipped my two front teeth. Dad was away so he was no help in this situation. When I woke up the next day and Mum saw my face, she said, "What happened to you?" I said, "You did."

If my child had said that to me, I would have been mortified and stopped drinking then and there. Not Mum. She accused me of making it up and if anything, drank more to cope with it all. I told people that I was running in the house, slipped and hit the door. Even when Dad came back from his trip he did not react as a father should have. There was no comforting, no reassuring me that everything would be all right, no loving hug. He just put his head in the sand as usual and pretended it would all go away.

While my Mum was on the phone during one of her rants, I remember getting the phone book out, circling Alcoholics Anonymous and putting it down in front of her. That didn't go down too well. One time Mum rang Dad to say my brother and I were fighting. Nothing unusual for brothers to do that; it's been happening since time began. He was working about four hours away and I'm not sure what Mum said to him but he drove home that night, came straight into my room, didn't say a word and gave me the biggest hiding of my life. I was 11.

I turn 50 this year and I still feel the pain of each whack when I think of it today. Another time he pushed my head through my bedroom wall. From the look on his face, I knew he regretted doing it as soon as he did it but it was too late. I kept the hole in the wall there as a reminder to him and it was still there the day I moved out.

As a father now, I question why Dad did nothing to protect his sons from their mother and his wife from herself. Out of pure frustration one night I took the wine she was drinking and walked out the front and smashed it on the road. Dad just got into the car and went to get more. I loved my parents but did not particularly like them.

I hated school but at least it was better than being at home. Home time was the worst, not having any control over what was behind our front door every time we entered. It wasn't until I was 49 that I realised the reason why I played up so much at school was because I wanted detention. That meant staying at school a little longer, prolonging my journey home.

One of the good things to come out of school was the friendships I made and still have today, 45 years later, especially with the guys. We are all fathers in our own right now and have been through the merry-go-round that is fatherhood. I was the last to get married but the first to have children.

There are some fond memories of Mum working nights for a short while and Dad would put us on his back and take us for horsey rides around the house before bed. We would go to sleep with him playing Neil Diamond or the Shadows on the record player but those memories are few and far between.

As time went on things did not get any better. My studies suffered, no one nurtured me and no one asked me if everything was OK at home. People knew what was going on but nobody did anything. Nothing, just silence. I found solace at my friend's house and would spend as much time as I could there.

After a while Mum did not have that night job anymore so she was at home. The nights were the worst. I recall several occasions when I had to open the door because the neighbours had called the police. No 12-year-old should have to deal with that. How could he or she function the next day at school? Clearly they couldn't. I would walk around in a kind of fog knowing that tomorrow was going to be just the same as all the others. Most of my time was spent in my room crying. Today you would have DoCS and all sorts of agencies involved but not back then.

I had always wanted to be a policeman and I knew that I wanted to make a difference in other kids' lives, if indeed I was one of those who knocked on the door to see a scared 12-year-old open it. Unfortunately, I didn't do well enough at school. I have a couple of regrets and that's one of them.

When I was old enough to get a part-time job I worked as long and as hard as I could to save up to buy a car. That was my ticket to freedom. The guy across the road had a mustard-coloured Toyota Corolla panel van with a cream vinyl roof and mag wheels. It looked like a million dollars. I had always wanted to own it but the boy next door to him, who was a year older, wanted it also. So it was a race to see who could save up fast enough. I asked my parents for a loan and Dad said no. If you want it badly enough you will work for it and that's what I did. Eventually I was able to save the $3000 and became the proud owner of the biggest piece of crap on the road. Hey, but it was my piece of crap. Although it allowed me the freedom to disappear, I still, eventually, had to go home. I would drive around until all hours waiting for the lights inside the house to go out before going inside. Sometimes I would fall asleep in my car.

One night I had had enough and decided to end my life. The pain was just too much to bear. I drove to a nearby park that was out of the way and placed a pipe from my exhaust into the rear window of my car. This was carefully planned for months trying to find the right place, then going and buying the things needed to do it. All the bits I needed were just sitting in the back of the van for ages, ready for when I needed them. I didn't leave a note or anything like that, I just went ahead and did it. I closed my eyes and went to sleep. I was abruptly woken by a tap on the driver's window and a bright light being shone by a policeman. I had made two critical errors.

1. Never put a rubber hose on a hot exhaust pipe. Sometime after affixing it to the exhaust pipe, it melted and just broke away, leaving the fumes to go into the atmosphere.

2. I picked a place that turned out to be a popular spot for that sort of thing.

That policeman took the time to talk to me and ask what led

to my taking such drastic measures that evening. He was the first person in 18 years who had asked me that question and he only knew me for 15 minutes. We both sat there in the cold night air while he listened to a young man with a broken heart and no reason to go on.

When I have mentioned this to people in the past, they all ask me the same question. What was it that he said that stood out to me the most? It wasn't like that. It wasn't what he said but what he didn't say, just the fact that he listened. That's all it took. Someone to listen. I found out that he would always drive back to the police station that way at the end of his shift just to check that all was good in the world, so to speak.

Some may say I was lucky the hose melted, others may say the luck was when the policeman came and tapped on the window. Looking back on it over the last 30 years or so, I have had different takes on it. Whether you are a believer or not, someone or something wanted me to hang around. In my case, I firmly believe that God had a hand in keeping me around.

Strangely, growing up we would attend church every week and yes, there were times when I would question if indeed there was a God and if there was, why was I in so much pain?

I moved out of home shortly after that and began to live my life. At first I had to couch surf for a little while with a family. Even though they already had a full house, they knew that I needed somewhere to stay. This was a turning point in my life as a young man. The father, let's call him Paul, had no sons of his own, only five daughters. However, he took the time when he had it to listen and more importantly, to love. He had an enormous effect on me. I watched him and learned from him what it took to be a husband and a father and a man.

Growing up I always thought I needed to prove something

to someone. I was always second guessing what people may or may not think of me but I am extremely proud of my work ethic and would spend long hours at work. Something I realised after that night in the car park was I could continue life as a victim, as some people do, or I could be the agent of change in my life. I chose the latter.

As I began to navigate life as an adult, it was apparent that I had missed out on some vital lessons in life from my Dad. I was lacking in the ability to love, really love – girls, friends and myself. There are some rites of passage that a father should pass down to his son. Teaching you how to catch a ball, ride a bike, drive a car and those sorts of things. Dad did some of those. I taught myself to drive but the biggest thing I missed out on was the sex talk. That I had to figure out myself. I'm not talking about the actual act of sex, I'm talking about respect for a woman and the morality of it.

One thing that I have always had is a highly active imagination. My brain is constantly working overtime. I had been working in the transport industry for nearly ten years and became the youngest professional driver in the country for two of the biggest companies at the time. I soon ended up starting my first business, mobile truck washing. It was hard work but I had found something I was good at and that was making money. The more I made the more I wanted. I would drive between sixty and seventy hours a week and then wash trucks on the weekend.

During this time, I came to know my now wife, who went to the same church. She has this beautiful smile that would light up a room. Still does. I don't know what she saw in me because most of the conversations we had started and ended with me saying how great I was at whatever – but thankfully, she persisted. I quickly had to adjust to sharing my time and life with her and her two young daughters, who at the time were eight and five. Instant family: Brady Bunch 101. I must say I loved being part of the foursome we had become. I valued enormously the unconditional love of two little girls wanting and needing to be loved, hugged, kissed and shown that they matter. These were all the things I wanted at their age.

One of the happiest moments of my life was when my wife's younger daughter asked if she could call me Daddy. My heart skipped a beat and my eyes filled with tears because there was nothing more I would have loved than to be called Daddy. Walking through the park or a shopping centre and hearing someone call out 'Daddy', you instantly know the relationship between the child and the adult. I had to say to her as much as that was a very nice gesture and that I would love nothing more, I wasn't her real Daddy and as she was still part of his life, it wouldn't be fair on him. It killed me to say that.

My wife is a few years older than I and had decided in her previous marriage that two children were enough for her and her husband. However, she then decided that it wasn't fair that I didn't have a child of my own and shortly after getting married, my wife fell pregnant with our son.

The day he came into the world was a bittersweet moment for me. On one hand the instant I saw him for the first time I fell head over heels in love. I knew then and there that he was the most important thing in the world to me and there's nothing I wouldn't do for him for as long as I lived. I was his protector, provider, the one who would form him as a boy, young man, and ultimately an adult. On the other hand, feeling this way made me think about what my Dad felt when I was born. Did he have the same thoughts and if he did, what happened? I would like to say that everything from then on was a bunch of roses and that in fact if that was the case, the chapter would end now – but that's not the case.

Not having had my father show me what fathering was all about when I was growing up was evident in the way I was raising the girls. I was used to doing things my way and I began to benchmark myself against their Dad. The unconditional love I mentioned before that the girls had for me, they had for him also and rightly so; after all, he was their father – but it drove me mad. I was the one putting a roof over their heads. I was the one spending all my spare time and energy with them. I saw that I was raising his kids. It was clear I was in over my head and instead of asking for help, I began to create an environment just like the one I had growing up. This led me to work longer and longer hours, come home tired and snap at whoever, whenever. I had created the family life I had grown up with, without the drinking and physical abuse but nonetheless, the result was the same. It was something I told myself I would never do if I was lucky enough to have a family of my own – but I did. As with my childhood, the scars take a very long time to heal and with all my children, hopefully, time will ease the pain.

In the most important phase of their development as little humans, when they were looking to me for guidance and direction, I failed them. The Stepdad title was something I struggled with. Why? I am not completely sure. I certainly was not the first nor would I be the last. Blended families have been around since time began. There were glimpses of brilliance, but they were few and far between and I began to resent the fact that the kids would always confide in their Mum and not me. Looking back now, would you blame them? They had a choice of either a grizzly bear or a kitten. We all know which we would choose but I began to feel like the outcast in my own family, so I did what I knew best – I started more businesses and threw myself into them.

I thought that a father's role was to provide for his family: a roof over their heads, warm place to sleep and food on the table. That's true, but it's not everything a father should do or be. I knew in my heart I could do better but for whatever reason, I didn't try to be better. If a client asked me to do something, I would give 150%, no problem at all. Why couldn't I give that same 150% to my family?

Remember watching television programs from the 50s and 60s? They always showed family members sitting around the living room looking at each other lovingly with smiles on their faces, listening to the radio or watching a black and white TV. Was that how the family dynamic worked back then? I reckon not. It certainly was not like that for me and I don't think it would have been like that for many others.

I have spent the best part of my adult life trying to live two lives; the life of a husband and father and the life of a businessman. For most people, these work well together but not for me. I kept looking over my shoulder to see if people were scoring me on my failures and successes. I was more interested in the successes but that comes at a cost. My wife was a rock through all these difficult years. She had already left one unhappy marriage, so what was stopping her leaving this one because it was less than ideal? She once told me that love was the reason she hung around. No matter how many times people told me that, I always felt uncomfortable.

I learned how to be a good father mostly from my wife. As most wives do, she would lovingly point out where I was going wrong and how I could improve, all through the eyes of love. She would be the buffer between me and the kids, trying to comfort them I suppose and explain that I didn't mean to say that or I didn't mean to do that.

One thing I did do and have done from day one is to tell my son I love him every day. He is nearly 20 and still lives at home so it is extremely easy for me to do. I would lie next to him when he was little and watch him sleep. I was devastated and angry when we found out when he was four that he was hearing-impaired. I realising I had been telling him I loved him since he was born and he couldn't hear me.

The first time I recall hearing my Dad say that he loved me was in 2001 when my brother passed away suddenly. I was 41. He was rushed to hospital on a Saturday night and passed away nine days later. I hadn't spoken to my parents or my brother for more than nine years and they only lived ten minutes away from me. It's funny but even though my upbringing was the way it was, I knew then that my parents needed me, so I was there.

I am the only one in my family who doesn't drink. My Dad was a happy drunk and I think it was his way of coping but my brother was just like Mum; abusive and violent at times. When Dad told me he loved me it was difficult to hear because it came across as forced, not natural as it is when I say it to my children. I have come to realise over time that those words were not part of the everyday vocabulary when he was growing up.

I decided to make my way in life and didn't need to have the added pressure of dealing with the past, whilst I was trying to navigate the present or even plan the future. However, I was not the only one to suffer through all of this, many people paid a price. My son did not have a relationship with his grandparents nor they with him. Mum and Dad did not have a relationship with my wife or the girls either. No one won.

I once gave my parents an ultimatum. If they wanted to see their only grandchild then they needed to make a choice, him or drink. They chose to drink. I'm not sure what else I could have done. You can only bash your head against a brick wall for so long before it begins to hurt.

I was three when my grandfather, Dad's father, passed away so I do not have any recollection of him at all and I cannot tell you what kind of man he was or what kind of father he was to my Dad. Was he loving, caring, gentle or nurturing?

I cannot tell you what type of role model he was to my Dad, whether he lived his fatherly life by example or if he showed him the love and affection we all crave. Even though I was not there to see this myself, I can hazard a guess that was not the case. Don't get me wrong, my Dad taught me that to work hard and to give back were very important attributes. He worked two, sometimes three jobs and if you needed someone to give you a hand he would be the first one to call. I was just at a loss to figure out why that same dedication to his work and others was not paralleled in his family life.

Those very same words were said to me not so many years ago. The apple did not fall far from the tree. I was fortunate enough to have been able to see what disaster lay in wait for me and took steps to lessen the pain and grief that was being caused at the time. My DNA is my DNA, there is nothing I can do about that. What I can do is decide if it defines more of me than is necessary. For a long time, it was easy for me to blame my anger and selfishness on my upbringing but there comes a point when I have to look at myself in the mirror and take ownership of the man looking back at me, warts and all. Not easy to do after living that way for more than 40 years.

Every father should be humble enough to sit his children down and ask them these two questions.

1. As your Dad name one thing I am good at.
2. As your Dad name one thing I am not good at.

These questions are better asked of older children so they can appreciate the importance and the seriousness of such questions. Then you need to be prepared for what comes next. The answer to question one will make you feel all warm and fuzzy but the answer to question two, not so much. You may score 100% for question one but as we are only human, there will more than likely be some pain associated with the answer to number two. The truth hurts.

I do this every so often because sometimes we become complacent and slip back into our old habits. It's what makes me a better father, not a perfect one but a better one. Now I benchmark myself against myself, not others.

I now relish the gift that it is to be a father. The girls at the time of writing are 31 and 28. The elder is married and has a successful career in the US; the younger is just about to get married and is eager to make me a grandad. This is something I am looking forward to very much. It's great to be given a chance to undo the wrongs. I could not be prouder of either of them. It has been a blessing to watch them grow into the beautiful women they are today and to see them choose the partners they have. It has also been fun torturing the guys. That's just a perk of the job, right?

Having them come to you for advice with some of the most important decisions of their lives is not only a beautiful feeling but important as well. What career should they pursue, where should they live? Who will they live with? Even if they don't take on board what you say, at least they loved you enough to ask. These decisions I had to make on my own. I would have loved nothing more than to share those experiences with my parents, to have their advice and love and support.

I look at my son and am so proud of the young man he has become. I am not afraid to say that he has taught me more about what it takes to be a good man than I have taught him.

In 2014 I was lucky enough to sell the largest business I had at the time to one of my competitors. This allowed me more time to spend with my family and more time to think about what I wanted to be my legacy when I eventually leave this earth. It also allowed me to work on saving my marriage because I had become caught up in the importance of material things. There is nothing wrong with wanting nice things but if it's at the expense of those you love, then we need to re-evaluate what is important in our lives. I had always told myself that I would not have a mortgage by the time I was 40 so I was driven to achieve this. Unfortunately I lost focus on what was important – my family! There's no use having a nice big house or flashy car if you're sitting in it alone. I recall a conversation with my wife when she said to me she didn't care if we lived in a tent as long as we were together. But I did.

I thought if I couldn't provide all these things then I would somehow be looked upon as less of a man, husband and father; a failure. In some ways, I had failed. I may have been successful in business but not when and where I needed to be – at home.

I began a journey which led me to find myself in front of 350 men, in another state, working through all the baggage I had carried for 40+ years. I attended a men's retreat weekend in Queensland. I did not know a soul. With nowhere to run it was a turning point, a definite 'line in the sand' moment for me as a husband and father.

Until then I was focused more on myself and making money, because that's what I thought made me a man. I wasn't a very nice person, definitely not a nice husband or father. Sure I was making money but was I happy? No, not really; in fact I was miserable. The purpose of attending this retreat was to give me some time to think about what I was going to do next, where my life was going and what part my family was going to play in that journey.

The first thing that hit me was the vast number of men all in one place and the fact that they all seemed to be there for the same reason – self-discovery. Some even looked to have found it and those guys had been there before. That didn't stop me from feeling a little out of place and uneasy. Having booked a return flight home for the Sunday was the only thing stopping me from leaving on a couple of occasions.

The point of the weekend that had the most impact on me was when I went to what Catholics call the Sacrament of Reconciliation; Confession. I hadn't been in a long time because I wasn't prepared to lay bare all the faults and failures I knew, deep down, I had. Nor was I prepared to take responsibility for those faults and failures.

As I sit here writing these words tears are falling from my eyes as I remember what happened when I entered the room to face up to those faults and failures, not as a child would do but as a man should, consequences and all. I remember walking in to see the priest sitting there. He looked straight at me and said, "Hi Stuart, how are you? Let's have a chat." In that instant I didn't see a priest sitting there, I saw Jesus. He was talking directly to me and even though I knew he would have been disappointed in the way I was living my life, all I saw were eyes filled with love.

I mentioned earlier that every father should be humble enough to be open with his children. You also need to be vulnerable. In front of those 350 men whom I didn't know, I read a text message I had sent my family saying that I had failed at being the husband and the father they all deserved and needed me to be and asked them to forgive me. I promised to be better and do better and I didn't want to be a failure or a disappointment in my children's eyes. I chose to send them all a text so they could keep what was written and I could be kept accountable for what was said when I would inevitably fall. Every time I fell it was a learning experience for me – and continues to be. This process didn't start and end on that weekend in 2014.

It's a long and sometimes slow process but at least the wheels are grinding away. There were men I met on that weekend who have been an integral part of my transformation, some of whom are playing a part in this book. Their non-judgemental love, support and guidance are truly gifts from God. There are things that only men could relate to and understand. Having those sounding boards has been a blessing.

I did have to face one thing that I didn't want to but ultimately knew I had to. Recently, after 49 years, I went to my parents, sat them down and forgave them. It wasn't easy. I found that over the years it was much easier for me to hang on to the hurt and anger and deal with it in my own way. The problem was I wasn't dealing with it. I would tell my story to people and there wasn't an effective ending, no 'bookend'. It wasn't until I heard one man's story of forgiveness that I even entertained the idea. I actually remember saying to him that I wasn't at that point in my life and doubted I ever would be. He said he understood exactly what I was talking about but encouraged me to think and pray about it and that the result would set me free.

I had over the years tried to do this on several occasions but I would set off in the car and would chicken out on the way – or even get to their place and just continue driving. What I was afraid of was that I would say I forgive you and the response would be – for what? Then what would I do? Thankfully this didn't happen but it was hard.

He was right though. I sat there in my parents' lounge room, a room that seemed so big when I was a child but was a lot smaller than I remembered. As I started to speak I could see unrest in both my parents' eyes. They didn't know why I was there. I just turned up. I prayed all the way there for God to be sitting by my side and to hold my nerve and my hand. He did. The relief was immediate.

Over the last couple of years, Dad's health has had its challenges. Recently I spent five hours in the emergency room with him after a fall at home. He laid there covered in blood from face planting the concrete. While Dad was lying there he opened up to me about some things that he had never said to me before and I commented on the fact that this is what should have happened a long time ago. I was happy that we finally have this time though. He was always a strong guy but now time and age are catching up with him and I see he is scared. The roles are reversed now and I will become the one who looks out for him and looks after him in the last phase of his life, however long that is. His memory is fading, he looks frail and that upsets me. How do you cram 50 years of life into whatever time he has left, trying to make better memories, ones that I can look back on fondly? Ultimately, it's not about me, it's about him. He is my Dad and I love him, failures, faults and frailty.

It's been a challenge to put down in words what life has been like, lived through my eyes and the eyes of those around me. You may recall I mentioned I haven't read too many books. That is not quite correct. Every time I would go to the airport to fly to one of my interstate offices, I would buy all the 'how to grow your wealth or succeed in business' books. Although I'm sure they have points that are valid in running a successful business, they don't mention what it takes to be successful in your life as a father. This is where the riches come from, not success or wealth from business. I am forever grateful for the opportunity to reassess the way I was living my life and I know some aren't so lucky.

Stuart's tips

A takeaway for me from this experience is: you can't be all to everyone until you are all to yourself.

Surround yourself with like-minded men who support you, challenge you, encourage you and love you. Men who, out of love, aren't afraid to call you out when you are less than you should be or could be. If you don't have those men in your life, find them. I did and I'm all the better for it.

Love is about giving and growing. The receiving is just a bonus.

There are two quotes I have found over the years are my 'go to' when I think I have it all sorted and begin to go back to the way I used to be. One you may have read before, one you may not have.

"As a Father you must have the mind-set that being a Dad is your most important job." Mark Merrill

"One night a Father overheard his son pray. Dear God make me the kind of man my Daddy is. Later that night the Father prayed. Dear God make me the kind of man my son wants me to be." Anonymous

Movies are also a great source of inspiration and a way of self reflection. Two I have found to be of great personal benefit are *Courageous* and *Fireproof*.

Courageous is about a father and his relationship with his children and his accountability.

Fireproof is about marriage and the relationship one man has with his wife. It depicts how we can sometimes be one person inside the home and another outside.

It took me 43 years to figure out that it wasn't Stuart against the world. Nor was it the world against Stuart. Through the love and support of my wife, friends and children, I made it out the other side. I pray that you too find the love and support to do the same. Or be that love and support to someone just like me.

6

Michael Forbes
There is no normal

Introduction

When I was in primary school we had a Friday night tradition where my siblings and I would be waiting for Dad to come home. We lived on the Gold Coast and he would be driving back from Brisbane. Even then, Friday night traffic meant a wildly variable arrival time. But even if the time stretched on, we would all still wait. The Cadbury Snack Block had just been released and for some time Dad always brought one home with him on a Friday. I suspect even without the chocolate we

Michael with his extended family.

Michael with his grandchildren, Harry and Maddy.

would have waited for Dad to get home and the weekend to commence.

When I became a Dad, it was always great to get home from work to my young children who would often run to greet me. In the morning before I went to work they would spend time with me, helping me pack my lunch or even just watching me shave.

For young children, good Dads fill their world like amazing mythical creatures – large, strong, wise. Initiating the craziest games, flinging bodies in the air and catching them, with all sorts of amazing skill and knowledge. Then, sometime in their teenage years, children realise their parents, even Dad, are just humans like everyone else – flawed and limited. If you are a lucky child, or a lucky parent, you survive these years and come to rich and mature relationship between adult child and parent.

In this chapter I want to focus on this relationship – both my experience as an adult child with my father, and my experience as a father to adult children. But first...

My story

I am the second of seven children, fortunate to be born into a family where Mum (Pat) and Dad (Alan) loved each other, loved us and where there was food on the table every night. I married my university sweetheart, Lisa, in 1985 and we have three fantastic children: Chris (born in 1989), Libby (1991) and Claire (1993). So far we have four grandchildren.

If this book was one of those self-help or inspirational books that are so popular, I could weave a grand story of my bright shiny life: high achievement, great success, the great love of my life, brilliant children, etc. And you would all wish you had been so lucky, or that I would just stop already. In the Facebook and Instagram age we have developed the skill of projecting the life we want people to see. We can forget that everyone is just trying to live life and most of us have no real idea of what we are doing. We compare our real lives with other projected lives and feel inadequate, while at the same time contributing to everyone else feeling inadequate by projecting an idealised version of our own lives.

My story, and my life as a father, is a little bit bright and shiny. But I also want to show you some of the other bits – the difficult decisions, the grinding hard work, the painful and embarrassing moments that we don't put on Facebook.

My early life really was very happy. I was born in Brisbane and then lived in Hughenden and Charleville in outback Queensland, with most of primary school spent living on the Gold Coast and all of high school and university back in Brisbane. The moves were all for Dad's work, including running his own civil engineering business on the Gold Coast and light engineering business in Brisbane. Despite going to five primary schools, my life felt very stable with the constant presence of my parents and growing numbers of siblings. It was only in later life that I realised how desperately close Dad had come to bankruptcy a couple of times. I understood the effort that Mum and Dad put into shielding their children from that desperation. All we knew was that one Christmas was a little light on for presents – we were well brought up enough not to complain. Then the next Christmas there were bikes for everyone and more! There was always someone to play with as our house was often the hangout zone for the street.

Mum and Dad were the youngest in their families by some way so all my grandparents were gone before I was a teenager and we had limited contact with any cousins. This meant we had a very close family life, something which has continued to this day. My siblings all get on pretty well.

Times were fairly tough financially when we moved to Brisbane, but we lived close to Nudgee College and I went there on a scholarship. This was when I started to realise I was better than most people at mathematics – a lot better.

Two very important things happened just as I finished school. The first was that I decided to study mathematics at the University of Queensland. Dad was very business-oriented and he wasn't too sure about mathematics until he realised that it was one pathway into being an actuary – a respectable business career from his perspective. The second important event was that I asked Lisa on a date – the first girl I had ever asked out. I think Lisa's parents didn't know what to make of me at the time. Val and Russell are both English and Lisa is their only child. I was tall, skinny and wild-haired back then, from a big rowdy family and studying mathematics of all things. Pretty soon I was letting the world know that I intended to do a PhD and become an academic. This was not something that particularly impressed Russell, who is an engineer by trade.

These two changes – studying maths at uni and dating Lisa – also marked the real transition to an adult relationship with my father. With maths it was now clear that I knew things he did not know. And in meeting and marrying my first girlfriend I was following his lead.

Lisa and I were married straight out of university and I was invited to join Opcom, a startup mathematical optimisation company, while studying a PhD part time. Then we hit the 'growth' years. The business grew, our family grew, I finished my PhD, the business kept growing. These years can be a very busy time in a man's life, but not necessarily a great time for reflection. Life becomes mainly about providing, doing and achieving. And I did just that, with very little reflection.

As I said in the introduction, one of the joys of this stage of life was our young children. I enjoyed homecomings, family holidays, even children's sport. As a bit of an all-sports fan I loved attending all our children's sports, even learning the rules, tactics and strategy of netball, hockey and water polo so I could follow those sports as well as Chris' more familiar rugby and cricket.

Then through a series of fortunate events from 2005 onwards, we sold Opcom, our first software company and I helped start some new software companies including Biarri, another optimisation company. We also became involved in more church activities, including development and charitable work in Uganda, and I started working part-time in academia at the University of Queensland.

Meanwhile, our children grew up. Chris, our eldest, married Jordan and has four children. He is a star mathematician for Biarri. Our older daughter, Libby, is a doctor specialising in paediatrics. And our youngest, Claire, served as a missionary with NET (National Evangelisation Team) Ministries before marrying another NET missionary, Caleb. She's well on her way to being a midwife.

I told you some bits were bright and shiny. Happy marriage, successful business career, three great children, four grandchildren so far. What a successful man! What a successful father!

But there is more to the story: a turbulent side of unexpected surprises and a darker side of tragedy and betrayal.

First, the surprises. In one year, Chris and Jordan had a child out of wedlock, my older daughter Libby came out as gay and my younger daughter Claire converted from being a strident atheist to being a fired-up young Catholic, including doing two years with NET.

Chris and Jordan's unexpected pregnancy has turned out to be a great blessing to the family. They are very happily married and well settled.

Libby's sexuality has also been a good journey for Lisa and me, as we deal with our own assumptions that all our children would 'naturally' be straight. Sometimes people, well-intentioned people, ask me if I would prefer if Libby was straight. My considered answer to that is no, because that would mean I wish someone else had been born in her place. And I can't imagine life without my beautiful, brilliant, ambitious doctor daughter, or indeed without any of my children.

There were several business struggles. Hard financial times when we thought Opcom might not last through the slow summer months. Difficult meetings where I was harassed and abused by clients with little ability to fight back because of the importance of the client. Some of these meetings are on my 'permanent tape'. I think most people have their own 'permanent tape'; that internal recording you can never erase and which sometimes pops into your mind out of nowhere. You're having a perfectly nice day and then you remember – oh, that happened – and then a little bit of the shine goes off the day.

And there was tragedy. In 2010 my father died after a short struggle with cancer. My father was a great and good man and pretty much the worst thing he ever did to his children was to die at only 70. A few weeks before he died there was a day when I was the designated carer. Everyone else was out. It had been a very difficult day for him, a difficult few days. He was asleep. No one else was there. For about 30 minutes I considered smothering my father with a pillow. His sleep at that time was equivalent to being in a coma, so there would be no question of struggle or pain. There was also very little chance of my being caught. It was mainly a theoretical exercise on my part, but it was a dark road to walk down. In the end I decided life and death belong to God and thank God I did. In the last two weeks of his life Dad was in a very large room in hospital. My brothers and I took turns sleeping on a sofa bed in the room, and when Dad woke up in the middle of the night, we had long conversations with him about all sorts of things. These were the real farewell.

Then, at the beginning of 2013, my mother died, after more than 30 years of fighting cancer. In her case death was less of a tragedy, as her health had declined over a long time. But it was difficult seeing Mum bereft of the love of her life for the final two and half years, as well as fighting gradually declining health.

And in the middle of those deaths was betrayal. A mathematical and business protégé of mine, a man who I regarded almost as a son, whose PhD I supervised, whom Biarri employed through my initiative, left Biarri under the most difficult of circumstances. After legal action and recriminations all that's left are the shattered remains of a once great relationship. It is easily the saddest thing that has happened to me in business, and perhaps in any relationship.

And remember, all the bad stuff has gone on the permanent tape. I have a great memory. There is no erasing that tape this side of dementia or heaven.

What I learnt from my Dad
Throughout our lives we are learning, being shaped and

formed. Much of that learning and formation happens as we are watching and being influenced by other people in our lives. If we are lucky, those influences come from good men. And I was lucky.

Some of the things I learnt from my Dad include...

Love the Lord your God with all your heart, and with all your soul, and with all your mind, and love those God has given you to love. When I was around ten Dad was very busy with his own business, Rotary, being president of the school Parents and Friends and a couple of church groups. When Mum had baby number six, she suggested to Dad that maybe it was time to drop some things so he could concentrate on his family. And he did. He went back to all those other good things later in life, but he concentrated on his family when he needed to do so.

Be optimistic, be prepared to take some risks and try to make the best out of adversity. Dad was very entrepreneurial, despite a couple of setbacks. He passed this on to his children in a big way.

Be present for your children, even when they become adults. Dad's father died of a sudden heart attack when Dad was 18. I know he felt this loss. When I was in my thirties I started walking with Dad for an hour or so a couple of times a week. This is long enough to get past the news, and to move on to what's really happening in life.

You can teach, form and shape your children right up to the moment of your death, and indeed beyond. Dad did this by the manner of his dying. He talked of how he was excited about the next step of the journey. And I had some great conversations with him over his last few days. His short term memory was going so he knew he was probably repeating himself, but we both found the humour in the situation. The whole process brought me closer to Dad, closer to the rest of my family and closer to God.

What I learnt from other father figures in my life

Hopefully any boy, young man or even older man has many good male role models in his life. One of the jobs of a father, and indeed a mother, is to ensure this is so. I was fortunate to have many great male teachers at school, especially at Nudgee College. These men variously encouraged me in my talents, pushed me out of my comfort zone, helped me laugh at myself and generally took off the rough edges.

My father-in-law, Russell, was also a key influence. He had a talent for practical home maintenance and DIY that was not my father's strength. He tried his best, largely in vain, to hand it on to me. But I also saw his hard-edged business persona soften as he became a grandfather and especially when he became a great grandfather. This meant he avoided turning into a grumpy old man and instead became something of a sage for his great grandchildren.

My business partners in Opcom were John and Tony – two men who had taught me at university and both of my father's generation. It was only after we sold Opcom and became part of a bigger company that I truly realised how much they had taught me and what a great culture they had fostered in the business. There were several times in the early, leaner days when dodgy business practices beckoned: the customer who was obviously asking for a bribe but trying to package it so that it didn't smell so bad; the aggressive tax-planning option proposed by external accountants. This is all part of normal business life for a growing company. But on each occasion, someone – and it could have been anyone in the leadership group – said, "I'm not comfortable with this." And that was that. The culture was such that anyone could speak up and once someone spoke up it was clear to all that this was a path to be avoided. It was only after I worked elsewhere that I realised a culture of compliant silence is more usual in business, and indeed in official church life.

More recently, I have been heavily influenced by many of the older men I have encountered through menALIVE. These men have lived through many of the experiences that are new to me. Some of them have the wisdom that comes from enduring pain, suffering and loss and come through more or less intact, even if they have scars.

Lessons in being a father

Everyone thinks his life is normal.

Most people think they live their life more or less the same way everyone else does. And to some extent, this is true. We know about the obvious differences. In my family's case we knew that it was unusual to have a family of star mathematicians. But the rituals and rhythms of each family are different – sometimes in subtle ways. In some families the children might do the cleaning up after a big family dinner. In others it might be the adults, or the grandchildren, or the young men or the young women. It may be that birthdays mean one present, on behalf of the whole family, or a host of presents. In some families the ironing is done when the clothes are dry, in others when the clothes need to be worn, and many younger families may not even own an iron. Recently my grand-daughter asked "What's that?" when I got out the iron and ironing board.

And there are the bigger differences – family breakdown and blended families, children with a disability and elderly parents, difference in wealth and religious breakdown.

All these combine to mean *there is no normal.*

Never make the mistake of thinking you are living a normal life or that your family is normal. It is exceptional – one of a kind. If you, the father, is present and engaged, your family is already doing better than many families.

And if there is no normal that applies to everyone, it means you have the freedom and the responsibility to create what will become normal for your family. So, go for it. Create habits and rituals that will define your family and that your children will remember forever. It is never too late to do this, even if your children are adults themselves. If you were a great figure in their lives when they were young, an echo of that myth lives on and you can build on that. If you were not, there is still time to start something new.

Surround yourself with good brothers.

No one can complete the journey of life, and especially fatherhood, on his own. You need to surround yourself with good men who will walk the journey with you. In my case, this started with my brothers. We've always been a close family, but I became much closer to my four brothers during our Dad's final illness. My brothers have been a big influence on me, but also on my children, especially my son. My youngest brother is about halfway between me and my son Chris in age. Chris knows that he can talk to his uncle – or to other men in the family – anytime.

As well as good close male family members, you also need to surround yourself with a strong Christian brotherhood. In my case, this is now the men of menALIVE – those who are older and those who are younger. A small group of Christian men, a band of brothers, meeting regularly to pray together and to share their highs and lows, is a powerful force for God's kingdom.

You have more influence than you think.

When your children are young adults, and maybe casting off some of the values and culture of their family of origin, it can seem like you have little influence on their lives. We can see the lack of influence of our words and beliefs and think we have lost all control. But you still have the influence of your actions. Once they are adults, forget about trying to *tell* your children how to live, that time is past. It's time to *show* them how to live.

This has come home to me dramatically in a way I would never have predicted. A few years back I started running more seriously. I had always run, but decided I wanted to get faster for my annual 10km race. So I joined a running club. If you hang out with runners you turn into a runner. Pretty quickly I was training for and running marathons. It used to be that 20km was a good week's running. Now it's just a good long run and 50km per week is the low point of my training. I lost a lot of weight and got a lot fitter and faster. Then something strange happened – my children all started running. Even my wife runs a bit.

The transition from early adulthood into late 20s and early 30s is often a time when young adults lose a lot of fitness and gain a lot of weight. This had started to happen with our children. We could have talked to them about the importance of fitness and losing weight. But we didn't need to, because they saw how much difference it had made for me. The added benefit is that I go on regular runs with my children and their partners. This is great catch up time.

Be intentional.

'Be intentional' means decide what outcomes you want and then act so as to achieve those outcomes. It's about longer-term planning. It means that when the moment arises, you are ready to seize it. By now you have probably worked out that I like running, so let's use another running analogy here. In the last ten kilometres of a marathon it gets very tough, for everyone. Everyone knows you need to be brave and dig deep, give everything. And it is important to be brave in that moment. But being intentional is about doing the hard days in training – early starts for long lonely miles when no one is watching. Being intentional means that when the moment arises you are able to perform as you want to perform.

A couple of examples from my lived reality. When our son Chris was about 15, I spent a fair bit of time travelling. And like most sons of that age, he started to test the boundaries. I had just arrived back from a trip and Lisa asked him to put his washing away. Back came a surly, "Yeah, yeah, whatever" and Chris turned his back on Lisa and walked away. I wasn't having that, so I quickly got in his face, up close, and said, "Don't you ever talk to my wife like that again." He still remembers to this day that I said "my wife" not "your mother". I'd like to claim that I was inspired and came up with the words on the spur of the moment, but I wasn't. I'd read them years before and stored them away for such a moment – I was intentional.

My other example of being intentional also involved Chris. A few years back he invited Lisa and me out to lunch. When he told us that Jordan, his then girlfriend and now wife, was pregnant, the first words out of my mouth were, "That's great, we're going to be grandparents." A lot better than, "How did that happen?" Again, I had thought about the scenario beforehand and planned my first response – I was intentional.

On the downside, I reacted poorly when Libby first told Lisa and me she was gay. I was dumbfounded, and my responses for some time were variations on "Are you sure?" What was I thinking? She is an extremely intelligent woman who had been raised a Mass-going Catholic with parents who were very active in the church. If she was telling us, then of course she was sure. It was only when my youngest daughter Claire challenged me about my attitude towards Libby's sexuality that Libby and I had a long talk and I moved from tolerance to acceptance. I had never imagined the scenario of one of our children saying the words "Mum, Dad, I'm gay". As a result, I wasn't really there for Libby for a few months at a time when I should have been.

Not everything about being intentional is planning for the unexpected conversations. There will be many conversations, so make sure you have something to talk about. This will mean knowing what's going on in your adult children's lives – what's important to them, what they are interested in. It may even mean doing some research. And of course, you can always take up running and encourage them to do the same.

Sometimes it takes time.

I remember a wise friend saying to me once, "Don't judge how your adult children have turned out until they are at least 30, maybe even older." In context, he was talking about children, especially sons, who have gone off the rails a bit.

So far I've had an amazing life, but even so there have been setbacks and troubles. And often these things have just taken time to fix, or in some cases time to heal, as there is no fixing them this side of heaven – especially true for the loss of loved ones. A good relationship with your adult children is worth the effort. Be intentional, surround yourself with good brothers, remember that what you do matters much more than what you say, and pray. Then wait.

Challenge Questions

You are reading this book because you want to be a better father. While I don't have the answers for your particular situation, I do have some questions you can work on that might help.

1. What does 'normal' look like for your family life? What could you add or subtract that would make it better?
2. Who are your 'brothers'? What type of influence are they on you and your children?
3. How have you influenced your children in the past? How would you like to influence them?
4. In what ways do you need to be intentional for your children, given their ages and stage of life?

Useful Books

Manhood, Raising Boys, Raising Girls and more by Steve Biddulph. Steve brings professional skills and personal experience to his books. They are written in an Australian context and regularly revised. His books were great resources when our children were young.

He'll be Ok: Growing Gorgeous Boys into Good Men by Celia Lashlie. Well researched and easy to read, this book is close to mandatory reading for parents of adolescent boys. The research is from New Zealand so it translates well to Australia.

7

Peter Gabauer
"You have what it takes" – receiving the baton of fatherhood early

"I have not shown you all that I want to show you – or taught you all the things I want to teach you." These words are as clear today as the day my Dad said them to me. We were sitting alone together, he had tears in his eyes and so did I. I had just finished massaging his swollen legs and bandaging them to provide some relief from the Lymphedema. This was

Peter's parents and siblings, not long before his father passed away at 46.

The Gabauer family: Peter, Jo, Sophia and Olivia.

not the only issue – my Dad was losing his battle with cancer. It first attacked his bowel, then liver and continued to wrack his body.

I still remember the day I heard Dad had cancer. I was 21 and had not long returned from working overseas when I heard Dad had been rushed to hospital for emergency surgery. I raced to the hospital where he lay in an Intensive Care Unit. The nurse led me into his room and left us alone. Dad was still in recovery and not conscious. The scene was surreal. Here was the strong one of the family lying in intensive care with monitors beeping, oxygen being pumped and looking grey and sullen. I had never seen him so ill. He looked like he would not make it through the night. I am not sure what came over me, but I yelled at him, "You can't die now!"

I was not prepared for this; none of us was prepared. No one ever is. He was 46; I was just 21. Responsibility weighed heavily on my shoulders. There was so much still unresolved between us and this is not how the story is meant to end, I thought. I knew nothing of his affairs; I had seven younger siblings – two sisters who were 20 and 18, four younger brothers 15, 11, eight and six and a baby sister who was only a year old. My Mum was 44 and had a history of mental illness. Life was beginning to feel very fragile. In that moment I felt helpless and very much alone.

When I left home at 18, I was an angry and rebellious young man. The relationship between Dad and I was strained. I had not left home on good terms. His strictness with me was too much. I needed space to grow and find my niche.

I had wanted a motorbike since I was eight years old. Dad said, "You will never have a motorbike while you live under my roof." My motorbike adventures were limited to riding around my uncle's farm on the holidays. When I turned 18,

I bought a motorbike and two days later I moved out. It was his birthday.

For some reason I felt like I was not good enough, that I was a disappointment to him, that I did not measure up to the son he wanted me to be. I felt like I had to win his approval and prove myself to him. Looking back this seems like a repeat of my father's experience with my grandfather. As the saying goes, "We repeat what we don't repair."

My grandfather, Josef Gabauer, was an Austrian immigrant who came to Australia in the 1930s with very little; in many ways, he was a self-made man and very successful. He was a bridge builder, building bridges in regional New South Wales, and he then became a farmer. He was entrepreneurial and courageous. He had survived incredible odds – and he had grown up without a father.

My father, Joseph Gabauer, was born on 17 March 1943 in Armidale, a country town in New South Wales. The family eventually settled north of Coffs Harbour. It was here my grandfather established a banana plantation. This would have involved backbreaking effort clearing the land and then growing the bananas. This period of my Dad's life was filled with lots of hard work as the farm was being established. Cutting down trees and clearing bush meant he spent many long hours labouring for his father so they could start planting bananas. My Dad did not have a close relationship with his father; he found him impatient, unduly critical and a harsh disciplinarian.

I recall Dad telling me the story of his father sending him to get the tractor from the other end of the property. Dad had never driven a tractor; in fact he had never been shown how to drive. Eventually when he returned sometime later with the tractor, his father scolded him for taking so long.

He resented his father, and in some ways, felt his father was jealous of the opportunities he had for an education.

Dad was a bright student and a keen footballer. When he finished high school, he was awarded an open scholarship at Sydney University – he decided to study Engineering and not Medicine as he hated the sight of blood. While he was at university, he met Mum, Nancy; she was the sister of one of his classmates. In 1967 they were married and I arrived the following year.

My earliest memories of my Dad were of him being locked away studying for his Master's degree. I also remember being at church and sitting on his knee, cradled in his arms. Mum used to work as a switchboard operator in the evenings for PMG (the Postmaster General's Department) back when every phone call had to be connected manually. Dad used to take my sister and me down to the local corner shop after dinner for a treat. Life was pretty good.

As a young father, Dad was very strict with me. I recall being at a family function when I was four or five, and my aunties telling Dad not to be so hard on me. I guess he was repeating the fathering mistakes of his Dad – I did not feel like I had a close relationship with Dad, more an 'I-better-stay-out of-trouble' relationship. Dad had practised his father's method of discipline – the 'spare the rod, spoil the child' model. He was quick to correct me – the belt would come off, and I would get a strap across the backside. It was common in that era, but it did not make it any better or any more effective. It was hard to have a warm relationship with him when he had that power over me. My reaction was to try to stay out of trouble.

Unfortunately, as I grew into adolescence, I began to resent my father just as he had resented his father. Sometimes his chastisements left me feeling a deep sense of injustice. I felt unfairly treated and punished disproportionately to my behaviour. It just did not seem fair. Looking back now, I wonder if for Dad it was more about keeping things under control in a growing family than dealing with some of my childish misdemeanours. However, my reaction was to become rebellious and angry. I was expected to take on adult responsibilities as the eldest child with the care of younger siblings, yet I was not treated that way when it came to discipline. This was a particular frustration for me and left me feeling angry and despondent.

When I was six, we moved from Sydney where Dad had worked as a civil engineer, designing and building bridges just like his father, to Ingham in North Queensland where he worked as a civil engineer in a sugar mill. We attended the local Catholic schools and church on Sunday. My parents wanted to raise us in the Catholic faith. One of the reasons for the move was to create some distance between him and his father whom he still found to be demanding in his expectations.

Dad had a big job as an engineer with lots of staff and responsibility. He cared for those who worked for him; he was respected and well-liked. I remember Dad coming home in the middle of the day and collecting some clothes. One of his men had been struck with a vomiting bug and soiled his clothes. Dad gave him his own clean clothes to wear home.

Another time I heard that one of the men who worked for Dad had lost a child to Sudden Infant Death Syndrome (SIDS). A few days later, I was out with Dad in the car and he parked outside the funeral home. While I waited in the car he went inside. When he came back, I asked what he was doing. He replied that he was just checking that everything had gone all right for the family. I don't know why, but I pressed him for more details, and he finally told me that he had paid for the funeral for the family. These moments of kindness and quiet generosity impacted me.

Another time he caught one of his truck drivers stealing fuel. It had been going on for months when they discovered it. Rather than terminate his employment, Dad demoted him so he remained employed and could support his family. It would have been difficult for that man to get another job in a small town had he been sacked. "Everyone deserves a second chance," Dad said. To me, this was a powerful example of mercy and compassion.

When I was about ten, Dad went on a Catholic men's retreat weekend run by the Cursillo Movement. I remember clearly because when he came back, he seemed different. Firstly, he would walk around the house singing with great enthusiasm but with little regard for the actual key of the song! This very serious man had been through a transforming experience and joy was starting to emerge. Even as a child I could see it. The other thing I noticed was that he began to become more patient and less severe in his discipline. He was not perfect, but he was trying. It seemed as though he was fighting against the parenting style he had grown up with and was trying to do things differently.

As an adult it is easier to reflect and see what was happening then. He had had a powerful conversion experience, and his life would never be the same again. His conversion also brought about personal transformation. Dad was a disciplined man and daily prayer and meditation became a foundational activity. At 5.30am each morning, he would head to the garage where he could have some peace and quiet and read his bible. Sometimes I would sneak down and sit quietly with him. It would be dark, except for a candle and a small lamp to read his bible. My childhood experience was of this being a very peaceful place. I find myself doing the same thing 40 years later, rising each morning to pray and meditate.

I was 11 when Mum first got sick. It was not long after my second brother, number five in the family, was born. It was post-partum depression, they said. All I knew was that Mum was in hospital and occasionally we could visit her.

As a husband, my father's love for my Mum was strong. This was clearly demonstrated to me as Dad would visit her daily even though the hospital was a hundred kilometres away from where we lived. Dad cared for her and never gave up hope that she would get well.

As a child it was distressing to go to the psychiatric hospital to visit her. They had all sorts of people with mental illness in one place. Sometimes you would hear someone scream out from behind a closed door, occasionally a couple of nurses would run down the hall to settle someone down. It was not predictable in any sense of the word. We would sit with Mum in a kind of visiting room where patients also did craft activities. Here was Mum but she was not Mum. She did not have the bright smile and energy that I remembered. She looked sad and listless. She was heavily sedated and could not really communicate with us. In some ways I feel as though my childhood ended at that point. I needed to become self-sufficient. Mum's health eventually returned and she came home and life seemed to settle down for a while, until my third brother was born and sadly the story was repeated. These were difficult years for our family and we were very lucky to be surrounded by dear friends who cared for us. At one point my little brother and I lived at our family friend's house for some months. These moments of stability and routine really helped me through this difficult period. It is moments of kindness like this that I will never forget.

My childhood was cut drastically short in so many ways. At 11 years of age, while my mates were out playing, I was actively caring for my two-year-old brother, feeding him, changing his nappies and patting him off to sleep. He was my sidekick, and we did everything together. I was growing up fast. People used to say how mature I was. Adult responsibilities were expected of me yet I was still being treated like a child and this made me resentful of my Dad.

In August 1984, when I was 16, we relocated to Brisbane from regional North Queensland. Changing schools halfway through Year 11 was difficult for me; I found home life very stressful. At times it was chaos with a big family and everyone with their own challenges. Looking back, I can only imagine the pressure my father would have been under himself. Mum was pregnant with their seventh child, Dad was starting a new job well below the level of his previous work and he had enrolled all the kids in new schools. He and Mum valued our education and moved so we would have better opportunities than those that were available in a small regional town.

In September of that year, a new baby brother arrived, child number seven, and shortly after Mum had another episode of post-natal depression and ended up in hospital.

It was just too much. I thought my head would explode! With so much going on I could not concentrate at school and then with the noise at home I had no chance of concentrating there either. Some days I used to skip school, taking a change of clothes in my school bag and going to the local library to study. It was no use. I lasted six months at my new school then I dropped out. I felt like a failure.

My Dad and I were so different and I did not feel that I measured up. I was not good at the things he was good at and therefore I assumed I was not good enough. He was an Engineer, good at Mathematics and Science. I liked English, History and Art. I was also good at fixing things and enjoyed wood and metalwork at school. My Dad was an introvert and by all accounts, growing up I was a charismatic extrovert. My Dad was a brilliant student. It seemed I was an average student. It's not surprising given my difficulties concentrating and the stress I was under with everything that was happening at home and Mum's health.

Not long after I dropped out of school, Dad took me to see a psychiatrist. After an hour of talking with the psychiatrist he smiled and said, "Peter, in my line of work it's so nice to chat to someone who is completely normal once in a while. You have had too much responsibility from too young an age. You need to take a year off and do what you want to do!"

It was a relief. I knew it in myself. I needed time and space.

Soon after, aged 17, I had the chance to fly to Fiji and crew on a yacht that was sailing back to Brisbane. For two weeks we prepared the boat for sailing by stocking up on provisions. I also had the chance to work alongside the skipper and his wife, a doctor, as she called on some very poor families. Whilst the doctor provided medical aid, my crew mate and I would do any house maintenance tasks needed. This experience shaped me like nothing before.

Time and space were what I needed and time and space I had. Time and Space, Sky and Horizon, for the entire two weeks. It also showed me that I had capacity and that I was valued. As part of a small crew, I would take my watch. My favourite watch was always before dawn when I would be rewarded by the most spectacular sunrises. It was my responsibility to make sure the yacht was on course, with the autopilot doing its job, and to keep an eye out for other ships and any changes in the weather.

As a crew we were put to the test when we were hit by an unexpected storm in the early hours one morning. It was all hands on deck. As I headed up the hatch, I was hit by the heavy spray of a rough crashing wave against the yacht. My wet weather gear was now wet inside and out. The cold water was a wake-up call as was the anxious order from the skipper, "Get a reef in that sail!" he yelled, to reduce the size of the sail to something more manageable. As another crew member and I worked feverishly the boat turned suddenly. The skipper was on the wrong side of the boom when it swung, catching him in its deadly path. In that moment everything was in slow motion. I saw him grab the boom and hang on for his life as he was suspended dangerously over the ocean. Disaster was thankfully averted as my crewmate grabbed the helm and the skipper's wife and I grabbed the skipper, bringing him safely back to the deck of the boat.

You never know how you are going to react in a storm and there is only one way to find out. I learnt that day that I can handle pressure well and that I am not afraid of discomfort. That was helpful learning as a few days later I was badly sunburnt on my back. Sleeping in a bunk on a rolling boat with bad sunburn – now that is discomfort!

Soon after returning home, I was given another opportunity to step up to the plate as a young man, this time in Sydney. My Uncle John, Mum's brother, was recovering from a skydiving accident and needed a driver and someone to help in his business. It was a godsend. It was the change I needed. I surfed at the beach before and after work and in the evenings would have long conversations with my uncle and aunt as he worked through his long recovery. My uncle was a businessman and an entrepreneur. He was also an extrovert, funny and entertaining. It was during these conversations he affirmed me and identified some of my talents. Even though I was gifted in different ways from my Dad, it did not diminish who I was as a man. My uncle's fathering in this moment, at a critical time, encouraged me in a way that I needed. It was grace-filled experience. He also introduced me to good Cognac and showed me how to smoke a Cuban cigar. It has since become a tradition whenever we get together.

I returned to Brisbane like a man on a mission. I was going to prove myself to my father. Like many men, I felt I had to be worthy of his love and approval. I worked hard in every job I had, I worked long hours, and I was the first to start work in the morning and the last to leave. I was ambitious and determined. I did not say no to any challenge. When Dad was diagnosed with cancer, I decided I needed to return to study to improve my job opportunities. I completed Years 11 and 12 in one year in an accelerated course, I then saw a clinical psychologist and did some aptitude tests. I did not want to waste anyone's time doing any more study if I did not have the ability. The aptitude test results revealed I could be a lawyer, a marketing manager or a film director, among other occupations. It is hard having such a smart father and as it turned out I was not that dumb after all. Perhaps I can make it, I thought. So, I started my studies in Business. For once the subject matter resonated with me and I enjoyed study. I even got a distinction for my law subject!

A father's words are so powerful to a son. Words that are said or left unsaid can be profound. Even a look can be enough to show pride or disappointment. I know because I have seen both. At this moment in time, I was now 22 and my Dad and I had grown closer. I was not going to feel like I did beside his bedside in the Intensive Care Unit again with anything unresolved. I had done a lot of growing up since I had left home. I had been overseas twice, had some great adventures and was becoming comfortable in my own skin. I remember going home for dinner – I rode over on my third motorbike by that stage. By now Dad was more accepting of my choices. He even prayed a blessing over my bike that day and gave me a St Christopher's medal.

I knew he was proud of me and the man I was becoming. We had resolved our differences. I forgave him and he forgave me too. Sometimes in the heat of life there are too many misunderstandings and not enough communication. It is not only the things that are said but the things left unsaid that have an impact. As a child it was easy to draw my own conclusions. As a son I needed Dad to tell me he was proud of me. I needed to hear that he loved me. I needed to know he believed in me and that I had what it takes.

Dad had not received much affection or affirmation from his father. It was partly his culture and partly that generation. We vowed to change that. Whenever I visited home, Dad and I always hugged. I found that a pat on the shoulder or a welcoming, manly hug from my Dad was deeply affirming. This changed the culture in our family. My brothers and I all hug now. I did not realise how much this changed how we greeted each other in my family. Not thinking, one day, I put my hand out to shake the hand of my six-foot tall, bushy-bearded nephew as he was leaving my house. Smiling he looked at me and said, "Hey Uncle Peter, we are huggers in this family!" And so we hugged!

While I was comfortable that Dad and I were different in personality and gifts, there was one attribute that we had in common, that he had imparted to me – and that was character. The most important part of any man is his character and Dad demonstrated and imparted this to me through his actions.

We do not always choose the circumstances of our lives but they have the power to shape and form us if we let them.

I was 22 when I moved home to support my Mum with nursing Dad. I did not know it then, but Dad only had six months to live. It was a busy household, Dad was going to medical appointments and chemotherapy, kids were off to school and meals were to be cooked. Life does not stop when someone is gravely sick. It is painful to watch someone you have always seen as strong and self-sufficient slowly decline in health. Dad was always needed by everyone else, and now he needed us. We were not alone in that time and had an incredible community of support around us.

In particular, Dad had two mates who would frequently drop in to sit with Dad. These men were more like brothers to Dad and I could see how much strength he drew from their relationships. Sharing brotherhood with a few key men is a great gift. Some 30 years later one of those men and the son of the other are now counted as my closest mates and brothers. These are men of incredible character and wisdom and have been there for me as an example to follow.

As the cancer progressed in Dad's body, he developed Lymphedema – this is when the lymphatic system stops working, and a person's limbs start to swell. The process of caring for someone with Lymphedema is time-consuming. First, the massaging of the legs to assist the drainage of the lymphatic system, applying thick moisturiser to legs that were now nearly twice the normal size and then the bandaging – a special criss-cross method shown to us by the medical staff. We did this several times a day and then again in the evening. While this was not going to cure Dad, it seemed to provide relief and it was good to be able to do something to ease his suffering.

It was during these times we had many profound conversations. The conversation about the lack of time to teach me and show me all the things he wanted to show me was one example. Yet he had already shown me and taught me so much. Manhood is bestowed on us – drawn out of us even – and my father provided an extraordinary example of what a real man should be. It was during these times I felt I was being coached and prepared. At times, it felt as though something was being imparted to me almost by osmosis, and at other times, a baton of responsibility was being passed to me. It was not always in the things that Dad said but by the example of his life. In the end, our actions endure beyond what we say. His quiet, consistent action was a powerful example.

I remember asking Dad what God would ask him when he arrived in heaven. Without overthinking, he said, "I bet God will ask me if I loved my wife." This is so simple yet profound. Dad saw his marriage to Mum and being a father as his vocation. He loved Mum and he loved his children intensely. When Dad was diagnosed with cancer, he was only 46. With a new baby in the house, he used to tell Mum to let him get up to my baby sister in the night as he said he wanted as much time with her as possible.

Since my father's conversion experience, he had been on a spiritual journey of deep inner transformation. He had forgiven his father and let go of resentment and bitterness. This 'inner' healing brought about 'outer' changes. Not all immediately but slowly and surely over time. We all prayed that Dad would be healed – he certainly was a worthy candidate and he had enough people praying for him. In some ways it was a miracle he survived that first surgery and lived for another two years. Early one morning, I woke up before the rest of the house and was praying in silence. I sat quietly, as Dad had done for all those years, my mind filled with all the worries of my current situation; Dad; Mum; my brothers and sisters – what would happen? My current situation was really tough. I prayed earnestly, "Lord, give me hope for the future!" In that moment I was filled with incredible optimism and hope. It seemed such an enormous contrast to my circumstances at the time – yet this was not momentary. I can say now, 30 years later, it was permanent. This hope sustained me for what was coming in the days and years ahead.

After a fierce two-year battle, my father passed away. Our family was crowded around his hospital bed when he took his last breath. The pain his cancer caused was enormous, but this paled into insignificance to the pain it was for him to be leaving such a young family.

In the days that passed following his death and funeral it was as though a weight was lifted. The time of seeing him suffering so much had ended. As I was feeling this I was overcome with emotion. I just broke down and sobbed, it seemed like I had bottled up the sadness and was keeping an eye out for everyone else and organising the funeral and now there was nothing left to organise, no task to hide inside. The tears flowed and the grief could no longer be contained. It was heartbreaking. My younger brother heard me, came in, sat on the bed beside and put his arm around me and we cried together. I was not alone in my suffering.

Following Dad's death, I stayed at home for another six months to make sure Mum would be all right and to support her and the family. Looking back, Mum did an amazing job continuing to raise the five children still at home. She is a courageous woman and never let the grief of losing Dad impact her care for the family. My parents lived their marriage vows, "in sickness and in health". Dad cared for Mum when she was sick and she cared for him when he became ill. They loved each other until the end. I admire and love my Mum. She is whip smart and laughs easily. She is courageous and has raised eight amazing children and now has eighteen grandchildren. She is imperfect, like all of us, but she has taught me so much in the way she accepts people and loves them.

My father was wise, considered, humble, warm and loving. He was reliable, steady and strong. He was always interested in other people and generous if anyone needed help. He made sacrifices and was truly a man for others. He loved greatly and was greatly loved by all. He treated everyone he met with dignity. He was a brilliant engineer according to his co-workers – able to simplify the most complex of problems and arrive at a solution. He was an avid reader with an astute mind yet he was accessible to everyone. A 'bushie' at heart, Dad had a great love of the outdoors and exploring in our four-wheel drive.

I was 23 when Dad died. He was just 48 years old. When I turned 48, I realised just how young that is. At different points in my life, I have looked at where Dad was at the same age and thought about what his journey must have been like. Yes, indeed, he had not taught me all the things he wanted to teach me or shown me all the things he wanted to show me. But perhaps that would always be the case — there would be more wisdom to impart and share. I have missed. many times, not being able to pick up the phone or sit with him and ask the big questions, or even just to sit and drink beer together. I would have liked him to have been at my university graduation, I would have loved to hear him make a speech at my wedding, I have missed his meeting my wife and being a grandfather to my two girls.

I also felt grief for my younger siblings – especially my younger brothers. They needed a Dad and I could not be that for them. I could, however, do many of the things that Dads do for their sons for my brothers. That in part, is the baton Dad passed to me. I took them to their football matches, on some occasions I attended parent-teacher interviews at their schools, took them camping and four-wheel driving and even taught some of them to abseil. I joined them on their scout camps and one brother came and lived with my wife and I while he was in Year 12. I always wanted to be available for them and encourage them in any way I could. I am so proud of them in so many ways. They are all adult men now with their own children. I know Dad would have been very proud of them and the men they have become. I am humbled when they seek me out for advice and even more delighted that they are men I can seek insight from, too. My interest in the well-being of my siblings will probably never leave me and nor should it. I now find myself invested in my nieces and nephews like a grandfather would be – although I am way too young for that title!

One of the best decisions I have ever made was asking Josephine Mitchell to marry me. Twenty-five years later I am so grateful for her influence in my life. We have been through many joys together and many hardships too. She has been supportive of me in my entrepreneurial journey. She is wise and insightful and I could not think of a better role model as a strong articulate woman for our two daughters, Sophia and Olivia.

Becoming a father changed me in ways I did not expect. The week after Sophia was born I had a Tai Kwon Do grading. This involved full contact sparring and even though you are wearing shin pads and gloves, you can still feel the power of your opponent. After holding a baby in hospital for the last week the last thing I felt like was full contact sparring! Something inside me had softened – this little bundle of joy had unlocked something inside me. Here I was lining up with a gorilla for our sparring and I am all soft inside. Not until he landed a few good hits on me was I able to fire up!

I have learned as a parent, you can't hide from your kids, they see you night and day, in the good and the difficult. For a parent, this can be humbling. My kids have seen me at my best and loved me at my worst.

No one sets out to be a bad parent – but it is easy to slip into the patterns and habits. The wake-up call for me was when Sophia, our eldest, was three months old and I realised I had been travelling for work for six weeks out of the twelve. Half of her life! This realisation set me on a pathway to be more present. Being present was something I really struggled with. Early in my career I was so focused on work it consumed me. Here I was still trying to prove myself.

In my work I was also 'proving myself'. I would continue to take on more responsibility and was not very good at saying 'no'. I would just put myself out and at times, others, to get the task done. When I completed my business degree I worked as a national marketing manager for two companies before starting our first business. In one of these roles I found myself stepping into the breach between the managing director and my team. Prior to my joining that company the marketing team had not been paid overtime. In those days it was not uncommon for people to work some additional hours on an *ad hoc* basis, but when it's sustained for weeks on end it's not a fair and reasonable expectation. I was able to bring justice to that situation for my team and then overtime was paid. During this season of work, I worked seven days a week for three months to meet a deadline. Looking back it was madness, as I did not want to disappoint anyone but it also showed me that I have a great capacity for work. It just needed to be balanced.

I remember coming home late from work one night to find the house in darkness. Jo had packed up the girls and gone to visit her parents. Her comment, "You're never home anyway", struck a chord. Even when I was home I was not present. This was a big wake-up call for me about my priorities. I was not going to sacrifice my marriage and my family on the altar of work. It was then I decided to start my first business to have more control over how I would work. This time allowed me greater flexibility with a young family.

When Jo and I met we were both students and did not have much. We joked then that if all we had was each other, a bottle of wine and some fish and chips on the beach, life would be OK. We are stronger together. Adversity brings us closer together – and in business there are always challenges. She calls out the best in me and hopefully I do the same for her. I want everyone in our house to flourish. Jo grew up seeing her Dad bring her Mum a cup of tea in bed in the morning – a beautiful ritual that I have adopted. Every day I make Jo her morning cup of tea and then make her a coffee to take to work.

I wanted to be intentional and have great relationships with my two daughters and not miss their growing up because I was distracted in my own world. I remember coming home from work one day and Sophia was playing with her dolls in her dolls' house. I was standing in my world, and she was sitting on the ground in her world. I changed out of my work clothes and got down on the ground to venture into her world; the world of a dolls' house, dolls, tiny furniture all neatly ordered and in its place. She told me all her dolls' names and I learnt them all! It was important to her, so it was important to me – and she would get cross if I mixed them up! This was a great lesson for me. I was getting out of my world and into hers.

I called it 'ground time.' In fact, for me as a Dad, it was very grounding. Often ground time would turn into wrestle mania and pillow fights. It was fun and playful. As a Dad, I have always encouraged my girls to be adventurous – whether it be mountain biking, surfing or climbing a mountain or training in martial arts. They have grown up with an imperfect father who has been mostly accessible and present. If I am not, they have no hesitation in telling me so! They know I love them and would lay down my life for them.

I recall one of my daughters who would have been around 13 or 14 years old, berating me and telling me in no uncertain terms what a terrible father I was on a particular occasion. She was really mad at me and was not holding back, expressing her frustration with some rather colourful language. Rather than getting mad at her for the way she was speaking to me (which would been well justified, although it would have served just to shut her down) I had the presence of mind to shut up and listen. I thought that even though she was so angry with me, at least the channels of communication, while a little strained, were still open. Even though I was in the wrong, I was secretly happy that she felt able to tell me about it. When I was her age, I would have just shut down on my parents.

Dad was active in the home – cooking and washing up, hanging out clothes, fixing things. An enduring image is of my Dad in the kitchen with a tea towel over his shoulder. More often than not one of the kids was drying up while Dad washed. We had many great conversations while doing the dishes together. Dad served our family. This has provided another great example for me in our home. At times I struggle to change gears when I get home from work – I was kindly reminded by my wife one day when I arrived home that I was not the General Manager! The kitchen is a hub in our house and you will often find me with a tea towel over my shoulder and doing the dishes. I actually like it now. It helps me change gears from work into home life.

A humbling part of the fathering journey is when you fail. I have fallen short many times as a Dad – I have been impatient, checked out, preoccupied and stressed. I have said things in the heat of the moment that have been hurtful and that I have regretted immediately. In those moments, I have not been the father that I want to be. I have had to ask for forgiveness. My girls have been gracious in forgiving me. They know, at my core, I love them more than anything else. I hope that in our marriage, Jo and I have provided a good example of the loving and equal partnership that our marriage strives to be.

Both of our daughters have an entrepreneurial flair and I joke that one day I would like to work for them. Our eldest, Sophia, has worked with me in our business and it has been such a gift to work side by side with her and see her flourish. I am proud of how our daughters are growing up and the people they are becoming. I like hanging out with them and finding adventure – hiking or having coffee after a bike ride. Most of all I like listening to them. That gives me the greatest joy of all when they want to hang out and chat. They are growing into wise women and I learn so much from them.

Being a father has not been limited to my two girls. I have had the honour of being a father figure, brother and mentor, to many others too, inside my family and out. This has been done simply by journeying with people over time – my sisters and brothers, young men seeking mentoring and guidance, men who have worked for me in our business. I too, have been fathered. I have been very lucky to have a number of key men who have been in my life as mentors and friends for the last 30 years. Men who have encouraged me – and seen more in me than I would have ever seen or believed.

The journey of fatherhood has been more about who I am becoming rather than what I am doing. As men, it is easy for us to take our self-worth and identity from what we do rather than who we become. I have been guilty of this and may keep battling with this for a while longer. I remember looking at my kids when they were babies - I loved them so much! All they could do was poo and cry and feed. This love is unconditional. Now they are teenagers I love them still, and it has nothing to do with what they do (although a little cleaning around the house would not go astray!).

Having been a father for nearly 20 years I am still on the learning journey. I am on the journey of transformation, just like Dad was. I have followed in my father's footsteps as a man of faith. God's grace guides and strengthens me. It is transforming and healing. I have grown up in an age of self-help. I read *The Power of Positive Thinking* by Norman Vincent Peale when I was 18 – it changed my thinking forever. Since then I have read many books and made many changes in my life. The wonderful thing about the human condition is that we have the power to change. The inner faith journey I have been on has brought about deep interior transformation and healing that was beyond the reach of what I could do myself. I believe God is still at work in me, shaping me into the man he created me to be. I hope to be a legacy man like my father, a man for others. A man who lived a life that was beyond himself.

Rather than offer fathering tips about what other men should do, I will share what I am trying to do and plan to do more of in the future:

1. Listen and be present.
2. Encourage always.
3. Love wholeheartedly.
4. Be available.
5. Continue to be adventurous.

Some recommended reading

Richard Rohr, *Falling Upward*

Mark E Thibodeaux, *God's Voice Within: The Ignatian Way to Discover God's Will*

Simon Senek, *Start with Why*.

8

Jude Hennessy
The spark of the infinite

Just half a cigarette

I was born on the first day of summer 1968 at St George Hospital in Sydney. I was to find out many years later that I was only half a cigarette away, one or two deep drawbacks, from the realm of non-existence.

Just a few years earlier, Terence Jude Hennessy, my father, was waiting nervously for a mate of his who'd talked him into meeting a young primary school teacher. So, my fate was hanging on a blind date and Dad's mate was running late! Dad recounts that the smoke had been lit and if they hadn't

Kerrie holding Rachel, Jude holding Tara.

Jude and his wife, Kerrie.

arrived by the time he'd finished, he was off.

Michele Philomena Newman turned up in the nick of time and Dad met Mum on the steps of NSW Leagues Club in 1964. They talked and danced, shared stories, made connections, and the two discerning very good sorts stole a kiss and fell in love.

Mum and Dad married and I was on the way in double quick time, born on 1 December 1968, heading home to a single room in my godfather's house in North Cronulla. "We didn't have two coins to rub together but were ridiculously happy," Dad would often say. I joke often that Mum and Dad were obviously in a competition to come up with the most Catholic name possible for one of their kids. I think mine won – baptised Jude Augustine, names I have slowly come to love because of who they are in my broader family, the Church, even if they were the source of plenty of childhood scuffles.

A praying grandma

My Grandma, Lena, had been a teacher before marrying John Hennessy. Dad was the youngest of their four kids and they lived in multiple country towns throughout New South Wales and Queensland, running the family pubs, building each one up, selling up and then moving on – regularly. Their love story is amazing, and like many of these musings, could fill a longer story. My grandfather had died six years earlier, Dad finding him slumped on his bed, but well dressed and ready for first Friday Mass.

Lena looked after me during the days so Mum could quickly return to work. I'm told she would sit by my cot, praying continual rosaries. Mum has often commented that I didn't stand a chance of becoming too wayward or shaky in my faith as a result, and in the main I guess, she has been right.

Less than a year after I was born, on the Feast of St Jude, 28 October 1969, Lena had a stroke. Mum and Dad moved into her unit that very night to care for her. She would pass away a few months later, not long before the birth of my little brother Luke.

What a whirlwind my parents were caught up in. Joy and loss were all mixed together in a 'stop the world I want to get off' sort of ride and this didn't abate for the next few years.

The visitors' book

My first true memory is the leaving of that little unit on Shelly Beach Park in Cronulla on my third birthday to a little fibro house with a green tin roof in Caringbah. It was a magical place that had so many holes in the windows and ceiling that there was ivy growing on the walls in our kitchen and lounge room. Mum and Dad would laugh that it was only the ivy and strategically twisted coat hanger wire that held the place up, but this knock-down house on the rambling block was theirs. No doubt, my later love for the purchase of 'fixer upperers' was instilled in me by this little place.

A visitor's book was unfurled that very night. These days it is several books, joined together, showing a family history of parties, birthdays, wakes, drop-ins, graduations – whatever. It is full of thousands of names, a word here, a poem there, a thank you, a scripture verse, a joke or funny story, reflections and gratitude for good times, with good people in that house, and in the one that would be built on its site a few years later.

Life seemed to bounce from one barbecue to the next, with Mum on the piano, Dad on the guitar, relatives joining in, all of them seemingly able to play an instrument, sing something or spin a yarn, and no one got off without contributing, this was an all-in affair. The music certainly drew a crowd, it was the spark of the infinite, according to Dad, a line he stole from his much listened-to mentor, Archbishop Fulton Sheen. Mum and Dad were seemingly the pied pipers of fun, that was the way they were going to do life, and to put it into today's language, that is how they were going to share the joy of the gospel.

Hard yards and loss

In the midst of all this easy to recall fun, were the hard yards, the stuff that kids don't always see and rarely remember. Here were the routines that build character, that establish patterns for both discipline and security. When the time came, Mum and Dad knew how to party, but they worked hard and prayed harder. Dad was working long hours. This happy-go-lucky larrikin had considered priesthood, had studied but not completed Law and Medicine at Sydney University, but left to take on the running of a family bar in Kings Cross. At age 22, he was the youngest licensee in Australia. After his father's death, he got a job with the Post Master General (PMG). I get the sense now that he frantically made up for lost time and opportunities, applying a fierce intellect to move quickly up the ranks with what would become Telecom and later Telstra. If you spend ten minutes with my father, even now at 87, after brain surgery to remove a tumour the size of a mango, you get a sense of the vortex that is his mind.

My father was proud and unwavering in his love of and trust in the Church and its teachings. In the late 1970s he came to a deep personal relationship with Christ via the Catholic Charismatic Renewal, a heart conversion that when combined with his already well-honed intellectual grasp of the faith, meant that he had the passion and capacity to share his faith – when the time was right. I wanted to be like this too.

Described by her peers and students as a brilliant teacher, Mum, or Mickey as everyone calls her, worked hard but kept priorities in the order she wanted. God and Dad were first, family second and work, somewhere below that. She loved the classroom, never sought promotion, was adept and organised.

Mickey had been school captain in 1960, the year in which her Mum would pass away in an instant, the night before she was to start her final exams – the 'Leaving'. A brilliant pianist, always humming, always a peacemaker, she is clever, particularly in reading people. She has been deeply blessed for sure, but she has needed every bit of her steely resilience, especially in her 47 year career with the Department of Education where she often felt the bigotry of her workplace as a fiercely Catholic woman. I was learning in what I saw and heard that living your faith authentically meant making yourself a target.

Outside the principal's office

I started school in 1974 at Our Lady of Fatima; however I really just wanted to be at home with my brother Luke and Aunty Kath who looked after us when Mum went to work. Then Angela Mary, my sister, was born. What a joy, a little girl and she seemingly came with a new car, a white Valiant with red leather seats! Each new baby seemed to come with a new car, how excellent! In all this, new games were to be learnt like soccer, cricket and rugby.

My wife-to-be was a pretty, dark-haired girl in the next grade up. I remember her from Legion of Mary meetings at lunchtime. She apparently doesn't remember my being there, but, of course, remembers me regularly waiting outside the principal's office to explain another refereeing dispute that I'd sorted out decisively. Let's just say I was pretty competitive and had a heightened sense of justice!

Blue skies turned to grey. In the space of three years, we lost Dad's older brother Tom and sister Kathleen. Both had cerebral haemorrhages and were gone in an instant in their mid-40s. Tom had the irresistibility of a black hole, stylish and capable. Both were incredible musicians, on display at what felt like weekly parties at someone's house. Kath was like a second Mum. I was five and seven when they died, and Dad and Mum were so sad. I remember developing a strong fear that Dad was next, with good reason I suppose, so I liked keeping him in my sight.

Joseph Bede was born in the middle of these two losses and my sister Kathleen, not long after Aunty Kath's passing. It was a cyclone of happiness and grief, of dreaming futures and remembering losses.

Marking middle stump

At about the same time that Kerry Packer started the cricket revolution, the concrete was laid in our backyard for the cricket net. I reckon I spent more hours standing on that painted crease hitting cricket balls than anywhere else on the planet. We boys were all fairly decent players as a result, but it became a huge part of my identity. "Jude - oh, you're the cricketer" became my identity as I came to set new club and then association records for runs and averages, some set by Test Cricketers.

By 13, I found myself a boy amongst men playing grade cricket for Sutherland, captaining rep sides, and at 15, playing Green Shield, just like my Dad had done, scoring a stack of runs and winning this prestigious comp. Still, a growing nervousness was becoming part of who I was. I started throwing up before games, fair enough too, I was 15 and training with men who played at the highest level, having bruises the size of dinner plates to prove it. Other bruises were taking longer to heal though. I was taunted a lot at training, for my name, my quiet nature, and also for my faith. I didn't know how to counter it – I was too damn polite!

When I was hit by a car just before turning 17, I was almost relieved to think that it meant I couldn't play for a while. That turned into two seasons as I excused myself so I could knuckle down to senior school. I thought it would devastate my Dad. It didn't, and he could probably see how the exposure of his boy to too much, too soon, was not turning out to be positive. When I finally told Dad I didn't want to play anymore, I remember him quite deliberately affirming me, saying, "No problems Gus, I love you whatever you want to do, cricket isn't who you are." In a way, he freed me from the pressure and expectation of being 'the cricketer'.

Laying on hands

During this time, Dad's sister, Pauline, had an operation. Something went wrong. I rushed to Canberra Hospital with Dad. Her husband Jack, who'd served heroically in the British Navy in World War II, was distraught. She was his life and together they had endured much, including the birth, and loss, of five children. She had the glamorous style and substance befitting her opera singer training, like her own father. Breathing machines did the work of lungs, but there were no machines to do the work of the brain. Doctors spoke of needing to turn the machines off as it was time for nature to be allowed to take its course. I just sat with Pauline, holding her hand and praying for her, while important discussions were held between the adults and doctors. After many months of visits, we were distraught as we said a final goodbye to Aunty Pauline, driving home.

Uncle Jack phoned a few days later and said he'd decided the machines would be turned off overnight. He would phone us in the morning to organise what would happen next – meaning the funeral.

Desperate, Dad jumped in the car and headed to the weekly Charismatic prayer meeting where he and Mum were now leaders. There had to be a way, he couldn't lose them all, in their 40s, all in the space of a few years. I was there as the crazy Charismatics prayed over Dad for his sister, for a miracle.

The phone rang early on Thursday morning with Dad adopting the voice he reserved for the sort of manly conversations you had with the tradesman who might come to fix a tap or a powerpoint. Then there was a lot of silence, pauses, a few questions, puzzled looks, then smiles.

Pauline had started breathing by herself. Not only that, she had woken up, the inactive brain had switched on, she had called out from her bed for some help, she wanted a shower and something to eat! Doctors came from far and wide with great disbelief.

Praying for miracles was one thing, but having one happen in such dramatic fashion – well, I was now at a point in my faith of never being able to be unconvinced. Joy ensued, great praise of God, much laughter. I remember looking at her from the bridal table at my wedding a decade later, still marvelling at the wondrous, miraculous nature of God. My faith became ferocious and 'Fr Jude' became my new nickname at school.

Finishing school

I was elected school captain in Year 10. Rather than being an opportunity and an honour, it was full of pressure and ridicule. A heap of stuff happened, including being maliciously set up for and accused of selling drugs, something funny to pin on the School Captain, Fr Jude. I would be exonerated on that 'charge', clearly set up, but still missed out on a place at the senior Catholic school I'd applied to attend as a result of the rumours. Apparently where there is smoke, there is fire. Eventually, I was given the chance to beg for entry from the headmaster, pleading my innocence, in tears. He eventually gave me a spot but with obvious doubt about my innocence and character, regardless of who vouched for me.

My confidence was rocked. I remember being asked to read by my history teacher from the textbook when they eventually let me into the school, now surrounded by girls at the co-educational De La Salle, Cronulla. I'd gone from making speeches and running assemblies every week at school the year before to not being able to make a noise. I just froze. "Go on Fr Jude,' someone taunted, kids laughed, but I didn't have any fight left in me at this point. The page was spinning with words and my heart was about to jump out of my chest. "Pick someone else", was all I could muster. It sounded rude, so I said it again as politely as Jude Hennessy would.

Thus began a period of going into hiding as far as I possibly could. The lack of confidence to read and speak in all but the most 'friendly' situations with my peers would remain with me for the better part of the next 20 years in a debilitating anxiety that became quite routine. I came to seek out Dad a lot during this time. I could talk to him about anything and he would pray with me most mornings. The nervousness that I had seen in him so many times was coming to be a part of me too.

A wonderful priest

On the way home from school, I would regularly duck into my Parish Church, Our Lady of Fatima, Caringbah. It was a place of great refuge for me, where I still came with Dad for the 2-3am Adoration shift on first Fridays. It was where I prayed from the prayer book of my grandfather, John Hennessy, seeing his annotations, really wishing I'd known him. Dad says I am him all over. Same build, same look, same style. He was an 'all rounder' in every sense of the word. He had been an incredible musician, doing all grades in the piano and voice at the conservatorium in Sydney, before being put into pubs by his own father. He is in the sporting hall of fame at St Joseph's College Hunters Hill, one of very few to be in the First XI Cricket, Rugby XV, Rowing VIII and incredibly, was GPS boxing champion. It seems like he could choose to put you to sleep with boxing gloves or operatic lullabies. He had a Papal Knighthood for service to the Church and by all reports an imposing presence, and yet Dad said he never heard him once raise his voice. When running the pubs, he only ever had to ask men to leave – and they did – no one wanted to mess with Jack Hennessy.

Anyhow, I was actually praying the house down at this point, and coming to experience moments of great joy and comfort in the midst of great confusion, a clear sense of 'hang in there Jude, I've got you and I've got this'. It was on one of those afternoons that the new parish priest, Fr Kerry Bayada, came in the back door to lock up the church and found me at the back of the church. I'd written to him when he was vocation director, when I was a very grown up 12 years old. I was now 16 and this was my first actual meeting with him. "What's doing?" he asked. Well, he got the full run down and I poured my guts out to him, finishing with something along the lines of, "I feel like the only person my age who actually believes this stuff." His response was, "Let's do something about it".

What ensued over the next few years was the development of some amazing youth ministry and youth Masses. I got to see the reach of peer to peer ministry, what an encounter with the kerygma, the Holy Spirit and the sacraments could do for the lives of young people. It was clear that the power of music and testimony were amazing. Lives were changed, friendships were forged and good Catholic marriages came about. Whenever I see Dr Ron and Mavis Pirola, founders of Antioch in Australia, I thank them for what it did for me, my family and for ensuring I met my wife, Kerrie.

Catching Kez

Kerrie and I first spoke in the school library at lunchtime. She was genuinely there to do some work, obviously very studious. For me it was just part of my hiding in the shadows strategy.

Thank goodness for her old Malvern Star. I was able to use that gearless blue bike to my advantage and would try to be somewhere she would run out of puff riding up the hill on our way home. She would slow down, say hello and we'd walk together, pushing her bike to the top of the hill. I would normally go straight on but would turn and walk alongside her. The extra ten minutes or so home was worth it, that's for sure, she was beautiful and gentle.

I asked her at some point to do the next Antioch Weekend. She said no, genuinely keen to study in preparation for exams, but in the end, she was there. She loved it, and I could see how beautiful, amazing and grace-filled she was! We were asked to lead the next Antioch weekend together. It meant doing a whole heap of talks and work together in preparing a team, planning, writing and praying together. All of a sudden, I had a bit of confidence again, or was able to fake it a little better with Kerrie around. I met her family; I'd always seen them at Mass. Her Mum and Dad ended up helping out with the weekend too, cooking for 60 young people.

Young love bloomed. We started going out when I was 17, just before Kerrie finished school. I would benefit from her meticulous HSC notes the following year – my goodness, how could anyone write so neatly? Thoughts of the priesthood remained for a while and led to breaks at different points, as did arguments here and there. I finished school and started teaching Religion in state schools as a volunteer while studying at Sydney University. On top of that I studied Theology at the Aquinas Academy in Sydney, and did a certificate in Youth Ministry, keen to be a teacher. Kez was too, ploughing through her course with great success and ridiculously good marks in preparing for primary school teaching.

God says no sometimes

At that point, a real test came the way of Kerrie's family. Her Dad, Paul, walking home, was struck by a car while on a pedestrian crossing. The family asked me to join them at the hospital. It was carnage, there was just so much blood. I led the Rosary on autopilot at Agnes' request. The hours and days that followed saw different strands of hope plucked out of their fingers. This fit man in his early 50s had a brainstem injury. He was in a coma.

I'd been here before though. Yes, God had come through with a miracle for Aunty Pauline. It's going to be OK, I believed with great confidence. Novenas were prayed, saints invoked, Holy Spirit called upon for miracles, the whole parish was involved. Wounds healed in his flesh, but not in the brainstem. They, we, my family too, were with Paul every day for almost 10 months, except one. He seemingly took that as permission to go – passing on 23 December 1988.

I found out that sometimes God says no. I found out that crosses are real and not to be shunned. Kez and her Mum remained full of faith, sad but trusting. I was angry with the driver, with God, wanted justice, an explanation, and for the girl and family I love, the miracle that was prayed for. I was not happy with almighty God and began a period of giving God pretty short quarter, because this is not how you are supposed to look after your kids, I thought, with all my infinite wisdom.

Plenty more where that came from – but never enough

Kez took some time off university to catch her breath and earn some money. Then she finished her teaching and went overseas, to London, travelling with a young woman who would a few years later become our sister-in-law.

I was missing Kerrie dreadfully, writing and waiting on letters. The heart would grow more aware and definitely fonder. I was having a good time and getting good marks pretty easily as long as I didn't have to speak, and took up cricket again, finding a whole bunch of people saying, "Hey, this bloke can play". I was awarded undergraduate Cricketer of the Year in my first season with Sydney University.

It was at this time I discovered I had something in common with Doug Walters, and it wasn't cricket-related. I discovered a penchant for smoking like a chimney and drinking a lot of beer – pretty damn quickly too. There was a period where you could be excused for thinking that I was doing my best to represent Australia in these pursuits. That combined with a great job at the Sydney Cricket Ground looking after the private boxes meant I was working hard, but playing harder.

No wonder our wise mother started to recount stories of her Dad. How she would go downstairs and pour his crates of whiskey down the sink, delivered with almost the same regularity as the milk for their milk bar-cum-betting shop. Grandpa Frank would say to her with a wink and a smile, there's plenty more where that came from dear girl, before eventually joining Alcoholics Anonymous.

Mum was wisely making us aware of what was in us. Dad's side too, with three generations of pubs, knew how to have a drink as well. It was something Kez feared too, having seen it in her heritage and she raised my need to ease my extremes and not make everything a competition. The ebb and flow between knowing what is moderation and what is not has been a journey for me, one that I got under control pretty early on, but not without some wreckage on the way, and the potential is still there.

Thrown in the deep end

After her return from London, Kerrie took a teaching job. I finished University and started teaching as well. I was invited to go and play some County Cricket in England. I said no, and while occasionally daydreaming about what that might have been like, I have never regretted it. I had wanted to marry Kerrie since we started walking home from school and we had been boyfriend and girlfriend for six years. Yes, there had been a few breaks along the way, allowing for testing of our hearts at different points. We were very different in so many ways, but the same in all the things we thought truly mattered. We loved God, and we loved each other. We spoke of our hopes for family and home, for a life together. We had next to nothing behind us financially but had some big hopes and dreams and a work ethic that was rare. We felt we could do anything.

We were married when I was 23, on 11 April 1992 by our priest who had become like a second father to us both, in the church where we had seen each other grow up from a distance, surrounded by family and so many common friends. This was the best day of my life, both for what happened on that day, and for what has happened because of this love and this union since – for better and for worse.

I started teaching at Freeman College, an amazing opportunity in a new school. I was surrounded by incredible practitioners. Not long after we were married, a bub was on the way. We were taken by surprise, but happily. We were living in a unit in Cronulla, driving a couple of old but reliable cars, saving as best we could. I started working a night job at Cronulla Leagues Club, behind the bar, on the door, cleaning dunnies – whatever. It was easy for me to get a gig there with Dad and my uncles foundation members of the Sharks. Things were going well; money was being scraped together.

I received a teary phone call from Kerrie one afternoon. She was on her way to hospital with a miscarriage, apparently not uncommon in your first pregnancy. The hour-long drive from Bonnyrigg to Sutherland Hospital was full of swirling thoughts and emotions. I've never felt farther from home. I was getting ready to be with Kerrie as she underwent some procedures that necessarily follow a late term miscarriage. Lo and behold, the ultrasound technician paused, said, "Hang on, no, the baby is still there, heart beating loud and strong."

Kez would have to take it very easy from here on in for a few months, but in what seemed like no time at all, Tara Kate was born on 12 June 1993. She had put her Mum through a labour that ended in an emergency caesarean, so I was handed this beautiful little girl for her first precious half hour, all on my own, whilst doctors looked after Kerrie.

I did what crazy Charismatics do when they want to pray but don't know what to say. I was a Dad, and something changed, immediately. I would do anything for this girl. Whatever it took. My mind shifted gear to all the things I would need to do, wanted to do for her, to show her, to teach her and to give her. I visualised putting myself in harm's way to keep her out of it and what I would ferociously do to anyone who ever hurt her. Dark hair and eyes stared back at me in some out of time moments. She still has them.

Tara was a much loved, continuously cuddled first grandchild. I have a treasured photo of her looking up at me wide-eyed while I sang and played guitar to her, my face freshly smashed in from a cricket ball that I was overly confident about hooking over the boundary. She was so alert and grew quickly, which was good, because before she was walking, she had a little sister on the way, and I dropped cricket faster than a low-down slips catch.

We looked at a house in Caringbah. No one else seemingly wanted it. It was a deceased estate. We got it at a very good price. The owner asked us what we were going to build on it when we knocked it down. What do you mean, knock it down? We would be living in it!

Baby Rachel arrived, 27 October 1994. What a cherub, with Hennessy red hair to boot, and plenty of it, straight out of the blocks. Another surge of protective, die hard, I'll do anything for you manhood juice rushed through me. How could they be so different, yet so the same? This little one was to be fiery, determined, hard to budge for good and for ill. I was busting with love and determination to be who I needed to be and do what I needed to do for her. More prayer and awe filled my heart, and a deep admiration for Kez who had endured another caesarean and was an amazing, nurturing Mum.

Blood, sweat and tears

Isn't it funny how the things you really want to remember, and wish were indelible, end up being a bit blurry because of how flat out you were going? I was working three jobs, loving as well as I could and took on the renovation of this falling down house single-handed. Through trial and error, I became 'handy,' serving a self-directed apprenticeship that would get me through three owner-builds. Walls were plastered, floors reinforced, roofs fixed, kitchen pulled out, bathrooms tiled, windows replaced, concreting done, gardens created from nothing. The place looked a picture – this was an awesome home, an incredible back yard, in our home parish. It put us on our feet financially, via buckets of sweat and some blood to boot.

Our place seemed to be the drop-in centre for everyone we had grown up with. It was barbecue central. I could run on fumes with this sort of a life. Kerrie, in fact most normal people, could not, and should not have to. It was the source of some big tests for us.

Another bub was on the way! A boy perhaps, here comes the cricket team, well at least half a cricket team. This time the miscarriage was for real, at home, taken in our stride. These things happen and we've been lucky and blessed thus far, we rightly thought.

The one that followed, however, required the hospital. It was dangerous, something called an ectopic pregnancy, where the baby grows in the fallopian tube, not the womb, and the pain alerted us to the miscarriage and the danger. My wife Kez is little but super tough. We were consoled by the explanation that these were rare, a one in 1000 chance.

Closer to home

I got a new job, much closer to home, a school expanding to take senior students for the first time. Then a number of things happened in the matter of months that rocked me to the core, and looking back, I was holding on by a thread.

I sang at the funeral of a student who died in tragic circumstances, the third time I had done so in twelve months. Then, a dear friend, someone who I studied and taught with, played sport with, died. I had a photo of him in our backyard holding Rachel after her Baptism, during his time of pastoral placement whilst studying for the priesthood. This was a good man.

He'd headed bush to teach after leaving the seminary with a real passion for Aboriginal people. He'd been accused of something, later proven and admitted as a mischievous fabrication. He was sent home with little explanation or support. He hung himself in his backyard. I sang at his funeral – too numb to look at his mother.

Julia, my assistant Year 10 Co-ordinator, was a rock for me during this time, looking after our 220 Year 10s like a mother hen. She looked after me too, always ready for a laugh, some encouragement, a listening ear. My girls would run to her whenever I took them on visits to the school. She was such an outgoing, joyful woman, who was even able to con me into agreeing to do a tandem parachute jump with her before I finished at the school.

I answered the phone after getting home from Sunday Mass just as a 'small group' of people was arriving for an impromptu post-Mass barbecue and we were frantically tidying up. Julia had been in an accident. She was in a formation parachute jump, "but - we are so sorry Jude – her chute didn't open." I sang at her funeral later that week and at the graduation Mass for 'our' Year 10s days later.

Within a month, I would have my last day at Freeman College. I made a speech, regressing into old anxieties, unable to say all I wanted to say, to much-loved friends. I loved this place and it had loved me back – healing many parts of me. I'd written the school song, with a friend, a song they still sing today. I didn't make it home that night. I'd tried to drink all the beer in Sydney and apparently came fairly close. I woke up on concrete to the sound of swimmer's arms slapping the water for early morning squad training – somewhere. I eventually got home quite battered and slept for as long as two little girls let you sleep.

Kez was very understanding of what was going on at this point, perhaps too forgiving, but she knew I was rocked, really shaken, brittle.

To turn the screws a little more, my two brothers, the lads I'd shared a room with just about every night before I'd married, had left Caringbah. One was in Perth and one in Brisbane. They were married to great girls but I really missed them, and at this point, I really needed some brothers, and would have grasped at anything vaguely resembling brotherhood.

My next school appointment turned out to be a great test for me, but a wonderful place in the end. There was much to do and little time to do it in. I worked most of those school holidays, trying to prepare for, and be ready to win over a staff who just wanted the bloke whose job I'd apparently stolen. Still, I did OK. I won little battles, little confidences, and again was surviving on a regimen of hard work and a heap of prayer. I learnt about cultural change here, which was good, because it has been part and parcel of every professional role I have taken on since.

Thank God for forgetfulness

The new school made a move possible for us. The idea of escaping the manic life associated with being a grown up in the place where we had been kids, amongst friends who still wanted to be kids, was attractive. Kerrie had time off work as Tara started her first week of school and we moved into a rented old farmhouse as part of our 'head south' adventure. Halfway up Bulli pass, I turned back, having left my guitar for the opening school Mass at home. Thank God for my forgetfulness. I came back in the door to see a little girl in her kindy outfit and pre-school Rachel, holding each other's hands and trying to help Mum off the floor.

I got Kerrie to Wollongong Hospital – wherever the bloody hell that was – into the emergency ward. By the time I'd parked the car and come back, I was whisked into a room. Kerrie was now in agony, then barely conscious, then unconscious within minutes. Alarms were going off everywhere, bags of blood were being squeezed into her frantically. I was just talking to her five minutes ago – but there was no talking now, just the frantic yelling of doctors with maybe eight people around her. It was an out of time experience for me as they rushed Kerrie into surgery. Doctors told me later, it was lucky we had arrived when we did. She had lost so much blood that heart failure had been imminent. The Lord was looking after us again, I thought – hoped.

It wasn't until later that night, that squeezing my hand Kez tearfully whispered, "Well – no more babies!" I hadn't given that a thought. It had been another one in 1000 chance ectopic pregnancy, but I was just glad to have Kerrie and had endured a number of hours that day not knowing if she would make it. Over time, both realisations began to sink in for us. We had two beautiful blessings in our daughters. There would be many more blessings and challenges to come, but no more children – not of our own, anyhow.

What followed was a time of great emotional ups and downs for us both, very much for Kerrie, and I kept the losses of the last few years, bottled up, very manfully – whatever the hell that meant. My Dad's saying of whatever isn't transformed will be transferred became a distinct possibility for me.

Soon after, I was asked to take on the role of Religious Education Co-ordinator at this new school. I was young to be taking on this role and was juggling weekend study to complete a Master's degree in Education. I was pulled in a whole lot of directions, kicking quite a few goals professionally but working some very long hours.

At home in the pub

I started playing squash and having a drink with some blokes from the parish mid-week. At one of these post-squash pub drinks, one of the lads grabbed a guitar, threw it at me and said, have a crack. It was walk up mic night – but I only played at church. A couple of beers in, I sang two songs, more to shut my mates up. The pub owner said, "You can sing mate – do you want a gig?" What? Seriously?

Within a year, I would be singing on my own in pubs all around Sydney and the Illawarra, at outdoor cafés and at countless parties. The money was amazing, which was great, because we had bought another house in Thirroul and I just hate being in debt. Thus began a ten-year stint of being an REC in two schools by day and a wannabe rock star by night.

It was great fun - at first, but by the time I packed up, drove home, calmed down and went to bed, it was regularly two or three am. If you ask me to describe this period, it would be 'sleepwalking'. No one was getting the best of me, the girls were faring better than most, but my wife sure wasn't. We started to grow distant. Arguing increased and became habitual.

My go-to point of attack and defence went something like – "I'm working my guts out here, do you even appreciate what I am doing?" – the opposite of servant manhood. Add to that, I was going through the motions with prayer, which fell back to turning up on Sundays, saying grace, not really having a personal relationship with the God who I knew was real. I comforted myself with the excuse that I was still pretty annoyed with what had transpired in the last few years, ridiculously pointing the finger at God. Patterns of sin started to become well-worn roads, particularly in my thinking, my judging, my words, my action – worse still, my inaction.

Do you want me to go?
One Saturday morning, with me sleeping downstairs and Kerrie upstairs after another late night after singing at a pub in Sydney, Kerrie came down and said a few things that I hardly listened to, half asleep. We were heading for a row, following a familiar pattern. I couldn't believe the words that came out of my mouth, even though I had rehearsed saying them in my head for a while now. "Do you want me to go?"

This was once unthinkable to me, but I was asking it – a combination of tiredness, brokenness, hurt and feeling used up. The same was true for Kerrie, and rightly, probably more so. She didn't answer, and that scared me, but I didn't show it. I had in recent years become quite hardened, I knew it – and Kez felt it. Eventually, she simply said, "No" but her answer didn't come easily.

Thank God for his grace in this moment, because, if she had

said yes, I would have gone, in fact, I knew where I was heading, such was my state of mind. I would have regretted it forever, but this was a watershed moment that I am sure will flash before my eyes when I die.

The next thing that came out of my mouth shocked me even more than the question I had asked only moments before. "Well, can you come over here, because we need to pray – together."

So we did as we should have been doing all along. Repenting in our prayer to God and in our conversation with each other. Our girls who were sleeping didn't stir, itself a grace, enabling us to rediscover a little of who we really were, what we were becoming, and figure out what we needed to do about it. We prayed and talked, talked and prayed – for hours. Grace entered at that point. Much would be worked through in ensuing months and years.

Brekky that morning was interrupted by a phone call from someone I'd met a handful of times who told me, "You've been on my mind this morning, I've been praying for you." He said it was a bit out of left field but he wanted to invite us to a Life in the Spirit Seminar. I told him I knew what it was, my Mum and Dad used to run them. That was just the kickstart that our faith needed – renewed by the Spirit, a deepening faith, one that our girls were drawn into as well, with an amazing group of young people. That phone call is one of the greatest gifts of my life. I will forever be in debt to this man on a pivotal day for our marriage and our family.

That experience was followed by a marriage weekend, led by Dr Byron and Francine Pirola. I had always admired this couple from a distance and Byron's parents too. We committed to never going down the path of forgetting the promises we made to one another; embraced simple techniques enabling men to communicate effectively and women to do so with limits, using rules that hit a good balance. We had fallen back on God, and so many aspects of our life were being renewed. We started regular marriage nights in our home.

Soon after, I attended my first menALIVE weekend in Wollongong. It was another transformative experience, bringing me together in an ongoing way with guys who would pray with and for each other every fortnight over an early morning coffee. This was the sort of brotherhood I needed and menALIVE would slowly become a huge influence on my manhood.

Runs on the board

Kez found a lump in her breast. It was probably nothing, she was only in her mid-30s after all. Nope - it was cancer. She was a trooper and we fell back on each other and God as she endured an operation and then radiation therapy. She is more than 10 years cancer-free now. Again, a blessing, as other friends have not been so fortunate. Still, even in saying that, our faith was maturing to endure this stuff with eyes and hearts that were more conscious of eternal realities. We knew that outcomes of even things such as this did not change the love or plans God has in store for us.

I'd moved to a new school too, St Gregory's College, Campbelltown. It again was pretty tough at first, a whole new team had been bought onto the executive to help bring about some cultural change amongst staff and to renew the place in buildings, academic results, and in faith and mission – this last one being my responsibility.

Again, there were some people who were hard work – change is never comfortable for most people – but it was my dream job in so many ways. It already had an amazing culture particularly in sport, a great Marian focus, and there were some people of deep faith there eager to participate in bringing these young men to an encounter with God through vibrant worship. We developed a genuine strategy for giving young men insights into what living a good, noble life might look like in our 'boys to men' program.

Coaching the First XI in cricket was a joy, and to be honest, aided me no end when it came to having some credibility when talking to the boys about faith and Christian manhood. If you could play sport with these lads, they were instantly pretty receptive to what you wanted to tell them. Over the next five years, we would win just about everything you could at a regional, state and national level. More importantly, they came to know what I expected in terms of the style and character of play and behaviour. It was to be honourable and classy and there was plenty of room in the lower grades for even the best cricketers, who thought I was bluffing.

That had been the mainstay of how I taught too, very high standards, giving, and expecting in return, honourable behaviour. They would get my absolute best and I expected it in return. When I see many ex-students today, I often get the remark, "Man, Hennessy – you were pretty scary, you were strict, but we loved you because you wanted the best for us, you taught us really well, and we knew you cared for us." Tick – that's job done, as far as I am concerned.

Other peoples' kids

I cut back on the pub gigs at this point, spending more time with my growing girls, preferring to jam with them as they became really proficient musos. Soon they were able to come to a few of my family-friendly gigs, we started playing together with another family, then for seven years at the Tamworth country music festival, brilliant fun, playing some awesome venues alongside some big names. These remain golden memories.

This 'slow down' enabled us to do something we'd talked about for too long – fostering. We decided on short to medium term placements, anything from weeks to a year, understanding that this interim placement was often difficult – for everyone.

It was gut-wrenching to have kids arrive with little notice and encounter their health issues because of neglect, psychological and behavioural issues, exposed to things that children shouldn't see or hear, often because of addiction.

It was no walk in the park, and it certainly tested the limits of our ability to love and serve generously. Each of us would falter at times but we could rely on each other to pick up the slack. I came to understand that love and service are a choice, not a feeling. We experienced the joy of seeing kids soften, feel safe, smile and laugh, and hardened kids calm down, relax, and begin to really bloom.

The experience again made me incredibly grateful for my own upbringing and environment and it did the same for our now teenage girls too. I was seeing up close and personal what research shows, that fatherhood or fatherlessness is a common denominator of so many things for good or ill, be it economically, emotionally, socially, but especially in the experience of feeling safe and loved.

This period in our lives, which we have only just finished, was one of great growth, coming to see the definite difference between the role of Mums and Dads, particularly for boys. Both roles are essential, but very, very different. Anyone who wants to push a line that says otherwise is constructing a false reality that may well aid their favourite 'isms' but does nothing to help kids.

Rumbling volcanoes

At the end of 2009, the nudging of God in a new direction startled me. I was, believe it or not, walking in the jungle in a place called Bougainville, east of Papua New Guinea. We were there as a family, helping to rebuild a school and train teachers after what was known as 'the crisis', as part of a long service leave trip.

There had been a generation of great brutality in this place, fuelled by greed, the power brought about by mining for gold and copper and the ravages of the ecological destruction it had caused. A lingering stench of violence hovered over the place still. I met many men who needed forgiveness and others who gave it.

Prayer was different up there. There were few distractions. God was doing something in me, and making me feel uneasy, unsettled – like there was something else he wanted me to do. It persisted, as did a strong sense of needing to trust God, that he had something else in store – and that I would say 'yes'.

In sharing this with Kerrie, she was surprised I was even considering the possibility, knowing that I was currently working in my dream job. But it was undeniable and became as loud as the rumbling of the volcano on my arvo walks along the river through the jungle.

Corridors of power

Be careful what you pray for, said my wife on our return, as she put the local paper with a job advert circled on the kitchen table. It was the position of Director of the Confraternity of Christian Doctrine, looking after the 600 catechists in our diocese who saw 10,000 students a week in around 140 state schools. This was the ministry that got me into this teaching caper in the first place.

I got the job with the bishop and kicked off in a new role. The catechists were amazing as I expected, because no one volunteers for this work unless they are 'sold out' for the Gospel. The political climate surrounding this work turned on a storm within weeks of my starting, and because of the particular responsibilities of my bishop, I was thrown into the deep end.

What transpired in a relatively short period was ridiculous and required me to surrender my anxiety and insecurities to the Holy Spirit. I slept little at first, head spinning as I found myself thrust into a world representing the Catholic Church, and increasingly all Christian Churches, in media forums, on radio, TV, quoted and misquoted in papers, identified as a target by secular atheists in commentary, speaking to forums of NSW bishops and other denominational leaders about strategies.

Now, one thing I love, and have a pretty fair knowledge of, is politics, being one of that strange breed of people who deliberately listen to parliamentary question time. I found myself walking parliamentary corridors, meeting with different groups, factions, ministers, advisors, the Premier and other church and faith leaders, advocating for retaining and strengthening this element of public education. We made this all about parental choice for formation in the faith and culture of their family, something that should be celebrated in our increasingly multi-faith society.

A parliamentary inquiry was called for and I was charged to be spokesperson for the Catholic Church across NSW. Two days before, I thought I was going to vomit, knowing that if this didn't go well, if I stuffed it up, we could quickly lose access to around 100,000 Catholic kids per week for formation in the faith of their family. 'What the hell am I doing here?' I was passionate about this ministry and its role in public education, that's for sure, but – I can't speak, I'll be a dribbling mess. The day before I asked my Dad and some trusted friends to pray for me – with me. Trust the Spirit – you know this stuff – he will give you the words when you need them.

I remember walking through the corridors of parliament, through a media scrum, and then being seated to give evidence. I had a steeliness in me that I was aware of and thought, 'OK, that's different'. I was allowed to read from an initial statement, something that I'd worked on with others which was brutal in its assessment of the political and media tactics engaged in this debate so far, but also of the important place of this work in schools. I went in hard – and didn't hold back.

After that, the real test began, being thrown questions without notice, from cunning politicians, the Greens and Labor left, in particular looking to sink this feature of public schools. The grilling went for well over an hour. In many instances, I didn't know what to say, but would pause, pray and then just start. I have looked back at the record of those questions and the answers in the Parliamentary Hansard, over 30 pages of evidence, and am dumbfounded as to where some of the answers came from. There was a clarity and vigour, even some quick wit that disarmed some of the protagonists. At a couple of points I strangely thought to myself, I'm actually enjoying this.

This wasn't me – never has been. Truly, the Spirit was taking my weakness, ensuring I surrendered, and taking over. That was the sort of stuff I'd read about in scripture – it changed me forever – preparing me to say 'yes' to whatever God asks of me – being scared, but doing it anyway.

As I walked out of that hearing, I noted a painting of a man on the wall, the first Member of Parliament in NSW for Bathurst.

It was my great grandfather, Henry William Newman. Mum had said something about this years before. I stopped, stared at the familiar features, and gave him a nod.

More and more speaking, my weak suit, came my way. I started a Catholic podcast called 'The Journey', on our local Christian radio station. It has grown steadily, now in over 25 Christian radio stations each week around Australia. I find this unbelievable. Still now, each time I am asked to speak at an event the pit of my stomach turns a little. I have required healing to be able to do so, from memories, ridicule and from seeing the same reticence and fears in my father. This playing small was at its base camp: prideful, fearing failure, avoiding criticism – and it needed to be surrendered to God. Truly, weakness was made strong – not a strength, just made stronger. There is a difference, one that requires almost daily surrender. My morning prayers always start with, 'I cannot – but you can.'

What now?

I find myself now in a role where after a review of diocesan operations, I am charged with the responsibility of focusing on a broad suite of initiatives as the Director of the Office of Renewal and Evangelisation in the Diocese of Wollongong. I love this job and embrace it as a privileged calling. It is incredibly frustrating at times, especially in a Church seemingly comfortable with managing decline. I've come to trust in the power of the basic gospel, which is the good and largely unknown news of our world. No one ever graduates from the basics – this almost too-good-to-be-true news. This is the fact that we are loved and known by God, who sent his son to save us, and who wants to be in a personal relationship with us now, in the Holy Spirit, through a deep prayer life as members of a Church that when firing on all cylinders, gives us all that we need. These things are our trump cards and it's time we started playing them.

What sort of father have I been?

Well, hopefully you have some decent insights already from what I have shared. Cutting to the chase however, I would say I have tried to be a father and husband who has modelled prayerfulness. I have always prayed with my girls, since their first moments. It is my right and responsibility to do so – fathers have a unique ability to bless, intercede and affirm.

I hope this prayerfulness has assured them of my love, but more so of God's love, and has led them to know that while I am their Dad and have plenty to bring to the table for them, I don't have all that it takes to love them, to protect them, to save them – not near enough – but I know the one who does. I guess I have always tried to take seriously the irrefutable correlation between knowing a loving father and being able to come to know and encounter The Loving Father – Our Heavenly Father.

I hope I have been a Dad who models unconditional love in the same way my Dad did. This is not a syrupy, get along at all costs type of love. That 'love' is gutless and apathetic. Unconditional love does not dodge setting a high bar, is a tough genuine love that sees who our children can be, co-operates with what is innate and gently instils what is lacking. Why? Because it is via both these elements that living life to the fullest is found, with God-given dignity and purpose.

Fathers generally put a high price on being respected, and they should; it is universally one of the biggest needs of manhood, seemingly in our DNA. I have found the best way to be assured of this is to learn how to apologise humbly. Perfection and faultlessness are not what is required of us by God or by our families. An authentic desire to love and serve is, and we need to double down when we don't hit the mark. We need to model saying sorry. Whatever good things we might try to give our own children, I have come to learn and witness in my own experience of raising daughters just how important love, high standards and modelling honesty and apologies are. That is the stuff that enables belief in and respect for the role of fathers, which is a gift that flows both ways.

Rather than build on this any further myself, I have asked my daughters to do so, and while retaining a certain level of anonymity in the combining of their musings, they have reflected on what sort of father they think I have been, how I've changed and how I am similar to or different from my own father. What they have written is a gift to me, and they and I hope it gives you some insights that help you in your own journey.

A word from my sponsors – Tara and Rachel

You have been an intentionally 'hands on' Dad. I have memories of you throwing me up the top of the linen cupboard in day-long games of hide and seek, always ready to play after dinner, our bedtime routine with prayers, songs, stories and maths, evening swims, countless hours in pools, teaching us to surf, to run, to play guitar, tennis, coaching our soccer team, trying so hard to teach us to hit golf balls and always being ready to help us with study.

I have never doubted for a second that you've always wanted to spend time with us and that has done more for our own knowledge of self than I think we can still yet comprehend.

You balance fun and banter with a constant greater depth. The way you model friendship, in spending time with people and having a laugh, yet always being willing to speak of Jesus and greater ideologies, has informed my friendships. My favourite time at parties has always been when most people have left and there's a few friends around having a quiet drink and a chat about purpose – and it's mostly because of you that I even know these conversations are possible.

The way you love Mum teaches me so many lessons. I will never settle for a disinterested husband who doesn't value prayer and service. You've set the bar high.

You have taught us the value and importance of hard work, and this has been instilled in both of us. I do remember you working so many jobs when we were younger and you were weary sometimes, but we knew you were doing it for us and while I think this is a truly good thing, it has skewed in my mind the value of productivity, it has sometimes been to the detriment of your own well-being, and I am seeing that now in myself. You never really rest. You need to.

I live with three girls now, and I have had many friends over the years, who do not have a father like I do, and I can see so clearly how it has hurt them and affected them. I can see how they love you and are surprised by your love and affection for your daughters, because they have never known that sort of love.

I know you have chosen your words over time carefully, especially at key times - the way you write letters and cards to us - I still have most of them, and always will. You told me once that you would never be the one to comment on our looks, when something was immodest, but would ensure Mum spoke, because you had read of the impact that could have on us coming from a father. Again, it is clear you have been very, very, intentional.

Your humility and absolute reliance on prayer is unlike any other father I know, and I believe this has only increased over time. You and Mum have both modelled prayer in such a way that I am so thankful for. You both often remind me of the important truth that nothing can truly be accomplished without God. You've never been afraid to talk about intense things around the Holy Spirit, family history, apologetics and so on, always displaying faith and good works and leading this family spiritually.

You have become a more patient man in my lifetime and respond to situations with greater empathy and mercy. I learn so much from how you allow yourself to grow, in all humility.

I am conscious you have experienced a lot of hurt and sorrow, especially through miscarriages as a couple and the loneliness now experienced because your two daughters keep moving to different continents. I know, though, that you allow these things to draw you deeper into prayer. You have clearly been at points of real sadness, even depression at different points in your life. You have been man enough to let us see you cry – sometimes often, and when you apologise.

You are similar to your Dad in the prioritising of quality time, prayer and reading, sport and music, occasional bursts of anger. I've seen you learn to control and harness your anger or maintain your cool and peace much better over the years.

You are more patient than your Dad. You have a wicked sense of humour, and while really opinionated about a lot of things, especially politically, you are softening to the views of others, whilst not budging on what you know is right.

You feel things very deeply, extremes at both ends, joy and sadness. You are physically protective and love cuddles, which I think helped us a lot with just feeling safe, comforted and comfortable around people and physical touch.

You would always be teaching us, in the simple things, and it was often a school of tough love. Everything's an opportunity to learn. We learnt how to do all things: camping, yard work, basic tool use, quizzes on long drives, very thorough with teaching and having us know the power and responsibility of being a driver – knowing what happened to Mum's father.

Sometimes you're hyper-critical of yourself. I've seen you at different points have low self-esteem concerning looks, weight, food, your abilities at work and socially. For someone so obviously talented and capable, whom other people look to for leadership, you've often severely underestimated yourself and can sometimes go to extremes to combat it. Often, I have seen you be either 100% or nothing at all. This 'all or nothing' approach has taught me lots of good things but has perhaps also taught us to beat ourselves up. We don't want you to beat yourself up. We literally think you are a superhero!

As far as what type of father, I think the best way I can put it is that you are a humble teacher. We know you've been honest with your failings, but you've always striven to lead by example, even in those failings. (Tara and Rachel)

Some final tips from my mate Rudyard

I have written probably too much already, giving insights and sharing things that in some instances have been known only to me, my God and my confessors. I believe the best learning and teaching happen in the context of story, so hopefully delving a little into mine, you have gained some insights that speak into your own story.

So, to finish, I simply wish to share my favourite piece of poetry – I have it taped to the chains holding up my punching bag. I aspire to be this sort of man. I might put it to music one day – an anthem for good men and strong Dads!

If – by Rudyard Kipling

If you can keep your head when all about you
Are losing theirs and blaming it on you,
If you can trust yourself when all men doubt you,
But make allowance for their doubting too;
If you can wait and not be tired by waiting,
Or being lied about, don't deal in lies,
Or being hated, don't give way to hating,
And yet don't look too good, nor talk too wise:

If you can dream—and not make dreams your master;
If you can think—and not make thoughts your aim;
If you can meet with Triumph and Disaster
And treat those two impostors just the same;
If you can bear to hear the truth you've spoken
Twisted by knaves to make a trap for fools,
Or watch the things you gave your life to, broken,
And stoop and build 'em up with worn-out tools:

If you can make one heap of all your winnings
And risk it on one turn of pitch-and-toss,
And lose, and start again at your beginnings
And never breathe a word about your loss;
If you can force your heart and nerve and sinew
To serve your turn long after they are gone,
And so hold on when there is nothing in you
Except the Will which says to them: 'Hold on!'

If you can talk with crowds and keep your virtue,

Or walk with Kings—nor lose the common touch,
If neither foes nor loving friends can hurt you,
If all men count with you, but none too much;
If you can fill the unforgiving minute
With sixty seconds' worth of distance run,
Yours is the Earth and everything that's in it,
And—which is more—you'll be a Man, my son!

Some reading that has really formed me
Rudyard Kipling, "If" (above)
John Eldridge, *Epic: The story God is telling and that you are a part of*
Dr Meg Meeker, *Strong Fathers, Strong Daughters: 10 Secrets every father should know*
Alex and Brett Harris, *Do Hard Things: A teenage rebellion against low expectations*
Fr James Mallon, *Divine Renovation: From maintenance to mission*
Fr Larry Richards, *Be a Man: Becoming the man God created you to be*
Jason Evert, *St John Paul the Great: His five loaves*
Michael Gaitley, *33 Days to Morning Glory: A retreat in preparation for Marian Consecration*
J. R. R., Tolkien *Lord of the Rings* (best fiction story ever, mirroring the one in the Bible)
C. S. Lewis, *The Screwtape Letters* — (a classic, creatively breaking open the world of spiritual warfare)
Ravi Zacharias, *The end of Reason: Discounting the new atheism and the new atheists*
Greg Sheridan, *God is Good for you: A defence of Christianity in troubled times.*

9

Torrien Lau
Let's call this one Grace!

Welcome, my name is Torrien Lau. I am 51, a father to five girls, grandfather to three children, a husband, a brother, a son – and this is my story.

I want to take you on a tour of some of the key moments of my life and how these moments led me to where I am today. There will be times when together, we will go back and forth in time, move forward and sideways and as your guide, I will bring you along for the ride. Don't get hung up on any experiences that might appear sad or hurtful as they are only subplots to

Torrien Lau with his father, Perry, and his older brother, Nivan.

Torrien Lau with his father, Perry, taken in California in 1999.

a greater plan for my life. The real story of my life is not just about events and I hope that by the end of the tour, you will understand, as I do, that there was so much more on offer for me than I could have ever imagined.

My earliest childhood memories are waking up to the sounds of my parents arguing. By the age of three I had already experienced a household that was tense, sometimes violent and unhappy, which set the tone for my own disposition for many years to come.

My father was an immigrant from mainland China and my mother one of the many who came by ship from England in the 1960s; a curious match to say the least. My mother was only 18 at the time she married my father and I believe he was around 24. I am still not sure how the two came together as knowing my mother, I can see that she would never have been able to fit the cultural expectations a Chinese husband would have of his wife and marriage. My mother has always been open-minded, strong-willed and free-thinking, as she would have had to be to marry a Chinese man in the 1960s. I am told that my father was a resourceful, determined and hardworking man who never let fear stop him from doing anything.

My parents had a Chinese restaurant that was apparently very successful and I have clear and vivid memories of the hustle and bustle of restaurant life. I recall the sounds of the woks clanging in the kitchen, the amazing smells, the Chinese chefs talking in their mother tongue and sitting at the table on which you could spin the food around. All these memories are as clear as if they happened yesterday. I can even remember my father eating the crispy fried tail of a fish and being totally disturbed that he seemed to really enjoy it!

At some stage my parents separated and I remember staying overnight at a flat near the restaurant with my father, sleeping in his bed, the smell of his breath and the safety of being next to him when waking up in the morning.

They divorced when I was around four and I cannot remember ever saying goodbye to my father. In retrospect I realise that I experienced a deep sadness and loss. My hero was no longer with me, this special person was gone and I didn't understand why. The deep wounding of abandonment was developing in my heart without my knowledge and it would take me decades to recognise and come to terms with it.

He then moved to North America and became a distant figure, a fading memory. For several years my father wrote and sent my brother and me expensive gifts on our birthdays. This was always exciting. It was harder for my brother as he was nearly two years older and had more time to bond and develop a relationship with our father.

When I was eight my father made an appearance with the intention of taking my brother and me to live with him in America. My mother had never spoken badly of my father. She intended me to know him in my own time, without her influencing the relationship and I have deep respect for her approach. The decision to go to America with my father was left to me and my brother which is almost an unfair pressure to place on an eight-year-old. This was a very stressful time for me, for this is when I had essentially to choose between the family that I had and the potential of having a relationship with a person who was now a stranger but still my father. The decision to leave the safety of my mother, brother and stepfather was too much and I decided to stay in Australia.

After my father returned to America we soon lost contact and our letters began to be returned to sender. I can remember being worried about him because in my mind something must have happened for him not to stay in contact with us. Mother tried to source his whereabouts for us through some of his friends but to no avail. It was 16 years before I would hear from him again. The feelings of abandonment were compounded and the wound was deepened by this absence of contact.

My mother came from a very working class background in Sheffield, England, and her father was a silent, inwardly unhappy man. Nonetheless, I was drawn to spending time with him even though he hardly spoke. Affection, sharing of feelings and affirmation were not part of the family make-up; a narrative of deficiency, of critique and stoicism was the norm. Coming through two world wars, poverty and migrating to a new country, this family dynamic is not surprising and has been passed on through the generations to me. My mother was incapable of telling me how proud she was of me, of showing affection, of saying that she loved me and that she thought I was a good son, although I have no doubt she did feel these things.

She then began a relationship with a man who eventually became my stepfather. He was a tall, strong, hairy policeman. I was immediately drawn to him and quickly adopted him as my new father. He was the product of an authoritarian, military type of fathering and I experienced his father as a stern, distant, unapproachable and serious character. My stepfather was a firm disciplinarian who suffered from a chronic back condition and subsequently lived with clinical depression. He was good to me in so many ways. I will always be grateful for his influence and we are growing closer as we get older.

He was extremely active in my life, performing many fathering roles such as taking me to sport, going camping, teaching me to shoot and to change oil in a car. I knew that he loved me but he was not the type of father to say 'I love you, I am proud of you, you are a good son', much the same as my mother and maternal family. Please don't misunderstand me, he was and is a good man and I love him dearly.

He was instrumental in teaching me good moral standards and provided my first experience of someone who believed in God. I was not raised a Catholic but through school and his influence I had an introduction to faith. Due to this exposure and my desire to feel like I belonged to something worthwhile, I decided to become a Catholic at the age of 14. I didn't belong with the Aussie kids or the Asian kids but there was something really honourable and good about the teachings of the Church and I felt that I was accepted for being me, despite my appearance or funny name.

Now let's go back in time to when I was five. At this age, I was sexually abused in front of four other people, an experience that would shape my entire life. I don't know how it came to be but I was blamed, although I was the victim, by our neighbour's parents and this actually added another layer of deep shame on top of the wounds of the abuse. The shame, guilt and humiliation of this event has shaped many of my behaviours for years and even to this day, I have to be conscious of the impacts and how I respond in certain circumstances.

So from that point until I was 16, my beautiful stepfather was a part of our family and played an important role in my upbringing. Unfortunately that didn't last and he and my mother separated with his moving out to live by himself; not his choice. Shortly afterwards, my mother had a new partner who moved into the family home. My loyalty was to my stepfather so I moved out with him while completing the last two years of high school.

This was a very difficult time as my stepfather entered a dark place of depression and the stable family life I was used to became disjointed and disappeared. My stepfather threw himself into work and I was essentially independent at 17;

supporting myself financially, emotionally and physically. I will never forget the first Christmas after the separation. I was alone at home, my stepfather was working, my mother was with her new partner and my brother was with his friends. I was totally alone, immensely sad, felt completely abandoned and cried tears of sorrow until no more tears would come.

At the age of 18 I was lost, without purpose. I had broken up with a girlfriend and made a feeble attempt to take my life. In essence this was a cry for help. Help was provided by my parish priest in whom I thought I had discovered a valuable friend and confidant. For a short time I experienced God's love and mercy. I managed to do a partial reset of my life and threw myself into work, career and earning money – and I was good at it.

Remember I said that my birth father was a good worker and that my stepfather threw himself into work when it got tough? Well, here I am at 18 now doing the same as my role models, distracting and numbing myself from the painful events of life. This became just one of my many addictions.

I married at the age of 23. I chose a woman whom I thought was the opposite of my mother but in many ways she ended up being very much like her. I was seeking normality, social acceptance, the appearance of a happy family and material success. We had two children and outwardly, we were the picture of the perfect family. My marriage was built on distractions, money, status and appearances but by the age of 26, my marriage was in trouble. I started to self-medicate with alcohol and drugs to escape my inner pains.

This might not make complete sense but hang in there and I will help you to understand. I realise that my actions, both as a husband and father, were based on control, authority and the use of words that made me feel safe and in control. This had the opposite effect on the people around me; they felt oppressed, unsafe and controlled. I was carrying suppressed memories, anger, shame and guilt without being consciously aware of it. I was living with a feeling of self-loathing that was so strong I couldn't stand to be in my own company. I had also stopped going to church as it felt like a waste of time.

My father called me when I was 24 and asked, "Do you know who this is?" I knew immediately who it was and replied that I did – in a dispassionate tone. I didn't want or need him in my life. I was a man and didn't need a father. I could manage on my own – at least that was what I thought. He had reached out to me which couldn't have been easy but I was in no state of mind to respond and didn't reciprocate contact. He sent expensive gifts that held no value to me as I was angry with him for abandoning me without an explanation. Forgiveness was not in my heart and I had dedicated my life to the pursuit of material goods, wealth, building and paying off my first house by the time I was 25.

After a couple of years of drinking and escalating drug consumption to numb the self-loathing, I had started to read *Manhood* by Steve Biddulph. I was reading the chapter on being a good father and Steve was suggesting that it was impossible to be a good father without resolving the issues with your own father.

I immediately put the book down and called my brother who had retained contact with our father to get his phone number. I called my father and asked him if he knew who it was. He said "Yes" and I asked what he was doing in the next fortnight. He said that he would be at home in California. I said that I would come and see him.

Two weeks later I was at San Francisco airport watching a short Chinese man from a distance while trying to muster the courage to go and introduce myself. Despite not seeing him for more than 20 years, I knew it was him.

I had three half-sisters, a stepmother and a father who was culturally very Chinese, while I was as Aussie as a pie and sauce at the football. Despite our differences it was scarily undeniable that genetically he and I were very similar, even down to the way we walked and our mannerisms. Many a time a shiver went down my spine when I saw myself in this man who was my father – although I didn't him know personally. I had the same 'can do' attitude, no fear of failure and the ability to create something with hands and mind.

I went to America with serious questions I wanted answered. Where did you go? Why didn't you let me know where you were? Why did you leave your sons? I eventually accepted that as a 60 year-old Chinese man he did not have the capacity or skills to share his feelings deeply and honestly with me, or maybe with anyone. None of my questions was answered and other than seeing what type of man my father was and where my genetic influences came from, I left empty-handed.

After returning to Australia I did not hear from him again. By making the effort to seek him out and travel halfway around the world, I felt that he would reciprocate by maintaining some form of relationship but I effectively experienced the loss, hurt, abandonment and rejection of my childhood all over again.

I reached out again when I was 44 as a last ditch effort to have a relationship – and had a terrible response. This ended my desire to be connected with him and I surrendered to the fact that we would never really bond. It did not heal the wound and to this day, I am still working on some type of healing for myself and contemplating what, if anything, I should do for his healing.

My first marriage broke down and I went through a very messy divorce. Our two beautiful daughters became victims of the actions of two selfish adults and this was to be one of my deepest hurts and biggest regrets. The relationship with my mother was one of distance and resentment while my relationship with my stepfather was average at best as I started to resent his depressed and negative outlook on life. I was unable to accept him as a broken but beautiful son of God. This went on for another ten years.

So let's now go back a few years to my early to mid-twenties. I had always sought the company of older males; perhaps I was trying to find a father-relationship to fill the aching void in my heart. My stepfather had done the best he could but still, I searched for more.

The priest friend who had helped me through that painful period of my late teens and the half-baked attempt at suicide had become an important person in my life. We were having one of our big drinking nights when I had yet another encounter with failed manhood and pseudo-fathering. He made sexual advances to me. I held him in such high esteem, had probably put him on a pedestal and thought that I had found a fatherly role model I could respect and aim to imitate.

This changed at that moment and betrayal is the only word that I can use to describe the feeling. I had been deceived into believing the relationship was something meaningful but it was actually based on a lie. I don't define my friend by this one action as I still consider him to be more than was revealed that night. I respect him for the positive influences he had on me over the years but none the less I cut this relationship out of my life as the trust between us had been broken. More on this later.

I was very good at cutting people out of my life. The moment

I felt someone didn't have my best interests at heart, that I didn't have their loyalty, I was gone, never to return. It was safer for me to do the running than for someone to run from me.

Around the age of 30 I consciously recognised that I had no real male or father figures, none that I felt I could look up to or model myself upon, so I decided to go it alone. I turned further to drugs and alcohol as my coping techniques and my life began to gather speed and spiral downwards. For the next several years I dedicated myself to achieving in my career, distracting myself from relationships and numbing the pain of my life experiences. My relationship with my family and children suffered deeply at this time as my subconscious self-loathing and feelings of worthlessness confirmed by my addictions created impenetrable barriers.

I was not the father I was determined to be, I was emotionally unavailable and may as well have been in a different country, just as my own father had been for me. The guilt was overwhelming and it drove me to consume more and more alcohol and drugs so that I didn't have to feel the pain and disappointment. For some reason, I was blessed enough not to lose everything as many do in this situation. I continued to work hard and provide for my family but I was hanging on by a thread.

By my early forties no matter how much I consumed, the emptiness and pain just would not be silenced. I had remarried by this time. I had two beautiful stepdaughters and a new baby girl had not long arrived. My wife was like no one I had ever met and I knew that she had come in to my life for a significant reason, even though I was unable to see what the reason was. After being married for a couple of years, I knew that if I didn't change then I would be destined to make the same mistakes and lose the very people I loved the most; my wife had said as much to me. I still didn't know how I would change or even if I could, for the pain and unease seemed to be overwhelming each time I tried to do something about it. I couldn't understand why I was so unable to be happy, couldn't love as I desired to, couldn't be the father I so desperately wanted to be.

One day a friend spoke to me about a men's group he and a couple of others were forming. It resonated with me immediately. He said to wait until they had begun and then he would like me to join. I was impatient and insisted that it was fine for me to start now. Every time I took a drink or a drug, I would feel a whisper from somewhere that I didn't need to do it. This time I heard a whisper that told me I needed to join this group. Finally I responded to the call without a moment's hesitation; let's call this one Grace!

I had joined a Catholic men's group that I knew nothing about. I had never prayed openly or shared my pain with anyone. I felt inadequate, too sinful, reeked of shame and guilt and saw myself as a pretender not worthy of love. These men who became my brothers accepted me without judgement, prayed for me, loved me even though I sometimes saw their jaws drop at the content of my sharing. Attending the weekly meetings was extremely challenging and one of the hardest things I have ever done, but something kept me going back through all the tears and all the anger. I had been absent from the Church for fifteen years and did I have some stuff to get through! Statistically speaking, the odds of making it were stacked against me; second marriages frequently fail, PTSD, child abuse, substance abuse, all preconditions that usually lead to more misery, failed relationships, pain and suffering.

Remember that period of about 16 years where I was self-medicating? I stayed like that for far too long because I was afraid, afraid of changing, of what I might become. I held on to the belief that it was easier to stay the same than to do the impossible and change. This was the stage where I felt like I tried everything, that I had nothing to lose. I had hit rock bottom so I turned to forgiveness, compassion, self-acceptance, tolerance. To do all this, I had to face my past hurts, failures and experiences. Changing from a coward to a brave-hearted man was hard, really hard, but man was it worth it!

Now come with me as we have a look at some of the good stuff. In short, the last ten years has been nothing short of miraculous and if someone had predicted where I am today, everyone, including me, would have just laughed. I share the following to give thanks, show gratitude and to convince myself it actually happened, not to big note myself.

Over the course of just a few years I went from clearing tables at a restaurant to being a successful CEO of a large NGO, contributing to multiple charities, posting on my own website and speaking on national radio. My marital relationship continues to grow beyond my wildest dreams and my relationships with my children are being restored and deepening in love. This is the same guy who made some really dumb choices that left a trail of hurt behind him wherever he went, so what was it that led him down a different path?

The most important thing I need to share with you is that the key influence in all these changes is that I turned to Love. My faith journey was supported by Jesus. This brought healing and I continue to turn to him each and every day. It has not been an easy journey but it has been an entirely blessed one.

Understanding how my past experiences shaped my thoughts, beliefs and behaviours has been a process of surrendering to God speaking to me through his questioning, provoking and to put it simply, showering me with his grace. The key to much of my growing awareness and healing has been based on leaning in to the questions: how did this feeling start? Where did I first experience it? What are my emotional and physical responses? How have the relationships with others, my father figures and parents affected me? What are you saying to me, Jesus, and what do you want me to do?

My 'good boy syndrome' of wanting to be liked by everyone originated from a lack of affirmation from my primary carers and the fear that people would leave me if they knew the real me.

My controlling attitudes and behaviours come from the abandonment issues of my father experience.

My fathering model was based on the experiences of my own father figures.

My addictive behaviours originate from a lack of intimacy and the need to fill a void which can only be filled by God.

I couldn't love because I didn't love myself and I didn't even know how to love from lack of healthy modelling.

My anger came from a lack of self-acceptance and my inability to forgive myself and others.

My guilt and shame needed to be treated so that I could put myself in a position to love myself – and so the list of revelations and learning goes on and on.

Another way to describe this technique would be to say, look up to heaven and God asking for help, look back to where an issue may have originated, then look forward with God to healing and progress. Look up, back and forward, look up, back and forward, over and over again until God has informed, instructed, renovated, restored and supported and you are more in union with him. The results are more peace, more joy and more love.

It's simple and easy.

It's simple and not so easy.

In fact, to be faced with answers that offend your senses, your pride, your ego; to hear something that goes against everything that you feel is justified, then to receive it, accept it within you and make a change is one of the hardest and bravest things that you could ever do. This is my definition of real courage, something perhaps impossible to do by yourself – but God supports and blesses with his grace. I practised this over and over and still do it to this day: look up, look back and look forward, all with God.

So when I stopped drinking and taking drugs in my early forties, I felt that all was good in the world and everything should be about the new me.

Boy was I wrong!

I had no idea of the damage I had created, the deep wounds I had inflicted on my wife and children. Many times when my wife and I were at loggerheads and she was obviously angry and frustrated with my lack of understanding, I would go outside, take a breath, and ask Jesus what he wanted me to do because I had nothing. It was the same answer every time; 'Just love her.' So I would go back inside and ask for a chance to listen, to understand and to hear what my wife was trying to say. She would be surprised and shocked but none the less, she would graciously continue with the new me and ultimately the outcome would be another step towards healing and restoration. Grace!

The lessons learned from this process were to listen twice as much as I spoke and be genuinely interested. Wanting to know more and asking questions is the best sign that you value someone, that they are important, that their opinion and ideas matter to you. Grunting and nodding are not enough, your interest needs to be intentional and most importantly, it must be genuine and authentic. If you fake it, people will pick it up in a heartbeat. With all your heart, with all your mind and with all your strength, listen.

When you have failed someone's love or failed in your responsibilities of being a trustworthy person in caring for a wife, a child or family member and you apologise, making amends does not stop with a one-off gesture. I remember when I first told my children that I was sorry for being emotionally unavailable to them and for being such a poor father figure, they looked at me with stunned silence. I came to learn that to change the existing and historical belief that I would continue to disappoint them was going to take a significant weight of evidence. I needed to make repeated efforts and continuing demonstrations to my loved ones that my professed change was real and permanent. This restoration of trust would take years and continues to this day but, as time goes on, love and loving actions that match up with loving words are closing the gap I created. The 'repeat entry' of acts of love and contrition proved not only to others, but importantly to myself, that I had permanently changed.

There were other broken relationships that required not just healing but restoration.

I was reading the daily scripture as I do every day since I returned to God. It was the reading where Jesus says to forgive seven times seventy times. I put the reading down and I heard Jesus saying he wanted me to forgive my childhood abuser. What? Impossible! Not going to do it JC, forget about it buddy!

After taking more time to digest what I had just heard, I bent to the request and agreed with Jesus to do it. So I found the contact details of my abuser, called and spoke the words, "I forgive you". There is obviously more to the story, but the most surprising thing was that my forgiveness was received and that person reached out to me to try to establish a relationship. I haven't taken up the offer but the message that I received loud and clear was that God wanted not just forgiveness but restoration of myself and this person to God.

The same thing happened with my priest friend. I found him, met him face to face and spoke the words, "I forgive you." It didn't stop there. I was running an event in his parish at my instigation and throughout the weekend, every time I tried to create space for moments of silence and reflection outside the program, he would appear and we would connect. The job was not done with the one-off act of forgiveness; no, I was being put in the situation where restoration was on offer. There is so much more than we can ever imagine and it only leads to more love and peace.

While I will always refer to the scriptures for the plans, lessons, guidance and restoration that God has for me, one important contribution to my healing and growth has been surrounding myself with good men. Some of these good men and one in particular, love me so much that they are prepared to call me out when they think I am just being dumb and will question my thinking and actions. This is not an easy thing to accept, just as when a good wife asks the difficult questions and confronts our behaviours and beliefs. The way in which another man does this loving act can illicit feelings of anger, withdrawal and resentment. I have found that if I respond by asking myself the questions – is this real? is this the truth? is there another way to look at this?– then more than likely I am allowing myself the space and opportunity to grow and learn. I cannot understate how valuable this has been and I am eternally grateful for this brotherly love.

Another technique I have been practising and found very

helpful is once again simple and easy – but hard. This is about accepting my human-worldly-self and my self-as-God's-son-created-in-his-image, two parts of me that if accepted completely, allow me to be in deeper union with God. Some might call it non-duality, books have been written on this and I am in no way an expert on the topic, so I will simply describe my technique.

I look at myself when experiencing a difficult emotion from any time of my life, from the position of love and compassion. For example, I shared with you that I was abused at the age of five. Sometimes when I feel the pain of my abuse, I look down and see little five-year-old me and I visualise me at my current age, holding him in my arms, comforting him, loving him with compassion as Jesus would do. There I am, two of me, not separate, loving myself and allowing acceptance of the things that the world brings, not judging my emotions but just treating them with love. Simple and easy but hard; love myself, love yourself.

All these things I practise are to be more loving, to come closer to Jesus, to accept the offer of peace and joy. I have the gift and opportunity of doing this within all my relationships. How much I have loved, not just how good a provider I am, will define me. As a father, I realised that I treated my children as a chore, a task, a duty, not as individuals or as God's children from the moment they were born. I thought they should be obedient, quiet, seen and not heard. They should receive me with respect as their provider and teacher. I try to break the generational programming of my family origins and I try to listen, validate, affirm and ask questions from a position of real and genuine interest. It is up to me to craft the relationships that I want, not for others to act as I think they should and come to me. I need to go to them, to reach out, to be available, to be patient and actively and intentionally offer myself to them.

They may not always want me there and that's OK too, but I can't turn away from the feelings of rejection or resentment as all that does is validate that I am not trustworthy, that I have an ulterior motive and I am just trying to get something from them for my own benefit.

A few years ago I became a grandfather. I practise this authentic questioning technique of being genuinely present with my three grandchildren and what a blessing I have been given in another chance to be a different and perhaps better father figure. I am in no way nailing it perfectly but I will make the repeat entry as many times as it takes. I can already see the difference in my Jesus-led parenting style and the improvements it is making in my relationships.

What is the most important lesson that I have learnt through the process of turning things around?

It is actually harder not to change than to make the change. There is a lie that says staying on the path without love and forgiveness is safer than accepting what God wants from me.

It was actually easier to stop drinking than to continue drinking.

It was easier to forgive those who hurt me than to hang on to the anger.

It was easier to go to my wife and ask for a second chance than to withdraw and accept defeat and failure.

It is easier to approach my children and grandchildren than to separate and isolate myself.

It was easier to accept God, Jesus and the Holy Spirit than to continually turn my back on their advances and love.

It is simple and easy but hard and worth it.

So what are my tips to being a better father?

1. Listen, ask questions, listen and repeat. Don't try to fix things or provide a solution unless you're asked for one!

2. Be compassionate to yourself and others. You are not defined by what you may have done or experienced in the past. For a man authentically to love others, he must be able to love himself, so own it and be gentle on yourself for you are a good man.

3. Be brave, face your past and man up to make positive changes; it's easier than not doing so.

4. Surround yourself with other good men; you are not the only one who might be experiencing the same feelings or experience. Do this and you will reduce the potential to experience loneliness, helplessness and isolation.

That's the end of the tour so thanks for coming along. Here are some of the books and resources that helped me in my journey and I hope they might help you as well.

Francis Xavier Nguyen Van Thuan, *Five loaves and two fishes*
John Eldredge, *Epic*
John Eldredge, *The One Minute Pause App*
Thomas Merton, *The Inner Experience*
Richard Rohr, *The Universal Christ*
Steve Biddulph, *Manhood*
C. S. Lewis, *The Screwtape Letters.*

10

Steve Lawrence
Fatherly approval is a very liberating reality

Introduction

"And he shall turn the hearts of the fathers to the children." Mal 4:6.

If there is anything most needed by children today it is their father's heart turned towards them. This chapter will attest to three key factors which, to me, seem crucial for fathers to live well if they wish to turn their hearts towards their children. These factors are 1) Presence 2) Example and 3)

Steve and his wife, Annie.

Rosary picture: Steve and his family lead the Rosary before Pope John Paul II.

Encouragement. Not exhaustive by any means, but these three qualities have proven vital in my own upbringing as you will see in the stories involving my father and my father figures. They also feature in reflections on the impact of my marriage with Annie, and on our six children – Hannah (26), Georgia (24), Dominic (22), Phoebe (20), Jerome (16) and Ambrose (13).

My Dad had three fathers

My Dad, Godfrey Lawrence, had three fathers. And yet it is only one, the least likely, whose influence has shaped my life.

Known as "Goofy," Dad played Test cricket for South Africa and held the record for many years for the most wickets (28) in a Test Series (1961-2) by a South African fast bowler. For this feat he was awarded his country's prestigious Sportsman of the Year prize. Born in Rhodesia (Zimbabwe) in 1932, his father left his mother at a very early age. She later remarried a Victorian-era policeman whose cold, distant manner left my Dad feeling unloved and lost. At age 13, at the time of the conclusion of World War II, his beloved mother, Irene, died. Dad's life went into free fall. He was alone, without direction, without support and without love. Tall, gangly and now an orphan with almost no confidence, having missed much schooling in the years of his mother's illness, he was a vulnerable and hurting adolescent. Thanks to one man, however, things eventually turned around.

It was the presence, attention and belief of a teacher at the boarding school he was sent to, at the express wish of his mother in her will, which ensured he proved to be Dad's truest 'father'. Dad's biological father had disappeared, his stepfather was distant and cold, but this man – Father Landreth – after whom one of my brothers is named, helped Dad to grow from boyhood to manhood. He did this by being present to him and paying him authentic loving attention, investing in his future and passing on the important values and beliefs that mark his life to this day. And he did it while teaching him how to play cricket.

I have learned many vital lessons of life, about manhood and success, from Dad. These include stories of my life as a professional footballer with the Hawthorn Football Club with whom I won a premiership (1991); of being a husband and father of six children, of having come from a broken family; of being a director of Australia's largest-ever event, World Youth Day 2008, as well as the adventures of travelling the world, teaching and encountering extraordinary people. At times these stories include very painful personal struggles that I've lived through which, hopefully, illustrate the truth that important victories often emerge from failure and that strengths can be born from weakness or personal wounds.

This man, Father Landreth, whom I've never met, entered Dad's life 75 years ago, and here I am, on the other side of the world, recounting the story of his vital intervention. Who will be speaking of you in 75 years? What decisions are you making today, through your actions, presence and belief in others, which will create an enduring impact in their lives and the lives of their children? What kind of father do you wish to become?

Fathering by presence
The Race: A recollection
I felt very nervous. It was just me and him. The race. Last week he and I had tied equal fourth place in the 100-metre final at our high school athletics carnival. Next week our school would be up against the other schools in the region, and our 4 x 100-metre relay running team had three places secured.

One remaining position was to be filled. He – or I – would fill it. As men, Damian Smith would to go on to play rugby for Australia, and I would play top level AFL (Australian football). On this day, however, we were skinny athletic fifteen-year-olds, highly competitive and desperate to win.

I had told my Dad about the race and, even though it was taking place at 3.30, before he would finish work, he made a point of being there to support me. I could see him as I lined up. Bang! Off we went, neck and neck for the first 50 metres, then Smith started to pull away. I fell behind, and the harder I tried to catch up, the more distance appeared between us. It was over before it started and I was devastated. Puffing, I congratulated my friend, but inside I felt terrible. I had failed. Dad came over and consoled me. He said, "I'm proud of you, beloved son." (He always called me 'beloved son', and still does today even though he's 88 and I'm 51.) All of a sudden it didn't seem to matter that I hadn't won. The important thing was that he was there.

Beloved son

I discovered that my identity as someone profoundly loved by my father was deeper than any achievement or failure. Somehow, I had a sense of that in the moment, even if I couldn't put words on it at the time. This experience, still so vivid in my memory, teaches me even today the power of loving presence. Dad made a decision that day to do what is important at that moment. I don't know what other priorities he had to rearrange to be there, but he *was* there, and that was very significant for me.

What actually is success? How do we judge it? Is it simply a matter of accomplishment that we measure by achievement or financial gain? Is it the reputation we gain in the world, or the influence we wield? It was once wisely asked, "What is the value of gaining the whole world and yet losing our very selves?"

The presence of my Dad, his *real* presence, especially during the crucial teenage years when our family was in crisis, somehow gave me a deep sense of myself. I received my identity through his loving and warm presence. As he was by Father Landreth, I was often fathered by Dad through many hours in the cricket nets. It was a presence that was always approving of me, loving, and gentle. I caught a passion for cricket and became a very accomplished cricketer. Saturdays and Sundays throughout every summer were dominated by cricket (possibly too much so!) and Mum and Dad spent many, many hours both watching our cricket and also driving from one ground to the other watching my three brothers.

There is something about close proximity between fathers and sons, where the father is teaching the son something of his expertise. In my case it was cricket, where I was delighted to learn the tricks of the trade – how to be a fast bowler or an accomplished middle order batsman. Those 'how to' moments with Dad were offered in a way that sought the best for me as his son, were delivered with warmth and the challenge to become better, and in a manner that showed confidence in me. Those moments were always significant for me. Even today as a 51-year-old man, with Dad being 88, I know I have his confidence. The experience of fatherly approval is a very liberating reality.

As well as calling me 'Stephen' or 'Steve', or my middle name 'Thomas', which is always said with affection, Dad also often addresses me as 'beloved son', a practice I continue with my sons. It alludes to the baptism account of Jesus in the Jordan River where he hears the words of God his Father, "You are my beloved son" (cf. Mark 1:9-11), words that reflect the total approval of God in Jesus. And these words are followed by Jesus entering into his public life. Fatherly approval is a great enabler for men to take their place in the world, which is why we need other men, other father figures, especially if we lack a true father in our upbringing. I often reflect that Saint Joseph, though not his biological father, nevertheless fathered Jesus and taught him to be a man in every human way.

How can you spend time with your children? What interests and passions do you have that you can invite your sons or daughters into? In what ways do you express your tender love to your children? Who can help you better connect with your kids?

Father figures from afar
I have been blessed by the gift of several father figures who have been significant for me in different periods of my life. Their influence has shaped me in different ways, and their presence and guidance have come at crucial times. They have assisted me in my journey to manhood over the years, an adventure which continues to this day. I describe in this section two of these father figures: the first from my youth, a hero and a shining light, Pope John Paul II; the second, from my life in ministry and family, a lettered man of culture, Michael D. O'Brien. John Paul II is a father by example, and Michael O'Brien a father by encouragement.

Fathering by example: Pope John Paul II
On 13 May 1981, a Turkish assassin, Mehmet Ali Agca, probably employed by the USSR, shot Pope John Paul II. He was fewer than five metres from the pope, exposed on his open popemobile while it slowly toured Saint Peter's Basilica among the crowds, and fired bullets from a Belgian Browning Hi Power pistol, an attempt on the Polish pope's life that was

ultimately unsuccessful. This date marked both the feast of Our Lady of Fatima and the intended inauguration of the John Paul II Institute for Studies in Marriage and the Family, both of which have proved to be highly significant in shaping my life and mission.

My personal conversion in faith is intricately connected to the story of Fatima, where the Blessed Virgin Mary appeared to three children in Portugal in 1917. Dad, having been on a pilgrimage there in 1980, the year before the assassination attempt, began to implement the messages of Our Lady of Fatima in our home. He did so by introducing in an incremental way the prayer of the rosary, the reading of the Catechism (written by Servant of God John A. Hardon, *The Universal Catechism of the Catholic Church* being published in 1994), the lives of saints and a serious adherence to the living of the sacraments. The failed assassination attempt captured my 12-year-old imagination and, from that time onwards, John Paul II became my hero.

My teenage years appeared quite normal. At school I was an above average student who was well-liked by my peers and on the sporting field I usually excelled. Spanning this same period, however, were years of bitter conflict in my home, a conflict coinciding with my Mum's embrace of Marxism and radical feminist ideology after she returned to university to study political science. From this time, Mum levelled sustained attacks of verbal and psychological aggression towards Dad. Mum declared that she no longer accepted Christianity and stopped going to Mass. There seemed to me to be a spiritual hostility present during those days, months and years. Looking back, there is no doubt that Mum had had a nervous breakdown, and the fallout was horrendous for all – Mum was unhappy, Dad had a few heart attacks over this period, and my brothers and I were left with psychological and emotional wounds that still linger.

Through this period in the 1980s John Paul II personified the promised "triumph of the Immaculate Heart of Mary" made at Fatima in 1917. This was evidenced through the compelling witness of his life as a priest and bishop under Nazism and Atheistic Communism, the fall of Communism in the USSR when he was pope, the establishment of World Youth Days and the extraordinary light that shone through his preaching and teaching on the world stage. All this took place at a time when there was so much confusion inside the Church about what the Holy Spirit was doing through the Second Vatican Council and the new movements and communities. My mind and soul were educated and nourished by delving into the encyclicals and exhortations of this inspired man. His teaching on human love in the divine plan, in particular, his *Theology of the Body*, burst forth as vitally illuminating for me. It provided answers to my deeper questions about the meaning of human sexuality and especially God's intention for what constitutes a true man and a true woman, particularly important as a healing source in light of the anti-male rhetoric I had been subjected to so often in those years.

So, it was an extraordinary blessing to meet John Paul II on 11 April in the Great Jubilee Year 2000. I was in Rome on behalf of the Melbourne Archdiocese, where I was serving as the Director of Catholic Youth Ministry and preparing to bring a group to the Holy Land and the Eternal City for World Youth Day in August of that year. I was also acting as a delegate of the WYD2000 Committee for the Australian Catholic Bishops Conference.

It was my last full day in Rome and I was blessed to go to an early morning private Mass with the pope inside the Vatican. Thirty others were present, and after Mass we met John Paul II. When it was my turn, I took his hand and managed to say two of the three things I had prepared. "Holy Father, there are

1000 young Australians coming to World Youth Day [which was by far our biggest pilgrimage group ever], and they are very much looking forward to it," to which he replied, "Very good, very good." Then I showed him a photograph and said, "And this is my family, could you please pray for them," to which he responded by making the sign of the cross over the photo. The third thing which I didn't get to verbalise because he was moved on to the next person was the sentiment, "I love you, Holy Father," which I'm quite sure he would have seen in my eyes, anyway.

Later that same day, 11 April, I would be asked to come to Rome with Annie, my wife, to take up a three-year role as Director of the Emmanuel School of Mission in Rome. (I distinctly recall the date because it was the feast day of Saint Stanislaw and during this visit I had the chance to chat briefly with the pope's private secretary, Monsignor Stanislaw Dziwisz, with whom I had a warm exchange where I was able to wish him a happy feast day.) We moved to Rome in September that year with our four small children under six years of age, an extraordinary adventure of marvellous blessings. One of those blessings was to live in close proximity to my father John Paul II, often attending papal Masses and having the chance to see him preach the Gospel, both by his words and – as he aged – through his suffering.

I have taken on board advice he gave to fathers as to how to love their children. Every daughter needs to know from her Dad that she is beautiful, he said, and every son needs to know from his Dad that he has what it takes to do well in life.

By divine providence I was present in Rome for his beatification Mass in 2011 and his canonisation Mass in 2014, both of which took place on Divine Mercy Sunday, his final and perhaps greatest fatherly legacy to me and to the world. Alongside his papal motto, *Totus Tuus* ("I am all yours

[Mary]"), it is the Divine Mercy phrase that perhaps best sums up his whole life and significance: "Jesus, I trust you."

The event which best ties so many strands of my life together, however, is the rosary in Saint Peter's Square on 7 October 2000 where our family led one of the Mysteries of Light, representing Oceania. We were standing five metres from John Paul II as we led the mystery, and five metres from the pilgrim statue of the Virgin of Fatima, the one adorned with the bullet from the assassination attempt in her crown. Taking place only a few weeks after our arrival, this event launched our three years of mission in Rome and consolidated many of the graces I'd received throughout the previous years. Stunningly, the "Europe" decade was led via satellite by the Carmelite Sisters in Portugal, which included the 93-year-old last living visionary of Fatima, Sister Lucia dos Santos. John Paul II's pastoral message to open wide the doors to Christ at the onset of the third millennium, and to put out into the deep waters ("duc in altum"), has inspired me no end and remains at the heart of my personal vocation and mission. My leadership business of speaking, coaching and consulting, for example, is named Altum Leadership Group from this text.

If children learn more from what you do than what you say, how would you assess the example you provide yours on a daily basis? What priorities do you need to develop that you can make sure you implement to show the way? Identify one small action you can make today which will help you move forward on this.

Fathering by encouragement: Michael D. O'Brien

The first of these father figures I only met once and he fathered me from a distance, so to speak, and by example. The second, similarly, is a man whom I have met only twice, and he has fathered me first through his books when I didn't know him, and then later through his letters after we'd met, providing enormous encouragement. Bacon and eggs were also important!

Michael O'Brien is a world-renowned Catholic painter and novelist who lives in Northern Ontario in Canada. I first came under his influence when I was given a copy of his best-selling novel *Father Elijah* while responsible for Catholic Youth Ministry in the Archdiocese of Melbourne. It was 1997 and at the time I was 28, married with two children, and in my eleventh season of professional Australian football with Hawthorn Football Club.

I found *Father Elijah* to be such an extraordinary and captivating novel, profoundly rich in its understanding of the human person and of the spiritual life. It was at the same time a 'ripper' of a story, filled with intrigue, heroism and drama, and ultimately presenting a message of hope in the midst of darkness. So much was I enamoured of the novel I immediately sought out other books by Michael O'Brien and quickly came upon one called *Strangers and Sojourners*. I was struck to find that its chief protagonist was a man named Stephen who was married to a woman named Anne, who together had three children. It was just like us! By that time, it was late 1997 and our third child had been born. It seemed prophetic that God had made this connection for me, and offered an answer to a prayer that my brother Dave and I made in our early twenties, that God would place us in the truth through books, videos, people we met and by any other means to lead us on the way of freedom and salvation. Again, I was profoundly nourished by the book, and hence one after the other I devoured all his works, finding them to be sources of literary delight, inspiration and, in fact, an ongoing source of personal conversion in my life with God. I had been reading his works for ten years but it was not until 2006 that I had the opportunity to meet the man.

It was about a year after I'd started in my role as Director of Evangelisation and Catechesis for Sydney's World Youth Day 2008. I was one of a small team to present at a youth ministry convention in Las Vegas, USA, there to invite 3000 American youth ministers to bring their young people to Sydney for WYD08. While in North America I took the opportunity to make a detour to Canada to meet Michael and to make a proposal to him. The proposal centred on asking him to participate in a painting commission associated with the WYD08 event, specifically a painting of Our Lady of the Southern Cross, to be hung in Saint Mary's Cathedral, Sydney. The youth of the world would be invited to consecrate themselves to Mary in front of the image while praying for a new outpouring of the Holy Spirit during pilgrimages to the cathedral, an idea central to WYD08's Acts 1:8 theme: "You will receive power when the Holy Spirit has come upon you, and you will be my witnesses."

In the end, that painting was rightly put onto canvas by an Australian artist, and not by Michael O'Brien. That Ontario meeting with Michael, however, was very significant for me, as his subsequent friendship and support by letters became fundamental to helping me through a crucible. It was not only the two remaining years while serving in my WYD08 role in Sydney which were difficult. I went from that 'frying pan' into three difficult years of 'fire' in my role as Director of Identity and Mission for the Australian Catholic University, during which I experienced a different kind of crucifixion.

In that first meeting with Michael O'Brien, where he and his wife Sheila hosted me for a few days, I felt the extraordinary presence of a loving father. We spoke of so many things and the grace of mutual friendship was given to us. 'Kindred soul' is a term thrown about, often loosely, but this is exactly what I experienced in him. Remarkably, I discovered that he perceived something similar. Somehow, he too received encouragement and strengthening from me, which surprised and touched me very much. I was in my mid-thirties at the time and he in his mid-sixties and, like me, married to a wonderful woman. By that time I was father to six children; our sixth and youngest was born earlier that year, 2006. It was the beginning of a fatherly encouragement that sustained me in extraordinary ways through the crucibles.

On the first morning after my arrival, following a long night of speaking together, he made me what may well be the most delicious breakfast of bacon and eggs I've ever eaten. That long night consisted of a depth of sharing regarding the struggles I was going through, what I believed to be brutal and unjust treatment at the hands of a person in my workplace, which were causing me intense suffering. We also discovered a unique shared perspective of mutual concerns regarding the state of the Church, the condition of the world, the call to holiness and so much else, including my love for his books. It was a conversation through which a divinely given bond was formed.

We have often referred to the breakfast that followed, and the breakfast the Risen Jesus cooked his disciples on the shore of Lake Tiberias after the miraculous catch of fish, as "breakfast on the shores of eternity". It is not sentimentality since our writing of letters across the globe has become a dialogue of friendship, of communion, of fatherly and filial (as well as fraternal) love. His many letters to me, full of anecdotes and encouragement, wise advice and humble entreaty, are personal and real, and deeply spiritual. He addresses me as *Stefanos*, the Greek version of my name, and these letters have the gift of always – even with the shortest message – mediating God's grace to me.

During the World Youth Day period I wrote a book, later published as *Five Smooth Stones: A 40 Day WYD08 Journal* (Modotti Press, 2010), which I penned as daily emails to Michael O'Brien and compiled after receiving his generous edits and suggestions. Over the years I have also been honoured to read manuscripts of novels he has drafted and I am delighted to play a minor role in providing feedback and giving impressions.

Scores of letters have passed between us and, though we have only met twice, there is a deep, open, trusting and respectful exchange that is a life-giving source for me. Given that I live in Australia at one end of the earth, and that he lives like a prophet in the ice of Canada's Northern Ontario, it is likely that our father-son relationship will have to content itself with communication via email, at least until we experience the communion of saints with Jesus over breakfast on the shores of eternity. In the meantime, he has taught me how to father people, that is, bring them to more abundant life, by timely support, encouragement and affirmation of gifts and qualities to be given at the service of others. In this way he has helped me to be a father to my children, as well as a father figure to others.

What level of encouragement and affirmation do you think each of your children feels from you? What is one new way you can communicate your approval and your confidence in them? How can you use words to let your children learn from you? To whom can you be a father figure?

A great man, but Dad is far from perfect
I have always *felt* loved by Dad. Though he often labours over points and tells long-winded stories, and though he not infrequently laments the absence of love he received from his

own father and stepfather, and though he was quite absent during my youngest years due to his work as a travelling salesman with National Cash Registers, Dad has unequivocally offered warmth and affection.

Nevertheless, I am quite aware of character flaws in Dad that have influenced his fathering in ways which have affected me. I accept that this is true of all fathers, including the ways I father my own children, despite my best efforts. Acknowledging this fact is the first step to overcoming it.

'Name it and tame it!' is a helpful phrase underlying the truth that if we can identify the flaws in the parenting (in this case, fathering) that we have received, then we will more likely be able to overcome those flaws and they will have less power over us. Over the years I have grown to understand what I have inherited, both positive and negative, from my upbringing, and shared this as a crucial task when helping other couples. Annie's Dad, for example, is very careful about the choice of his words, and I have learnt from him to be more succinct, while retaining my Dad's passion and love of detail when telling stories. We need to be equipped to welcome the strengths and discard the weaknesses of our own childhoods. Annie and I have tried together to build a family based on the hybrid positive qualities we have received, along with a recognition of what we bring with our own capacities, gifts and opportunities.

Repeating the sins of the past

One of the ongoing difficulties I have experienced in the course of my life has been a struggle with negative self-talk. It is something my adult children, even today, bring to my attention from time to time. It has a touch of the victim mentality about it, a 'woe is me' attitude, essentially a form of self-criticism or self-condemnation. It is linked to fault-finding, blaming and putting down, which is an expression of a lack of mercy toward myself (and others). Thankfully, over many years of experiencing God's mercy, the gentle love and tenderness of others – especially Annie – and a deepening of understanding about who I am as a child of God, I have largely overcome it.

I seem to have inherited it from the six crisis years of my parents' conflict. There is a saying, "The child that lives with criticism learns to condemn." While I have worked on overcoming this fault over a lifetime, and seen much progress, there are vestiges of this sinful attitude that seem still to occupy a place in my being.

When I am in the presence of someone speaking with an acid tongue something in my heart sinks and I find it hard not to get upset. Consequently, learning not to take offence has been an ongoing point of conversion in my life. "Love does not take offence" is one of the statements made famous by Saint Paul in the reading so often proclaimed at weddings (1 Cor 13:5). That is the one thing in his list that I have probably struggled with the most.

Though Dad's general disposition is mostly joyful, and his recovery from the crisis remarkable, even miraculous, he has not been fully able to free himself from the hurt of the breakup with Mum, nor the experience of rejection which cut into him as a little boy whose father left him as a baby and whose stepfather seemed distant and cold. His overcoming of this hurt will help me to become freer too.

Aside from his strengths, what faults or weaknesses do you see in your father which you perpetuate? Name one fault and positive quality of yours that you see in your children? Who can help you to identify these more clearly? Choose one small act on a daily basis to overcome these faults.

Impact of our marriage on my fathering

One of the simplest yet most vital practices that Annie and I have committed to living throughout the course of our marriage has been to start the day with a moment of prayer together. When the alarm goes off at 6.30am, we find each other's hand and give our day to God, praying the consecration to Mary. This is among the most important things we do in our lives as a couple because it taps into the source from which everything else flows.

We then have a cup of coffee together. It is not a profound time of conversation or important planning, though it might include some sharing or the making of arrangements, but usually it is made of ordinary conversation. Small things. Even though it takes only ten or twenty minutes, this short moment of pause and connection is a privileged time which provides for both of us the chance to communicate effectively to one another, without using words, that "You are first in my life." I have found that, if ever we have allowed this short daily time to slip by, something seems missing, out of place.

Husband to cherish and serve wife

From the beginning, I was determined to make Annie feel loved and supported, especially during the 'parental emergency' years where, as a young Mum, she accomplished heroic tasks taking care of six small children. That meant being as present as possible during meal times and when the kids were being bathed and put to bed. During this time, I discovered that I relished reading the children stories or, better still, telling them stories. In doing so I developed numerous series of wonderful characters that the kids pleaded with me to revisit regularly over the years. Crime stories of "Bob the Bobby", an English policeman; "Aaron, Berty, Craig and Dave," a group of adventurous ants, and stories constructed with individual items whispered secretly into my ear, all feature.

It also meant that I decided to take a lion's share of cleaning the kitchen, something I've tried to do well over the years, and which I know corresponds to Annie's love language, that of being loved through acts of service. Things being done for her help her to feel loved, whereas my main love language is made up of words. I need to be told "I love you." Other key decisions I have taken over the years include always speaking well of Annie in public, as well as in private, being tender with her, holding her hand when we are arguing (reminding us that unity is the deepest reality we are working towards), and trying to humbly admit fault without excusing myself when we make up, quickly asking forgiveness and quickly forgiving.

It has been said that the best way for a man to love his children is to love their mother! Very recently I was delighted when my Dad said to me that he had had the best conversation with my Mum for over 20 years, even though they are separated. So I am sure that when I give flowers to Annie, or when we go out on dinner dates or take a walk together when we are at the beach, this has a wonderful impact on the kids. My love for Annie should be open and tender. I have no problems letting the children see our affection, and through that they know we have a profound intimacy. It gives them security and hope for their own futures.

Impact on children

When Annie is confident in my presence for her, then I find that she feels cherished, supported and loved. When she sees my positive and loving actions towards her, and that I'm focused on her wellbeing, helping her in her role as mother and wife, and supporting her various projects and missions, she feels valued and encouraged.

"Love seeks the good of the other for their own sake," and not because of any outcome that might emerge from it. It is not utilitarian or conditional. Nevertheless, the impact of her feeling loved does shape her attitude towards me, and I find that it puts order into our relationship. It helps her willingness to be served, therefore to do things with me, so we make decisions together. This encourages me to take my place, helps me step into my authority and leadership role, all seeming to emerge gently and naturally. It makes me feel that she wants me to step up and forward, and I feel respected and honoured in that, rather than in competition. It is my experience that if a man feels he is competing with a woman, especially his wife, it is a killer for male participation. He'd rather step away than enter the 'arena'.

I have also realised that men need to make sure that they have other men in their lives as real brothers with whom they can share deeply. Men need the fellowship of other men, but also to know that it is a valid need to find or create personal space. It took me a long time to give myself permission to do this without feeling guilty. At the same time, we need to be careful to avoid hiding out in the 'cave' and justifying substantial absence.

Annie and I decided many years ago that TV would have very little place in our family life and we have worked hard to ensure that dinner is spent as a family sitting at the table and that conversation is something we try to cultivate. After dinner every night we spend a brief moment praying together as a family, using various formal and informal methods. The kids are very accepting of this practice, and often pipe up to propose a preference, but it was not always easy. We have tried to find a balance between making them feel free to be part of it, focusing on keeping it short and attractive, as well as helping them to understand that this is what it means to be part of our family. We might pray a decade of the rosary one night, have a minute of silence in front of the fire, sing a song, each pray a 'thank you' prayer for something in the day or ask God to help people in need, for example. I have found that the time gathered together in the lounge after the dinner clean-up does require a bit of effort on our behalf. This is especially as we often have to work around homework demands, footy training drop-offs or phone calls. But despite the occasional opposition we are joyfully insistent and inevitably the kids hang around and often this leads to good conversations and peaceful moments.

I learnt that I also need to ensure that I am not 'absent' – still at work in my mind, for example, or in my own thoughts – when I'm sitting at the dinner table and thus putting myself outside the conversation. This is another way of opting out. Presence requires active and tangible interest. One of the things I did when driving home from work over the years was to pray that I might leave work behind me and be ready to be fully available to my family's need of my loving presence. It seemed easier when the kids were little and I was greeted with a king's welcome upon my return. It is, however, no less important with teens whom I've actively had to go to in their bedrooms, or be ready for their question late at night, when the last thing I felt like was a conversation as I was getting ready for bed. These are key moments that can't be manufactured by me but require my readiness and attention.

Greetings and farewells have always been something Annie and I have paid special care to, and whenever possible we have tried to offer a warm and heartfelt 'hello' or 'goodbye' – you never know if it will be the last! We have no problem saying, 'I love you,' and regularly, and have built this into the culture of our family.

All of these things play out into the family and in the man's role of father to his children. The more united the husband and wife are in their respective places within their loving communion, the greater the positive impact this will have on the children; the more integrated those children will be in their own sense of identity, sexuality and authority and the easier they will find entering into healthy relationships and making a positive impact in the world. This has been our experience.

What actions do you practise in your marriage which shape the life of your family? What do you see as the three most important things you do with your wife? What is something you do now to love your wife better than you did one, five or ten years ago? Identify a new inventive way you can cherish or serve her. Who can help you with this?

Conclusion: The heart of the matter

If there is one thing about fathering with which I wish to conclude, by drawing into a unity the reflections and experiences of this chapter, it is this: to be a father is to seek the good of your child, and to do what is needed to help your child to grow. Whether through tender, loving presence and approval, being an inspiring and virtuous example or a compassionate and encouraging support, the true exercise of authority is a matter of the heart. 'Authority' comes from the Latin word *auctoritas*, which means 'to make grow'. I highlight this point in my book *Make Your Mark: Five Hidden Keys to Great Leadership* (Wilkinson Press, 2019) and it is just as valid for leaders in business and public service as for fathers.

In order, then, for fathers to become good or to move from good to great, a man needs to attend to his heart. In order to reach the heights, he must go to the depths. It is there he lives with God, and – if he opens his life to grace – it is where

God changes him, little by little, and everything around him changes too: his wife, his children, his work, his community, his world. Ultimately, I believe, it is only God who can give a man a true father's heart. And that man is asked by God to accept it. Fatherhood, lived primarily from the heart, is both a gift and a task.

Summary

- **Presence.** When I look back and think about my Dad, one of the things I can say is that he was *there*. And the presence that was *there* was warm, affectionate and loving. This is the kind of father I want my kids to experience and remember. So, when I make decisions on a daily basis, I ask myself: is this the decision of a father who is present to his children? And when I try to put my wife first in the thousand ways I am called to do, I ask: am I being the kind of husband to Annie my children need me to be?

- **Example.** John Paul II was literally a 'holy' father to me. It was his behaviour, not his title, that motivated and inspired me to be the best I could be. My teenage years and youth were illuminated by his joyful witness, generous sacrifice and wise words. Even today he models to me how to be a father who keeps his promises, who builds trust and who acts with integrity. It reminds me that in the end my children will be shaped much more by what I do than by what I say.

- **Encouragement.** Understanding the gifts, strengths and passions of one's own child requires attentive listening, insight and the investment of time and energy. This is my experience of Michael O'Brien's fathering, an encouragement which I seek to emulate for my children. Encouragement is the affirming action that seeks the good of the other according to the way they are known and understood. It supports them to have the courage to take the steps that will bring about their unique purpose. I want my children to be encouraged in this way by me.

For further reading

Each of the following three books exemplifies in its own way the three qualities of fathering by presence, example and encouragement, and so much more:

Alexandre Havard, *Virtuous Leadership: An Agenda for Personal Excellence*

John Paul II, *Guardian of the Redeemer*

Michael D. O'Brien, *Father Elijah*.

11

Warwick Marsh
Turn the hearts of the fathers to the children

It was a fine weather Sunday in this small resort town. The café was full of people having their lunch. No one seemed to recall seeing the young man with blonde hair enter the café and order a meal.

Without any warning he unzipped his bag and produced an AR15 semi-automatic rifle and began methodically to shoot people dead. He had an amazing ability when it came to guns!

Warwick with his brother and father.

Warwick and his extended family.

There was a man there enjoying lunch with his wife of over 20 years. As Martin Bryant swung the gun around and pointed the barrel at his wife the man made the split-second decision.

Without any hesitation he leapt forward between the barrel point and his wife's head. His brains took the full force of the bullet and he fell dead on top of his wife, who lives to this day.

"Greater love has no man than this – to lay his life down for his friends."

We say it every Anzac Day as we remember those who gave their lives for our freedom. This man proved his love for his wife. Would you do the same?

If you want to know the truth, I'm not sure if I would. I hope I never have to find out. My big problem is proving my love for my wife while I'm still alive.

You know that song "What if God was one of us, just a slob like one of us?" I really identify with that song. You see, I am a slob. After 45 years of marriage I am only just learning to put my dirty clothes in the dirty clothes basket. I don't clean up after myself at home as I should. Thank God for a forgiving wife. That is my secret.

What's this got to do with fatherhood?

Children are born into the world through love. Love is the greatest force in the universe. If we are to turn the tide of fatherlessness in Australia, we must first learn to love again. What do I mean by 'learn to love again'?

Our relationships: husband-wife, father-son, father-daughter, are held together through love. Love is the glue that holds the nation together. You can have laws to promote love or you can have laws to destroy love. The challenge we have is to find out what love really is.

I was doing a seminar in Tasmania. I asked the question "What is love?" A lady in the group answered. It is usually a lady. Women understand this better than we men. *"Love is being committed to being committed."*

The man who died at the Broad Arrow Café, Port Arthur, that day demonstrated his love for his wife in the ultimate way. He proved his commitment beyond a shadow of a doubt.

If we are to turn the tide of fatherlessness in our nation, we need to dramatically improve the love relationships of the people of our nation.

How do we do this?

I believe we need top down, bottom up reform. We need to work at the top levels of government to bring justice and fairness. Love is being fair. We need the government to begin to invest in prevention rather than cure. One ounce of prevention is worth a pound of cure.

The 12^{pt} Plan estimates the cost of fatherlessness at $13 billion per annum with foundational figures from Dr Bruce Robinson from the University of Western Australia. I believe the true cost of fatherlessness in Australia to be closer to $30-40 billion pa.

Good relationships are better than money in the bank. They cannot be valued yet we pay for their failure, usually in more ways than one.

When we make mistakes as mothers and fathers our children usually pay the price. When we get it right as mothers and fathers and choose the way of love together, our children benefit.

Chris Miles MP, former Parliamentary Secretary to the Prime Minister, made a remarkably interesting and profound observation at the Fathering Forum organised on 10 February 2003 at Parliament House, Canberra by Dads4Kids.

Chris Miles said, "Fathers have to become a wellspring of life for their families, fathers need to be a source of creativity, a source of *giving, a source of guidance for their families and their children. You see, life's about giving. It is more blessed to give than to receive."*

The above words are taken from my speech at the National Strategic Conference on Fatherhood, 18 August 2003, which was held in the Main Committee Room in the centre of Parliament House, Canberra. Within a few years Parliament would enact much-needed shared parenting laws to allow fathers more access to their children after divorce. It was a powerful time of change.

So how did I, a nobody from Wollongong, end up convening a conference on fatherhood in Australia's Parliament? How did I become the co-founder with my wife of the Dads4Kids Fatherhood Foundation? I thought you would never ask.

Joyce Meyer says, "Your mess becomes your ministry." Henri Nouwen explained this idea beautifully in his book, *The Wounded Healer*. For Nouwen, those who seek to help others must be willing to go beyond their professional role and leave themselves open as fellow human beings with the same wounds and suffering – in the image of Christ. In other words, we heal from our own wounds.

I had a wonderful mother and father, but they just could not get along. My mother was a McLeod-McKay from Scotland. Strong-willed and determined, she was a highly qualified nurse who had travelled the world.

Dad was Australian born, but of English stock, and quietly proud of it. In many ways they were made for each other. My mother was careful and frugal with money and good at business. My Dad was an entrepreneur, highly creative, and yet he struggled to put food on the table. Had they been able to work together, our family would have been very wealthy, but the reverse was the case.

Dad was exceptionally good at telling stories. My brother and I would sing a song to Dad that was popular at the time, "Tell me a story, tell me a story, remember what you said. You promised you would. You gotta give in, so I'll be good. Tell me a story, then I'll go to bed."

To hear these stories, my brother and I would jump into Mum and Dad's bed night after night. I can remember my Mum being distinctly unimpressed as she was elbowed by two small boys who hung on to Dad's every word.

Yes, we had some great memories growing up, but Charles Dickens' words summed it up well, "It was the best of times and the worst of times."

By the time I hit high school, I had been to ten different schools with some 15 house moves. By the time I was seven my brother and I had been around the world twice to visit our grandmother in Edinburgh, Scotland.

Looking back, I realise that I was probably abducted by my mother to get us away from my father. For a while we lived at Castlereagh near the Nepean River in Western Sydney on a five-acre farm. It was an idyllic life for a six-year-old boy. That year I learned to ride a bike, started school and almost started a bushfire. Fire is something I have always loved, but you must be careful with your loves.

Boys also love hanging out with their Dads. I remember being with Dad when he was growing pumpkins when a bee flew into a yellow pumpkin flower, shaped like a small cupcake. I could not resist the urge to close over the yellow petals to trap the insect in the flower with my hands. The bee, realising his entrapment by these curious hands behind the thin petals, promptly stung the culprit.

My hand was burning and I let out a loud cry. My father

stooped down to pick me up with his strong arms of love and console me in my grief. I never tried to trap a bee again. Once bitten, twice shy.

Living on the farm was my last happy memory of my father for two years or more. Dad told me many years later that he came home and Mum had gone. The house was cleaned out and his two beautiful boys were gone too. He never told me so, but I am sure he cried himself to sleep that night and for many nights thereafter.

We eventually travelled back to Scotland, the second time in so many years, to live again with our grandmother. I survived and grew older, not realising the sadness that was growing in my heart. When we are young, we push the pain away but that does not mean it is not there.

This was the second trip to Scotland and the second long absence from my father. I calculated some time ago that approximately half of my first 12 years on the planet were spent separated from my father.

Coming back to Sydney from Scotland to be with Dad again was a very exciting event. In true Marsh fashion, Dad let off a celebratory tuppenny bunger on the wharf at Circular Quay.

Mum was unimpressed to say the least, but my brother and I were spellbound. Tuppeny bungers become illegal within the decade because they were just too powerful and dangerous. That was the beginning I believe of the Marsh family's love affair with explosives.

I was so excited to be back in Australia and with my Dad, but the volatility in my parents' relationship continued. After a few more hasty moves, we ended up living in Lavender Bay and attending Kirribilli Primary School. Mum and Dad continued their shouting matches and door slamming, so much so that the police came to adjudicate. I don't think it was the first time.

Mum had a fiery temper when she got going. Dad could get angry too. They had married older in life for their generation and were rather set in their ways. The ten-year age difference did not seem to help, nor did the dramatic difference between the Scottish and English/Australian outlooks on life.

In all the many fights Mum and Dad had, I can remember that my father never hit my mother, but my mother was not as gracious. She drew blood on him at least once.

I remember that my school friends at the time thought I was English because that is what Australian mixed with Scottish sounded like. That of course is the worst thing you can say to a Scotsman. The Scots have a derogatory word to describe the English, *Sassenach*, and I am sure that word was used by my Mum in relation to my father more than once.

One morning, my brother and I, after a particularly torrid week of fighting, were called into the principal's office at Kirribilli Public School. In the office was my mother with a man from 'child welfare'. They informed us that because of our troubles at home we would be put in a home and separated from our father.

My brother and I promptly burst into tears and cried so loudly and for so long that they relented. I firmly believe that if we had not vehemently protested with our tears and cries, we might never have seen our father again.

Sadly, in today's world, with our current family law system, that would have been the case. I know many fathers today, who through no fault of their own, have been grieving the loss of their children for decades. Australia's Family Law Court system has a horrific attitude to fathers.

We moved house again and again, and the fighting continued. Thankfully, my mother and father never divorced, but they lived separated lives, maybe out of necessity. We ended up living in Blackheath in the Blue Mountains so my Mum could travel more easily to a live-in job in Bathurst.

I remember as a young teenage boy lying in a ditch by the side of the road, crying. I was grief-stricken. I could not understand why my mother and father fought so furiously. I wanted to die. Perhaps if they were non-believers, I could have reconciled the fighting, but both held to a faith in God. My father in particular had trained as an Anglican priest for the ministry. Sadly, he had become disillusioned with the religious side of denominationalism and no longer attended church. Thankfully, he was still very committed to God and was an avid student of the scriptures.

Needless to say, my mother and father's continued conflagrations caused me great pain. I was mostly a straight A student and good at studying but in the middle of this family conflict, my interest in school began to fade and my ability to study too. In times of depression suicide became a consideration but thankfully not a reality.

Quite a few of my friends were involved with drugs and I was given some white pills wrapped in silver foil by one of my fellow students at school. Thankfully, I never took those drugs. I was living on the edge in so many ways. Deep inside, my heart was broken by my family's relational breakdown and my periodic fatherlessness, but I did not realise it.

Growing up, I had heard a lot about the love of God, but it was extremely hard to reconcile the love of God in a Christian family that was at war with itself. My struggles continued but one night I heard Billy Graham sharing the good news of God's love through Jesus Christ, that he came to seek and save that which was lost.

What was lost was a relationship with our loving Father in heaven. It was lost because of our innate ability to sin, which in the Greek, means to 'miss the mark'. The analogy in the original language was built around the idea of an archer, shooting arrows at a target but missing the bullseye every time.

The first man, Adam, with his wife, Eve, lived in a beautiful garden. Our Father in heaven walked with them every evening. When they ate of the tree of knowledge of good and evil, their voluntary decision betrayed the whole human race to the corrupting power of missing the bullseye of God's perfection.

Billy Graham pointed out that Jesus broke the power of sin and death by dying in our place, on a cruel cross. His blood paid the ransom for our sin, including our failure and other people's too.

That night I got down beside my bed and prayed the sinner's prayer. *Dear God, thank you for sending Jesus, who died in my place, whose blood forgave my sin. Thank you, Father, that your Son rose again and I ask Him to come and live in my heart for eternity. Amen.*

In saying this prayer, I found myself accepted into the heavenly family. Peace flooded my soul and even though I did not have all the answers to my many problems, I had found The Answer, and his name was Jesus.

At the time I was learning blues guitar, listening to great guitarists like Eric Clapton, Jimmy Page from Led Zeppelin and Jimi Hendrix, to name a few. I started writing songs and remember performing the Christian version of "Help" by the Beatles at a Youth for Christ meeting in Katoomba. It was my first big public performance.

It was the early days of the so-called Jesus Revolution and whilst my grades were still dropping, I was heavily involved in the Inter-School Christian Fellowship of my high school. In some ways I was winning but the pain deep inside had not gone way.

In January 1972, I attended a Summer of Service with Youth With A Mission in Wollongong. We used to witness to all the young surfers and drug takers in the main street, every Friday and Saturday night. Many young people came to Christ. Many would call it a move of the Spirit. Whatever the case, we were living in momentous times for many different reasons.

I dropped out of school, left the Blue Mountains and moved to Wollongong to serve in a local church called the Lighthouse where hundreds of young people were coming to faith and finding the Father's love for the first time. Interestingly, at the time, I was determined not to marry as all I knew from my experience was the pain and heartbreak of growing up in a broken home.

Sadly, I was not alone. Many of my friends had experienced the same wounding. The good news is that this loneliness did not last forever because I met a beautiful young woman called Alison who shared my deep love for God and a consuming passion to help others.

We were married in 1975, I was 21 and she was 20 and from an earthly point of view, it was the best thing I ever did. The song says, "Love will find a way," and it certainly found a way in my heart. The really wonderful thing was that I could go to her home and enjoy the beautiful atmosphere of love and peace which again gave me hope for my future family and marriage.

My big goal in life became loving my wife which proved a

lot harder to do than to say. The fact that I had no strong role models in my own family made the job that much more difficult.

It got worse a few years later when my wife's family, who could do no wrong, got involved in a Christian cult and effectively cut my wife and I, and the rest of their family, out of their lives, at the insistence of the cult leader. This was a double whammy. Now I was really struggling for role models.

There is a saying, "When the going gets tough, the tough get going", so I cast about for other older men who had good relationships with their wives and were good fathers, both naturally and spiritually.

Unfortunately, I do not think I ever had a formal mentoring relationship with any man, but I sure had many informal relationships with men of faith who loved their wives and treasured their families. Loving my wife was my big goal in life, because I had seen the devastation firsthand, in two families, in the lives of those who didn't put their wives and families in the place that they so deserved.

As our children were born my wife and I read books on marriage and relationships and we started to go to marriage retreats. I was also heavily involved in working with men through the Full Gospel Business Men's Fellowship. It was at one of these events I first heard Ewin Louis Cole, author of *Maximised Manhood*, speak. His teaching really challenged me to the core and helped me become a better husband and father, but I still had a long, long way to go. At the same time, my wife discovered the *Above Rubies* magazine which has a strong focus on mothering, family and faith. This was a godsend for her too.

All through this time, I was experiencing the ups and downs

of the building industry, which is another story in itself. Suffice to say, in the late nineties, my wife and I were playing in a Christian rock band appropriately called the Good News Band.

One day we were scheduled to play at a local boys' high school. Early that morning, I had a very unusual dream. I saw a man and woman walking down a long road against the setting sun. As silhouettes I was unable to recognise either of them. In the mother's arms was a little boy reaching out and crying out for Daddy, or was the little boy in the father's arms, reaching out and crying out for Mummy?

That detail escapes me. As I watched, this couple moved farther and farther apart as they walked down the long road. All the while, the child was crying out and reaching out for the other parent but the little boy's voice was not heeded.

Watching this dream just seemed to tear my heart out. I was sobbing uncontrollably. I woke up and realised it was a dream, and yet my pillow was wet with tears. I felt like yelling out, "What is this all about? Who is the little boy in the dream?"

A voice whispered, "You are the little boy!" and I sobbed all the more.

Here I was, 34 and still struggling with a deep father wound and now a father of four sons myself. And yet, the tears bubbling out of my eyes were bringing healing to my heart. I realised it was a holy moment.

Over the years I had simply buried the pain and pushed on as we all do, but the wound was festering deep inside and the still small voice was calling me home to find the unconditional love of my Father in heaven. It reminded me of the time my father picked me up in his arms after I clasped the flower and was stung by the bee.

That morning we played our loud music to a roomful of teenage boys in the middle of a teachers' strike. In more ways than one it was the opportunity for a riot, and it very nearly happened. I vividly remember telling the students halfway through our performance about the dream I had early that morning, my own tears and my own story of growing up in a broken home.

It was strange because the whole auditorium went quiet. You could have heard a pin drop in the silence. I have talked to people about the experience and we all agree that up to half of those boys knew that story from my dream all too well. The other half had friends who were experiencing family breakup and they were afraid the same relationship breakdown was going to happen to their parents as well.

Our relationships in our families are our greatest asset. We need to protect them for the sake of our future generations. The Preamble to the 12pt plan I quoted in my speech that day, 18 August 2003, at the first National Strategic Conference on Fatherhood in the Australian Parliament, says this.

> The greatest resource this country possesses lies in the families of our nation. At the same time, the strength of our families depends on the quality of the relationships between mothers and fathers.
>
> The quality of the relationships between mothers and fathers and their children will determine the destiny of Australia. The future of Australia lies in the character of her children. Equipping and supporting fathers and mothers in their relationships helps ensure that our children have the best possible future.
>
> The National Fathering Forum believes that every

child has the fundamental right to both a mother and a father. The best way to secure this right is to establish a loving and stable marriage between a man and a woman for life. This long-term relationship facilitates the rights of grandmothers and grandfathers to continued access and valuable input into their grandchildren.

The overwhelming conclusion of current social science research has shown that the best environment for children is a close, warm, sustained and continuous relationship with both biological parents. The best way to ensure strong families is to support strong marriages. This traditional family unit – a loving father, mother and their children – is the best way to nurture, educate and protect children. This is the best social security system the world has ever known.

Fatherlessness can be defined as the absence of an active, positive father influence in the lives of children. Fatherlessness is both a natural and spiritual problem.

It needs strategic and synergistic partnerships that should involve government, business, church, community, faith-based and secular charities and many others working together to strengthen and support Australian fathers.

Back to my story. In 1990 I left the security of a developing construction business behind to go on the road for a year with my family and experience the adventure of discovering Australia. We also wanted to share the good news of Jesus Christ through our music with all who would listen. That year became the first year of three decades of full-time service to the people of Australia.

Over the next decade or more we played music in over 100 Indigenous communities, hundreds of churches of all denominations and 20 gaols in every state of Australia except South Australia. We also played in many high schools and as I have often observed, the difference between high schools and gaols, sadly, is not immense. Of course, we also played in pubs, clubs, town halls, festivals and more typical music venues as well. We recorded several albums and our music was heard on radio and TV.

From 1996 to 1998, I was the main co-ordinator for the Praise Corroboree. This was a cross-cultural gathering in the Great Hall of Parliament House, Canberra as well as on a stage on the front lawn of Parliament House that spanned 72 hours.

During this time, I organised meetings of Aboriginal Elders from all over Australia with parliamentary leaders including cabinet ministers, the Deputy Prime Minister and twice with then Prime Minister, John Howard.

In 1998, I was at Parliament House, Canberra for an interactive seminar with a Federal Member of Parliament in a room of 50 people. I was in my blue pin-stripe suit, doing my best to look intelligent when the question was asked of all those in the room, "What is Australia's biggest problem and what is Australia's greatest need?"

The answers flowed quickly from the group: abortion (100,000 babies die before they even see the light); drugs; crime; pornography; divorce and family breakdown. They all seemed pretty bad and in need of attention. It was then that Pastor Ron Williams, whom we had first met at Kalgoorlie Gaol in Western Australia, stood up to speak. He had on a crumpled tweed jacket, his grey hair and beard looked a little bit worn and yet we were all transfixed as we listened to his gentle words.

"Australia's greatest need is for fathers. Fathers who will love their children and love their wives and look after them. Fathers in the business world who will put people before profits. Fathers in the political world who will be statesmen and not just politicians. Fathers in the local community who will care for their community as if it were their family. Fathers in the church who will do the same."

As he said these words, I felt the tears welling up in my eyes. They weren't just welling up, I was starting to sob and I turned my face to the wall to prevent people from seeing me. I was very embarrassed.

At the time, I didn't understand why I was crying but I remember the tears I shed when I had that dream as God revealed my own father wound. I wondered again why the words of this Aboriginal Elder had so deeply touched my heart.

At the time our family band, The Marshes, started to write songs for our new double album called *Fathers*. The album became our final musical *tour de force* with sixteen songs on disc one and ten instrumentals on disc two.

One day, while working on this album, I arrived at the recording studio and asked the main engineer, "Where's Jeff?" Jeff had been helping us on the project for several months as an assistant engineer with all our demo songs and had been a great help in seeing the songs come to fruition.

The chief engineer's reply shocked me, "Jeff's been put in gaol for molesting his young teenage stepdaughters." Sickened to the core, I immediately cancelled the recording session and did not return for several weeks. I was devastated. I felt like a failure as I had not realised what was going on. In fact, I wondered whether I should complete the project. I even thought about returning to the construction industry.

I sought counsel from wise men and women. The good news is they encouraged me to proceed with this project for the sake of the nation's children. I'm so glad I did.

One of the songs I wrote, which became the opening track for the *Fathers* album, is titled 'Daddy Doesn't Live Here Anymore'. It was written with a friend, who himself grew up fatherless, as both a form of self-therapy and also a means to help others, by sharing with our fellow human beings with the same wounds and suffering, as Henri Nouwen wrote. The song is as follows:

Don't come knockin' on my front door
'Cos Daddy doesn't live here any more
He's gone away, I don't know where
He don't live here no more

1. And now I cry myself to sleep
If only I could see him now
I'm sure somehow, he'd hold me close
And tell me …. and tell me …

2. And if there is a God up there
I'm sure You know, but I don't care
If only I could see Him now
I'd like to tell Him how I feel

3. And so please God, hear my prayer
Show me that You really care
I trust You now so hold me close
Don't tell me, don't tell me

Don't come knockin' on my front door
'Cos Daddy doesn't live here any more

He's gone away, I don't know where
He don't live here no more
Another song that features on the album is called "Hearts of the Fathers". It is an attempt to identify the problem and grasp hold of the Malachi mission.

1. In this nation, there's a cry of desperation
Suicidal litigation, families crumble from within
And they don't know where they're going
And they can't see where they've been
But they know they need some changes,
Some changes from within ... to turn the...

Hearts of the fathers
Hearts of the sons
Hearts of the children
Father make us one
Father make us one

2. Men look for all the answers
Taking chances with the dancers
Too many fleeting glances
Lead to faithlessness and sin
And they don't know what they're sowing
And they don't know where they've been
But they know they need some changes,
Some changes from within ..... to turn the.....

3. You know the Son is rising, by the Light that breaks the dawn
The morning stars are glowing, soon the shadows will be torn
And you know the wind is blowing
And you can't see where He's been
But you know the change is coming
And He is coming from within..... to turn the.....

The rest of course is history. We released the Fathers album in early 2000 and toured across Australia in the lead up to the Olympic Games, Sydney. It felt like throwing a rock in the ocean. Yes, there was a splash, but the ripples soon disappeared.

It certainly felt like a message that was barely heard even in the wilderness, similar to John the Baptist who fulfilled the words found in Malachi 4:6, to "Turn the hearts of the fathers to the children and the hearts of the children to the fathers lest the land be smitten with a curse of irrevocable destruction."

In May 2002, the Board of Australian Heart Ministries founded the Dads4Kids Fatherhood Foundation. We released the first TV Community Service Announcements for national free to air television. Later that year Dads4Kids started discussions with parliamentarians to work towards the first historic Fathering Forum on 10 February 2003.

The 12^{Pt} Plan was released in June 2003 as Dads4Kids prepared for the National Strategic Conference on Fatherhood to be held in Parliament House, Canberra, August 2003.

This brings me to the point of my speech, with which I started this chapter. We are making progress, but it is painfully slow. The work of Dads4Kids can be very discouraging at times. Often it feels like three steps forward and two steps back.

Sometimes I wonder if it really is worth it. But then I remember the 870,000 children who will go to sleep tonight without their biological father in the home, and the many other millions who have a father in the home but he is emotionally disengaged. He is still trying to recover from the wounds of his childhood, as I was in my mid-thirties.

Our society is filled with pain. Much of it is caused by the father wound. That is why the words of Malachi are so important. He was right to emphasise the heart and so must we. So, let me finish my speech as an encouragement to you.

The future is in your heart. Together we can make a difference. It is about you and I as fathers having a change of heart. It is about you and I valuing our relationships above our jobs, our position, our money, our career. It is about you and I being living examples of our words.

Our children will become what we are, not what we say. The greatest challenge we have as fathers is to change from the inside out. Yes, the laws need changing. But more importantly, we need a change deep within us all.

I have to stop being a slob at home. I have to not just be able to die for my wife, I have to live for her daily. We must do the same for our children. We must value our children more than our jobs, our positions and our money.

Men spell love S-E-X, women spell love T-A-L-K, children spell love T-I-M-E. We must all take spelling lessons together and learn how to spell L-O-V-E again. As the woman from Tasmania said, "Love is being committed to being committed."

Three Great Tips for Dads

1. *Guard your heart with all diligence for out of your heart flow the issues of life.* Live out of your heart because that is what is important and that is what your children need.

2. Reach out to your Heavenly Father for healing for your heart because we have all been battered and wounded in some way. The good news is God heals the broken-hearted and binds up their wounds.

3. Tell your children each day you love them because love is being committed.

Three Great Books on Fatherhood
Derek Prince, *Husbands & Fathers*
Dr Bruce Robinson, *Fathering from the Fast Lane*
John Eldredge, *Fathered by God.*

Three Great Songs About Fatherhood
Teach Your Children Well by Crosby, Stills, Nash & Young
Fathers be Good to your Daughters by John Mayer
Best Daddy by Cody Qualls

12

Brian Sullivan
Only the sacrament of the present moment

Introduction

It is true to say that fatherhood research is still in its early days, and it would be wise to keep an open mind about how mothers and fathers differ in their approach to parenting (or not), as well as about fathers' particular contributions. Much of the research into fathering has probably focused on western cultures, with other cultures' ideas and realities of fathering

Brian and his Mum, Marie.

Brian, his wife Elisa, and his Mum, Marie.

not being understood, or considered, nearly enough.

With this understanding, I launch into my chapter about the lessons that I have learned about fathers: from the fathering that I received; from the fathers who influenced me (positively or negatively) and from my own experience of being a Dad. This is my experience and my history, but my hope is that something of my experience will resonate with yours and together we may all be better men and better fathers. It seems now more than ever that our world, our children, need us to be better men and better fathers.

Please know from the outset that I am not an expert on fatherhood. I do not consider myself an exemplary role model or great example of fatherhood. I struggle, I battle, I win some and I lose some. I write this as a fragile and failing man, a man who has made mistakes as a father. Hopefully, I am learning from failures and mistakes and to me that is critical. My hope is that now I have more good days than bad days as a father for my children's sake, but it's still a learning journey, and they will tell the truth about that.

President Barack Obama, in a 2008 Father's Day speech, powerfully captured the significance of fatherhood, and fatherlessness in America and everywhere:

> We know the statistics – that children who grow up without a father are five times more likely to live in poverty and commit crime, nine times more likely to drop out of schools and 20 times more likely to end up in prison. They are more likely to have behavioural problems, or run away from home, or become teenage parents themselves. And the foundations of our community are weaker because of it.

While this may be statistically true, another famous quote comes to mind: "lies, damned lies, and statistics". Statistics reveal but they also conceal. I grew up without a father (Obama did too). Dad died when I was eight, the only boy with five sisters, three older and two younger. We weren't rich but we never went hungry. Families who don't have a father present and engaged can be less financially resourced of course. We were raised, cared for, nurtured and given opportunities by a kind and resourceful woman of faith, our mother. I never dropped out of school (in fact, if I may boast a little – I was school captain). Fortunately, I went to a great Catholic school and am now an academic. I have never been to prison (not yet anyway), although I have worked professionally with many men who have ended up or will end up there. I didn't have behavioural problems (not all my friends would agree with this), run away from home or become a teenage parent. I am no saint by any stretch of the imagination. However, I have been a schoolteacher and school counsellor and worked with children with all three of those challenges.

Before talking about fathers, I want to say that I owe so much of who I am and what I have done to my mother's influence. That is for sure. So, I want to acknowledge strong women who are left to carry heavy burdens of parenting solo and who courageously and conscientiously raise wonderful children. So let's not forget the many children who grow up without fathers but who are raised by resilient women (albeit not without challenges and difficulties) who see their children through to being strong contributing adults.

Please don't get me wrong, being without my Dad growing up was not easy. In fact, I still miss him, and I have missed him all my life, in many ways at different times. He was not there for the milestones; he never saw me play football, never saw me graduate, never knew me as an adult. He never knew my wife and my children. Yes, I miss having a Dad. I grieved that loss deeply but couldn't or didn't reveal that pain to anyone. In fact, I probably brushed it off, stoically believing that it was what a man did – never focus on your pain but get on with your life. Now I know that is not a good way to process grief.

However, our emphasis in this book is on fathering, and that is so necessary because of the magnitude of its absence. In our society, for many children, adversity, addiction, abuse, aggression and absence are the only experiences they have of their fathers. I will now look at my experience of my own father's absence.

Lessons learned from my father's death

As I reflect on my experience, I realise that my father taught me lessons through his death and through the terrible absence his death has left in my life:

1. Life is fired at us point blank – there comes a time when there is no cure; no second chance; no new beginning. Life is over – death may be the doorway to a new adventure, but for us who are left behind it means our lives are now different because the other is no longer physically present for us to hold on to. Dad told my mother he was not afraid to die and he made sure that she was able to buy a house and look after her children. He took care of business as a responsible father should. I am forever grateful for that. He may have been unafraid to die, but as a small boy I was afraid of his death. I was afraid of what would happen to me, to our family, to my mother. That fear of who I was, who I am, who I would be without him is still with me, but it has calmed over the years. His absence was an ongoing presence in my life, as a child and teenager. Death stung early and I felt that sting. But there was more than that.

2. Through his death, I learned about his goodness, about how highly people valued him. "He was one of the good guys" his work colleague told me many years after his death. Stories of his growing up, stories of his football days, stories of him as a Dad with my older sisters, stories of him courting my mother and their early married life, stories about him as an active Catholic parishioner, stories of his dying. Apparently, to my jealous sister's disgust, he would sing to me "Briannie is a good boy, Briannie is!" I love when they tell me that story. These myths and stories built my image of him. I felt I got to know him even though I had just turned eight when he died. I learned that his values, his personality, his love, his characteristics were still alive and were accessible to me. My mother armed me and sheltered me with wonderfully warm humorous stories about him. Admittedly, these are my memories of others' memories of him. That is still somehow consoling and comforting, and basking in the light of those stories, I gain strength. That was so important to me growing up and even now.

3. Because my father died when I was young, it meant I experienced some men who took a fatherly interest in me in ways that I might not have if my Dad was still alive. A couple of men went out of their way to seek me out and to include me and gift me with their kindness and goodness. One was a priest who taught me from when I was in Year 6 to Year 12. He died recently after a friendship we shared for 50 years. He literally was God-sent I believe. He instilled in me a love of music, literature, especially poetry, and sport. He was fun and funny. He baptised one of my children and was a family friend. In this fallout after the Royal Commission into Institutional Responses to Child Sexual Abuse, it is important to remember and to remind ourselves, that while perpetrators were so destructive,

statistically they were few and real pastors, so benevolent, were statistically the majority. I may never have met Fr Pat if my own father didn't die. So, I am so thankful for Pat's contribution to my life. When one door closes, other doors open.

Lessons learned from violent men and fathers

For the past 22 years or so, I have worked in some way or other with men who have been coercively controlling and physically, sexually and psychologically abusive to their partner/s and their children. These are men, partners and fathers, not monsters (although their behaviour and actions towards their intimate partners and children are monstrous and sometimes murderous). I challenge these men; I confront them about their beliefs and behaviour. When I hear their stories of the abuse and violence they suffered as children, I have compassion for that boy in them, but I will not collude with them, excuse, justify or overlook the horrific harm they are doing to women and children. I learn from them in a negative way. I learn what I should not be thinking, how I should not be responding and what I should not be saying if I want to be a respectful, responsible and resourceful father and man. Recently, I was asked to speak at an emotional gathering, remembering a family who had been killed by their recently separated husband and father…

"When anyone dies like this, especially children, there is an overwhelming sense of tragedy, unfairness and unnecessary loss. Tears that seem endless, unbearable pain, questions without answers, powerlessness and hopelessness. Just sheer exhaustion at the incredible work the domestic violence intervention sector does and then this. Maybe this is a brief glimpse of what a victim of domestic abuse lives with every day.

"If this is not a deafening wake-up call or turning point for this state and our country – then nothing will change the status quo. How do we transfigure and transform this death, darkness and despair into hope and life?

"Archbishop Desmond Tutu, speaking about justice in another violent context, said a situation will not change until we first speak the truth. Let's, as a society, tell the truth, be honest and face up to the reality of men's violence without listening to the uninformed ranting about this violence being equal between men and women. Without the mindless 'whataboutery' that distracts from the crisis facing women and children living with abusive men. I call it uninformed, but it is more than that – it is dishonest. We need to correct these false narratives and lies. Domestic violence is the most serious form of human rights violation in our country and it is men's violence towards women and children that is the core of this. Fact! No excuses! Where are the men of respect and non-violence standing against this behaviour? How can we do more to end this violence against women and children?

"These killings are not about a father being 'driven to the brink' – these wicked acts of violent cruel murder are deliberate, purposeful and planned, about winning the contest, winning the battle, winning the prize which is power over others' lives, about having the last word, calling the final shot. This is nothing more than brutal revenge and payback at not getting his way, and the cost of a woman just wanting to live an abuse-free life was a vicious ambush that murdered her and her children."

- A father sacrifices himself for his children – he doesn't sacrifice his children.
- A father respects his children's mother, especially when that intimate relationship between the man and women may be over.

- A father can never say he loves his children if he harms their mother.
- A father de-centres himself and centres those he loves – it is not all about him anymore.
- A father would rather suffer himself than see his children suffer.
- A father knows that his children are not his trophies, his property or possession – they are through him but not from him – they are not his to own.
- A father is an optimist for his children's futures, not a narcissist about his own superiority, entitlement, rights over others.

When I work with men who are violent and abusive, I want them to become aware of the harm they are causing for their children and their partners. I want them to reflect on what their experience of their fathers was like and the effect it had on them. I want them to understand how important it is that they grow to be respectful, safe and responsible men who can care for their children, and be a resource for their children, not a risk. That is what I want to be too.

Lessons learned from my children

In the beginning is the relationship (Martin Buber). Fatherhood is not just the passing on of sperm and fertilising the ovum. Any irresponsible fool with a penis can do that. Fatherhood is life-giving relationship, presence, engagement, nurturing, protection; much like motherhood, only different.

As fathers we can tread lightly through our children's dreams and hopes, or we can trudge and trample heavily and harmfully. We move through their soul-scapes and heart-scapes as risk or resource. We can face adversity with patience or pugnacity.

We can be adversity in our children's experience, or we can be their advantage, their resilience factor.

So, as a Dad, I want to learn – and have learned – from my children. They want me to be there for them – and be me. I want to let my children get to know me. This is not a dress rehearsal – I have only one shot at being a father to my children at the age they are now. I can't push pause or replay. I have only the sacrament of the present moment. I don't want to miss this time or opportunity and live with regrets and remorse about myself as a father.

So, when my daughter received her first high school award, it was no big deal for me to give up a work trip to San Diego to be at the presentation evening. San Diego isn't going anywhere but the opportunity to be there to watch her receive that award would never come again. When my son asked to go on a 'boys only' trip to Queenstown, New Zealand, earlier this year (just he and I), even though pressures of deadlines at work were weighing on me, I knew that I might never get that invitation again – so a no brainer, of course, and we had a memorable adventure.

I don't tell you this to self-promote, as I don't see myself as a particularly gifted or gifting father, but my children's lives are important to me. In fact I can honestly say they are more important to me than my own life. For me, that is what parenting is, a de-centring process where you choose to grow up and become responsible for more than just your self. Loving their mother, my wife, is integral to my fathering of them. It is the bedrock of our family. It is the fertile garden from which they grow into good human beings. The best thing I can give to my children is the love, respect and life I give to my wife, their mother. It is my gift to myself too.

Two things I have learned from having children – and maybe

children are necessary to learn these lessons (well at least for me they were). Firstly, I am not God – I don't have total control or command of others' lives, safety, decisions, circumstances. Secondly, my children are not me! They are of and through me and my wife, but they are separate human beings, with their own road, their own journey, their own calling, their own lives to lead. They have their own mistakes to make, their own lessons to learn, their own pain to experience, their own resilience to build, their own mountains to climb, their own victories and failures. Of course, I hope that my example, my presence, my 'wisdom' (when called on) may be of use to them and may influence them. I hope that who I am may not only be in their physical DNA, but in their values DNA, their moral DNA, their spiritual DNA and their relational DNA. That at least is my hope. They need me to walk with them, sometimes behind them, sometimes maybe even in the distance. They don't need me to carry them, or crowd them, or coerce them, supervising their every move. They are not children anymore. They are beautiful young adults with the world (all its promises, dreams, lies, threats, hopes and disappointments) before them. And they will sort and sift the wheat from the chaff, the gold from the tinsel, the good from the bad. I trust them to do that (not always without mistakes) because we, my wife and I, have parented them to be strong and resilient. When the going gets tough, they will show their toughness.

I want to share with you now two letters I have written to my children – I asked their permission to include them in this chapter and they both agreed. I thank them for their generosity of spirit.

My dear Son on your 18th birthday

Happy 18th birthday. Legally, you are now an adult. At least you are the legal age of maturity according to our society. However, you know that being a man is more than just reaching your 18th year! Being, or at least becoming a man, your journey to manhood, began with your first living moment and will not cease until the day you die. Please allow me as your Dad to write to you about my beliefs about manhood. Take what is useful now and keep the rest for later.

What does it mean to be a man? That is the question that you need to answer. You can find some helpful answers from good men you know (and I hope you count me as one of them), watching, listening, asking. You can find helpful answers in good books about good men. What does it mean to be a good man? Well, it is much more than achievements and accomplishments. It is more than status and assets. It is more than prowess and power. It is even more than being a doctor – although if you are a good man then I believe it will contribute to your being a good doctor too.

I believe that being a good man is critical for your life and for the life of so many others. We have a 'famine of good men' now in our world, as Fulton Sheen noted so many years ago. Maybe it is always the case. However, you and your life can break that famine! You are breaking that famine!

Being a good man is about character, compassion, courage and kindness. It is about being a man whom others can rely on to be honest, a person of integrity whom others can depend on, a man who lives up to his responsibilities even when the going gets tough. You can be courageous when you do the right thing even when it is not easy to do, even when others might laugh at you, or criticise you. It means being unselfish and thoughtful. A man of compassion and kindness is a guiding light for others. I love that saying: "Others are fighting a battle you know nothing about, so always be kind." A good man is always kind. As I see it, Jesus is the ultimate epitome of courageous compassionate manhood. He is more than that I know – he is our Divine Saviour and Redeemer, but as a man, what an inspiration!

As I see it, you are already on that journey of courage, character, compassion and kindness. Sometimes these are challenged in family life and it is not so easy to be/live those values – the way you treat those closest to you can be your greatest testing ground. But that is what a good man does.

Here are some truths that I have learned on my own continuing journey to manhood:

Remember who you are, where you come from, in terms of family, friends, school etc. You've been living in an environment where you've breathed in certain key values – these are a solid foundation. Now you get to decide and confirm your values and what is important to you and live them out. Don't be afraid to be an individual, but don't be afraid to call on others for support and guidance. Alone, you may travel fast, but together, with others, you will travel far. You need to belong to a community where good men belong too.

Respect yourself and others. Every human has dignity and goodness – the fact that they don't show it all the time doesn't mean you don't treat them with respect. Your treating them with respect may be what they need to realise their own dignity and goodness again. Never treat anyone, (girls and women especially) as objects or property or less than you. I don't need to say that because I know how respectful and responsible you are with your friends who are girls/young women. Our male sexuality is about respect, love, sharing life. Sadly, so much of sexuality today is seen as self-assertion, self-pleasure at all costs, disposable relationships and using others for selfish gain. That is never going to lead to faithful, lasting, loving intimacy. Augustine said, "Love and do what you please." Reflect deeply on that statement. It is not about licence to please yourself, but it is a call to a life of love with all that means: self-giving, self-sacrifice, self-surrender.

Listen more than you speak. Find out about others. Listen to their stories. You will learn more by paying attention to what others have to say and people appreciate being heard. You have two ears and one mouth – there are your percentages.

Always be grateful. An attitude of gratitude is so important. Gratitude makes you resilient, hopeful and less depressed. Count your blessings, your many blessings, every day. If you focus on what you don't have, you'll be miserable and ungrateful and grasping. When you count your blessings, you know deep down how fortunate you are and you can be at peace with your goals but content in the present moment too.

Be selfless. Let someone else have the nice chair, closer parking space or last slice. Let others go first. Ask others how you can help. Look for simple ways to help others. Seriously, you'll be happier this way. Fighting for superiority and status is exhausting and ultimately pointless. It is not energy well-spent and never the measure of a man. Life is not all about you or getting your own needs met. I believe you will never be happier than when you serve. A strange paradox indeed but deeply Christian and truly human.

Keep your promises. Doing what you say you will do is a rare thing in our world today. It is one of the easiest ways to stand apart. Be true to your word. Say what you mean and mean what you say – but never be mean!

Be confident but stay humble. You can accomplish anything you put your mind to, so don't doubt your abilities. On the other hand, don't think too highly of yourself. You have a wonderful contribution to make to this world and to your community, but remember others do too. Everyone plays their role. I love the story of the doctor, head of the hospital, who used to greet and talk with the cleaners whenever he met them, because their role in keeping the wards clean was crucial to good medicine and healthcare. He knew their value and knew they were all on the same team.

There is no substitute for hard work. The process of working toward a goal is often as rewarding as the achievement itself. You are motivated and you don't need to be pushed here. I am amazed at your drive for your goals, but don't forget others on the way.

Intelligence and wisdom are not the same. Intelligence is the ability to learn. Wisdom is using knowledge and experience to make good choices. You can have both, and you will need to have both as a man and a doctor. Wisdom means being open to learn from experience and listening to the wisdom that precedes you.

Never stop learning. There's a whole world to be explored beyond the classroom long after graduation. Never stop listening to wise and good people. I know how much you love and value learning so I know this one will not be a problem for you.

Search for, reach for, what is true. There is so much bullshit, so many lies and deception in our world. People promising this and that, false prophets and charlatans, people selling you their falsehoods. Have a good bullshit detector, talk to those you trust and value and know your own truth. That will steer you clear of going down wrong paths with sometimes nasty consequences.

Accept yourself. This has taken me a long time to reach – but it is important. You are a combination of nature and nurture – genes and environment in an amazing interaction. You were meant to be. You have been gifted in ways no one else has, in unique ways. You are a world premiere. Never has there been a YOU before. You have people who love you, care about you, support you and are there for you. God delights in you, his creation. You wouldn't be here if God didn't plan you, love you and bring you into being. These are all amazing reasons to be happy with yourself.

When you get knocked down, get up again. Life can be hard at times, and we all suffer, that is part of being human. When life knocks you down, for whatever reason – a failure, a disappointment, some bad news, a loss of one kind or other, whatever it is – get up, get over it, get on with it. It may take time to do this, you may take your time, but always work towards that. The sun will shine tomorrow, and you are still the person you were meant to be.

Know when to say sorry and mean it. You (we) are not perfect. We screw up and hurt others, we make mistakes, and we can do wrong – that is part of being human. We have a dark side. So, this is important, saying sorry and meaning it can heal relationships and heal yourself. It is hard sometimes to say sorry, but it is never unimportant. Learn to do it and your life will always be better. Know that no matter what you do, you are always forgiven by God. Saying sorry to God is knowing you live in that forgiveness. That is why the sacrament of reconciliation is so beautiful.

Forgive others. The flipside of saying sorry is learning to forgive others' mistakes and misdemeanours. It is the gift you give yourself. It means you won't be carrying hurt, resentment and anger around with you – they are heavy burdens to bear, they weigh you down and slow you up –

learn to let it go.

Embrace LIFE. Whatever life throws at you, embrace. Change, challenges, obstacles, accomplishments, difficulties, adventures, success, failure are all opportunities to grow. I've found failure the hardest but richest growth opportunity. Enjoy the moment. Success and failure are often passing and don't last forever. They don't determine you as a person. Sometimes it is good to take calculated risks (but never be reckless or foolish). You win and you lose – that is life and that is OK. Stay centred and balanced – ride the waves.

Live, love, and laugh! Value your life, it is the only one you have, and it won't last (in its present form) forever. Value your family and forge friendships that last. ENJOY YOUR LIFE, YOUR SELF, YOUR FAMILY, YOUR FRIENDS, YOUR PRESENT HERE AND NOW. It's been called the sacrament of the present moment and living in the here and now will take care of your future.

These last 18 years have been challenging for me on my journey learning to be your father. I am not and don't profess to be perfect. I have made mistakes and maybe even hurt you. My intention has always been to love you and support you to be the person, the good man, you are called to be. I am sorry for any hurt, any wrong I have done to you. These last 18 years have been the best of my life as well. Having a son like you gives me meaning and purpose and great joy. Know that I love you, and am immensely proud of you.

Forever, your father and friend,

Dad

To My Daughter on your 16th Birthday – A Letter from Dad

I will write you a letter on your 18th as I did for your brother, but please allow me some fatherly freedom, to write you as my daughter, for your 16th birthday too.

1. I love you more than you realise. That means I want the best for you; I care about you all the time; I will put you before me whenever possible; I will do what I can to help you achieve your goals and dreams. I hope you know that and remember that and feel that deep down in your heart always.

2. I believe in your capabilities and competencies. You are a gifted person: you are smart, quick to catch on, a good thinker and speaker, and emotionally sharp. So you will be able to pretty much choose your life's trajectory when it comes to careers. I am not worried about that for you, because you are talented and growing in confidence. After all, Sophie, your name means WISE.

3. You are a beautiful young woman, attractive physically and personally. You have a beautiful and sensitive soul and that of course is so much more important than external beauty. Always respect yourself and your dignity and worth and demand others do the same. If they do not, do not associate with them.

4. You have a wonderful and wicked sense of humour (I wonder where that came from?) and you make me laugh and you make others laugh too. That is a great gift. You can light up a room (and I don't mean as an arsonist! LOL).

5. When I see you dance (and yes I know you say I am biased) I have a tear in my eye, because I am so proud of you and you dance with such emotion and feeling and grace that you move me.

6. You are such a compassionate and caring person to those in need and to those who are hurting. That will always mean you will have friends and companions, because you

listen and respect others. Never lose that focus on others.

7. You know how much my faith (Jesus) means to me. He is the light for my path, a helper close at hand, strength when I feel weak, a refuge when I need protection, a friend when I need comfort, and the giver of life eternal. I pray that in your life you may know Him as your friend and guide and protector, the One you can always turn to and call upon. He makes all the difference. He is the source of life and life to the full.

8. I hope you know that whatever happens, whenever it happens, that you can call on me to be there for you (even though as you say I sometimes don't answer my phone – but I am getting better). I will stand by you and support you as your Dad for as long as I am able. And even after that.

9. I remember well 16 years ago when you were born, and you came out looking around as if you owned the place, how much I loved you and how much joy you have brought into my life. Thank you for being my beautiful daughter and happy birthday for today – I thank God for the gift that is you.

Love always, Dad.

To finish my reflections on fatherhood and fathers, I have concluded with a poem I wrote when thinking about myself as father and the impact, influence and inspiration I can have or be – or not. I hope it speaks to you.

What a father does

A father is always busy doing something, never nothing.
A father always does something,
whether he is alive or dead,
whether he is there fleshly, or his skin is long shed,
whether he is helicopter or dead-beat

whether he is sunshine or sleet
whether smiling or scowling,
whooping or howling,
whether memory in frame
or face to face blame,
whether he gifts you time, strips time away
whether he's there forever, never, or an irregular day
whether he is old, cold or warm,
whether he is new, calm or storm,
whether he loves, shoves, or less,
whether he forgive or confess,
whether he remembers or forgot,
whether he knows you best or not,
whether giving bread and fish, or snake and stone
whether tried and true, or false to the bone.

He is there, when he's there or not there
He is there, when he cares or doesn't care
He is there, when he's fair or not fair.
Insidious or inspiring,
Safe-haven or terminally terrifying.
A father always does something.
A father never does nothing,
whether kind-comforted or cruelty hurled,
A being is always being
knotted and twisted or nurtured and unfurled.

He emboldens and betrays,
beguiles and degrades,
beholds and builds up too
the being oh so human that is you.
and for the rest of your life,
lessons learning, unlearning,
in waves of uncertainty, hope,

peace and inevitably strife,
figuring out what he has done or undone
gratefully or ungratefully,
and, knowingly and unknowingly,
there's you, passing it on, and on,
son to father,
to father to son,
your son.

Finally...

I don't know if I would call these 'tips' but I do think that a wise, reflective father would consider these suggestions worthy of consideration.

- A wise Dad spends time with his children doing what they want to do.
- A wise Dad knows his children, knows what they like, knows who their friends are, knows what they're watching on TV, knows their phone and computer history.
- A wise Dad is patient and forgiving and gives second and third and fourth+ ... chances.
- A wise Dad says sorry for his mistakes and takes responsibility for them in the presence of his children.
- A wise Dad loves his children's mother – and if he doesn't love her anymore and they are separated, he respects and honours her as the children's mother.
- A wise Dad gives his children happy childhood memories to nurture and protect them in their adulthood.

Here are three books about being a father and about being a

man that have influenced and inspired me (in no particular order):

Frank Pitman, *Grow Up! How taking responsibility can make you a happy adult*

Lon Nease & Michael Austin [eds.], *Fatherhood: The Dao of Daddy*

Fernando Savater, *Amador: A father talks to his son about happiness, freedom and love*

And three spiritual books I tend to return to:

John O'Donohue, *Anam Cara: Spiritual Wisdom from the Celtic World*

Ronald Rolheiser OMI, *The Shattered Lantern: Rediscovering a Felt Presence of God*

Anthony de Mello SJ, *Awareness*.

Conclusion

In *Raising Fathers* we have proposed that fatherhood matters and makes a huge difference. When the work is done well, all flourish and when done badly, it is catastrophic. Our project is Raising Better Fathers. How?

So much treasure has been revealed in these pages that I am rich with challenges and tools to take into the trade of my life. I am not the same (who could be?) and my parenting, fathering and loving have been recalibrated by a new system of measurement. There is a new mirror that reveals the fresh and original me after these stories have stretched my substance and soul.

The hardy honesty was brutal at times and the vulnerability was breathtaking. Someone once said, "What is truth?" Let me tell you what I think! It is the intentional and authentic self-observation that yields a person's robust rendition of his narrative. The art of storytelling has taken on a novel power. It is like a parable in its message, yet it is not anecdotal but fresh and true. The impact is astounding.

An example is necessary.

Towards the end of the writing of this work, I asked all the contributors to send their manuscripts to their families, at least to those individuals they mention, to read. I wanted to close the circle and ensure there were no unhappy family members. (This process yielded some grief for one of the original contributors and he had to withdraw his chapter). Intentionally and importantly I wanted to see if there might be some responses which capture carefully what the author could not write about himself. I have several beautiful responses. The one below is from David, Peter Gabauer's (Chapter 7) brother.

> *Hey Pete,*
>
> *Thank you for sharing this with me. It brought a tear to my eye remembering how you selflessly stepped into the breach for our family and made yourself available to us. I really can't imagine what it would have been like at your age to go through this – I had the benefit of that childlike adaptability and freedom from responsibility. Thank you for being such a great brother, thank you for being a better father to me in your limited capacity than so many fathers are when they apply themselves full time to it! Thank you for being such a wonderful companion and friend – I love and appreciate you deeply. Written beautifully by the way, and a real treasure for me and for so many more when printed. I had to laugh about the tea towel over the shoulder as that is one of my strong memories of Dad – seeing him standing at the sink, tea towel over left shoulder. I often become aware at work of a rag I've unconsciously put over my shoulder and it will make me think of Dad and remind me that he is with me on my journey in life.*
>
> *David*

What can I say but WOW!

Somehow in the plethora of information and news we have become dislodged from the task of looking inward to discover the reflective realities. There is a sacred script inscribed into our generational histories. Our stories, left untold, leave society with only the 'now' to inform our how and why. This leaves us an eternal cycle of every generation starting from zero.

CONCLUSION

The grace of this book is that twelve men have taken the same topic and message and told their story in different ways. The experience for the authors in doing this has not only impacted us as readers, but irrevocably transformed the scribes.

For example:

To spend time with my younger self was both confronting and cathartic. I wanted to whisper, "Don't go there" or "Don't do that" but of course it's the falls rather than the successes that teach us and mould us.

Writing my story for this book has filled me with gratitude for the family and friends who held me, chastened me and checked I did not go under on their watch. I am a most fortunate man.

John Brady (Chapter 4)

This book has been a great gift to me at a precious time in the life of our family. When I found out my Dad had been diagnosed with an untreatable lung disease a few months ago, Robert was one of the first people I called, knowing he had ventured into the experience of fatherhood and sonship much deeper than I. I asked Robert for his advice on how to make the most of the time we have left and this book, now published, has been a precious part of that memory-making. This book has given me permission to talk to my Dad about things we have never openly discussed, that almost needed an excuse to push their meaning out of silence and into words. This book allowed me to ask my parents if they thought I had lost my mind when I decided to become a Christian. They said, 'No, never' and that they knew Christians when they were young and knew their goodness. So I've been touched by this experience, and I know my father has too. And that means the world to me.

Daniel Ang (Chapter 2)

I found the mission of writing my story for this book a therapy and a tender tonic. Some parts of my mind, heart and soul were soothed. A kind interior voice spoke life over my brokenness. The ruins are being restored. The process has given us all permission to be personal.

Others felt the same.

> *Writing this chapter has definitely been a cathartic experience for me but the greatest reward has been the beautiful and humbling responses I received from my wife and daughters after they had read it. I will cherish those responses for the rest of my life! I now realise that writing down my life story (warts and all!) and sharing it with my family has been another big step in my long learning journey as a father.*

Doug Black (Chapter 3)

In my work with men we regularly run into what is called the 'Father Wound' or 'Father Hunger' (in fact not just with men, women as well). An absent, addicted, abusive, angry, alcoholic and/or anonymous father will leave an individual wounded, with the experience of being unfathered and unfinished. The outcome is believing the destructive lie that one is unlovable. So much destructive behaviour stems from this. So much of our social crisis and chaos emanates from the damage of poor fathering.

As one of the authors said, "What is not resolved is repeated."

For example, Torrien Lau (Chapter 9) speaks to this issue.

> *When I was asked to write a chapter for Raising Fathers, I immediately said 'yes' before realising what I was committing to. It was one of those moments when you*

hear the words coming out of your mouth while your mind is still trying to catch up! It took me quite some time to put pen to paper and I was probably one of the last contributors to provide his work. Unbeknown to me, writing about my experiences as both a son and a father was going to be more difficult than I expected.

I felt that I had successfully worked through many, if not all, my father wounds and was I in for a shock! By going through the process of sharing my story, untreated wounds started to appear which I found quite confronting and an interesting by-product of the process. It lends itself to one of the purposes of the book itself, don't you think? By looking at our relationships we open ourselves to a greater awareness of our pain, vulnerability and the areas of healing that become exposed through self-reflection.

I was able to come to terms with the facts that I hadn't fully forgiven my father for abandoning me and I actually did love him even though I hadn't had much to do with him since he left when I was very young. I even ended up writing to my father telling him that I forgive him for not being present in my life and abandoning my brother and me. I certainly didn't expect these significant experiences when I first said 'yes'.

Overall, I feel completely privileged to be a contributor to this important work. I was profoundly blessed to experience further healing of my wounds and inspired to become a better father.

As we turn the last pages of this book, we would like to say it is not the end of the story. There is work still to be done and ground to be taken back. Humanity is still to be restored to its original glory.

There are two more things to say:

I want to encourage you to do the work now. Work on yourself. Please, go and find those old photos of Mum and Dad and any of your childhood. Try to remember how you felt at that time. Endeavour to recall experiences and stories. Then do something that might be life changing – begin to write and keep going. Just be you, write for you first and then see what happens.

You might churn out many pages, or it could be a slow process. Whatever the speed, stay with the task. This little work in the discovery of the real you may well change your family history and determine the future. It may well be destiny-defining.

Finally, many of the authors spoke about their faith in God and the importance of the Christian message in their journey. They implied there was an invisible force at work in the world and in their lives. They said that this power was the essential ingredient that defined them.

What if they are right?

My last word is this historical truth: A man named Jesus walked the earth telling stories and spoke predominantly about his Father. He gave God a new name – 'Abba' which means, in a tender way, Dadda/Papa. He said his Father was good –The Good Father! If you can, run home to Him.

Acknowledgements

This book is many years in the making and many people have influenced and directly affected this work. I want to name, declare their influence and express appreciation for what these people have contributed to my writing and my life.

As I stated in the preface, I have been deep in the trenches of the task of fathering from the front line for 35 years. My first and most important coach was my Dad, John Falzon. He taught me much about what to do and I also learned something of what not to do. I love you Dad. My Mum, Lucy, who is frail and aged, you are a big character in my journey. In so many ways you have shaped me. Thank you. I love you.

There have been some father figures who spoke into my manhood including Uncle Joe and Uncle Tullio, both of whom have passed to the other side now. You took time to notice, affirm and grant me permission to individuate and differentiate. You showed me what a man should be. You blessed me.

My community of like-minded men in menALIVE. My journeymen, my band of brothers, who have walked with me, laughed, and cried with me for nearly 20 years. You know who you are and be assured I know and respect who you are. There are none like you in this great south land of the Holy Spirit. Thank you. I love you. May we walk together a little longer.

To the brave men who co-authored this book with me. You gave much of your time, talent and treasure to write vulnerably and openly about your journey. You revealed your failures, brokenness and life stories. You humbly and honestly shared your victories and triumphs. You recognised the reason for this work and owned the vision and proposition that fathers really matter. Fathers everywhere are in debt to you. They now have a compass and a map. Thank you for patiently putting up with my pushing *you* with regard to deadlines and details. You smiled when I sent back your scripts for reworking or suggested some changes. You are generous, gracious and good men. You stand in the breach, you put up your hand and say, "Here I am" and "Yes I will". We all are in debt to you. I have grown to love you. I pray the readers love you too!

To Tracey, our editor who read every word with conviction and confidence in the cause. Your energy for the enterprise of *Raising Fathers* went beyond your engagement. Thank you.

Finally, and foremost to my wife Alicia and my children Isaac, Matthias, Chiara and Shem. You allowed me to experiment on you. You tolerated my imperfect husbanding and fathering. You trained and taught me in the way I should go. You helped me to discover how you needed to be loved. You loved me when I was absent, angry, selfish and neglectful. You are my joy, my delight, my prize and my life. I love you.

To Our Father, My Father – hallowed be thy name. Thank you, praise you for Fathering me.

Robert Falzon

August, 2020

Bibliography

Bennett, Wayne, *Don't Die with the Music in You*, Sydney NSW, 2007.

Biddulph, Steve, *The New Manhood: Love, Freedom, Spirit and the New Masculinity*, Cammeray NSW, 2019.

Raising Boys in the Twenty-first Century: Why Boys are Different and How to Help Them Become Happy and Well-Balanced Men, Mona Vale NSW, 2018.

Raising Girls in the Twenty-first Century: Helping your Daughter to Grow up Wise, Warm and Strong, Cammeray NSW, 2019.

Brown, Brene, *The Gifts of Imperfection: Let Go of Who You Think You're Supposed to Be and Embrace Who You Are*, Center City MN, 2010.

Casey, Michael, *Toward God: The Ancient Wisdom of Western Prayer*, Liguori MO, 1996.

Chapman, Gary, *The Five Love Languages: The Secret to Love that Lasts*, Chicago IL, 1992.

Covey, Stephen, *Seven Habits of Highly Effective People*, New York NY, 1989.

Dalbey, Gordon, *Healing the Masculine Soul: God's Restoration of Men to Real Manhood*, Nashville TN, 1988.

Sons of the Father, Carol Stream IL, 1996.

de Lubac, Henri, *The Splendour of the Church*, San Francisco CA, 1999.

de Mello, Anthony, *Awareness*, London UK, 1990.

Eldredge, John, & Brent, Curtis, *Sacred Romance: Drawing*

Closer to the Heart of God, Nashville TN, 1997

Wild at Heart: Discovering the Secret of a Man's Soul, Nashville TN, 2001.

Epic: The Story God is Telling and the Role that is Yours to Play, Nashville TN, 2004.

Fathered by God: Learning What Your Dad Could Never Teach You, Nashville TN, 2009.

Evert, Jason, *St John Paul the Great: His Five Loaves,* Denver CO, 2014.

Falzon, Robert & O'Shea, Peter, *The Father Factor,* Cleveland Qld, 2014.

Gaitley, Michael E, *33 Days to Morning Glory: A Retreat in Preparation for Marian Consecration,* Stockbridge MA, 2011.

Harris, Alex & Brett, *Do Hard Things: A Teenage Rebellion Against Low Expectations,* New York NY, 2008.

Havard, Alexandre, *Virtuous Leadership: An Agenda for Personal Excellence,* Cleveland OH, 2007.

Hybels, Bill, *Who You Are When No One's Looking,* Westmont IL, 1987.

John Paul II, Pope *Guardian of the Redeemer,* Homebush NSW, 1989.

Lashlie, Celia, *He'll be OK: Growing Gorgeous Boys into Good Men,* Sydney NSW, 2013.

Lewis, CS, *The Screwtape Letters,* London UK, 1942.

Mallon, James, *Divine Renovation: Bringing your Parish from Maintenance to Mission,* Mulgrave Vic, 2016.

Meeker, Meg, *Strong Fathers, Strong Daughters: 10 Secrets Every Father Should Know,* Washington DC, 2007.

Merton, Thomas, *New Seeds of Contemplation*, New York NY, 1972.

The Inner Experience, New York NY, 2004

Nease, Lon & Austin, Michael, [eds.] *Fatherhood: The Dao of Daddy*, Sussex UK, 2010.

O'Brien, Michael D, *Father Elijah*, San Francisco CA, 1996.

O'Donohue, John, *Anam Cara: Spiritual Wisdom from the Celtic World*, London UK, 1997.

Peck, M Scott, *People of the Lie: The Hope for Healing Human Evil*, New York NY, 1983.

Pitman, Frank, *Grow Up! How Taking Responsibility can Make you a Happy Adult*, New York NY, 1998.

Prince, Derek, *Husbands & Fathers: Rediscover the Creator's Purpose for Men*, Ada MI, 2000.

Richards, Larry, *Be a Man: Becoming the Man God Created You to Be*, San Francisco CA, 2009.

Robinson, Bruce, *Fathering from the Fast Lane: Practical Ideas for Busy Dads*, Mona Vale NSW, 2003.

Rohr, Richard, *Adam Returns: The Five Promises of Male Initiation*, Chestnut Ridge NY, 2004.

The Naked Now: Learning to See as the Mystics See, Chestnut Ridge NY, 2009.

Eager to Love: The Alternative Way of Francis of Assisi, Cincinnati OH, 2014.

The Universal Christ: How a Forgotten Reality Can Change Everything We See, Hope For and Believe, New York NY, 2019.

Rolheiser, Ronald, *Seeking Spirituality: Guidelines for a Christian Spirituality for the Twenty-First Century*, London,

1998.

Against an Infinite Horizon: The Finger of God in our Everyday Lives, Chestnut Ridge NY, 2002.

The Shattered Lantern: Rediscovering a Felt Presence of God, Chestnut Ridge NY, 2004.

Forgotten Among the Lilies: Learning to Love Beyond Our Fears, New York NY, 2007.

Falling Upward: A Spirituality for the Two Halves of Life, San Francisco CA, 2011.

The Holy Longing: The Search for a Christian Spirituality, New York NY, 2014.

Savater, Fernando, *Amador: A Father Talks to his Son about Happiness, Freedom and Love*, Melbourne Vic, 1995.

Senek, Simon, *Start with Why*, New York NY, 2009.

Sheridan, Greg, *God is Good for you: A Defence of Christianity in Troubled Times*, Crows Nest NSW, 2018.

Thibodeaux, Mark E, *God's Voice Within: The Ignatian Way to Discover God's Will*, Chicago IL, 2010.

Tolkien, JRR, *Lord of the Rings*, London UK, 1968.

Zacharias, Ravi, *The end of Reason: Discounting the New Atheism and the New Atheists*, New York NY, 2008.

www.ingramcontent.com/pod-product-compliance
Lightning Source LLC
Chambersburg PA
CBHW052102230426
43671CB00011B/1905